The Genius
of the
Roman Rite

Historical, Theological, and Pastoral
Perspectives on Catholic Liturgy

30. Ⅲ. 2010

*For Tamara, in memory of your visit to
Rome during Holy Week 2010.
With every good wish,*

Fr Michael

Uwe Michael Lang
Editor

HillenbrandBooks

Chicago / Mundelein, Illinois

The Genius of the Roman Rite: Historical, Theological and Pastoral Perspective on Catholic Liturgy © 2010 Archdiocese of Chicago: Liturgy Training Publications, 3949 South Racine Avenue, Chicago IL 60609; 1-800-933-1800, fax 1-800-933-7094, e-mail orders@ ltp.org. All rights reserved. See our Web site at www.LTP.org.

Hillenbrand Books is an imprint of Liturgy Training Publications (LTP) and the Liturgical Institute at the University of Saint Mary of the Lake (USML). The imprint is focused on contemporary and classical theological thought concerning the liturgy of the Catholic Church. Available at bookstores everywhere, through LTP by calling 1-800-933-1800, or visiting www.LTP.org. Further information about the **Hillenbrand Books** publishing program is available from the University of Saint Mary of the Lake/ Mundelein Seminary, 1000 East Maple Avenue, Mundelein, IL 60060 (847-837-4542), on the Web at www.usml.edu/liturgicalinstitute, or e-mail litinst@usml.edu.

Printed in the United States of America.

Library of Congress Control Number: 2009938656

ISBN 978-1-59525-031-5

HGRR

Contents

Acknowledgments

Thanks are due to the Benedictine nuns of St Cecilia's Abbey, Ryde (Isle of Wight) for translating Abbé Claude Barthe's paper from French, to Father Andrew Wadsworth for translating Don Nicola Bux's paper from Italian, and to Alexander Morrison for translating P. Gabriel Díaz's paper from Spanish. The editor is also indebted to Catherine Donner and Owen Curry for their help with preparing the manuscript.

An earlier version of Dr. Cristina Dondi's paper can be found under the title "Liturgical Policies of the Hospitallers between the Invention of Printing and the Council of Trent: The Evidence of the Early Printed Breviaries and Missals," in V. Mallia-Milanes (ed.), *The Military Orders. Volume 3: History and Heritage* (Aldershot: Ashgate, 2008).

Introduction

Uwe Michael Lang

This book contains the proceedings of the 11th International
Colloquium of CIEL (*Centre International d'Études Liturgiques*–
International Centre for Liturgical Studies), held in Merton College,
Oxford from September 13 to 16, 2006. CIEL was founded in
1994 to promote the study and appreciation of the traditional liturgies
of the Catholic Church, in particular the Roman rite. The organization's earlier colloquia were held in France, and since 2005 regular
meetings have taken place in Rome. The proceedings of the previous
colloquia were published in English translation by the UK branch
of CIEL. The 2006 conference was the first one to be hosted by CIEL
UK and has opened a new chapter in the history of these colloquia,
with most papers being delivered in English and many participants
coming from the Anglophone world.

The title chosen for the Oxford colloquium and for this
volume refers to an influential essay by the English liturgical scholar
Edmund Bishop (1846–1917), "The Genius of the Roman Rite":

> Some one a very long time ago described Genius as 'Son of the Gods and
> Father of Men.' It is thus that we speak of the Genius of a people—the
> French or the English, the German or the Italian; a something intangible
> and indefinable, it is true, but a permanent reality that we can quite
> well apprehend; a characteristic and distinguishing spirit that manifests
> itself in all that that a people says and does, in its history and its literature;
> determining the character of both, and affecting the general character
> even of its thought.
>
> An enquiry into the genius of the Roman rite is therefore an endeavour to
> get at, and to recognize, the particular, the native spirit animating and pen-
> etrating that rite, which differentiates it from others, Gallican or Gothic,
> Greek or Oriental.[1]

---

1. E. Bishop, "The Genius of the Roman Rite," in *id*, *Liturgica Historica* (Oxford: Clarendon
Press, 1918), 1-19, at 2; see also P. Bradshaw, "The Genius of the Roman Rite Revisited," in U.

The papers collected in this volume cover a variety of topics, ranging from studies of Latin liturgical prose and poetry, the music proper to the Roman rite, the development of the Church's sacred year, the liturgies of the military religious orders to treatments of important theological topics. However, all of these contributions capture something of the "genius" of the Roman liturgical tradition. As is evident from the opening paper by Eamon Duffy, this kind of scholarly reflection is very appropriate in the pontificate of Benedict XVI, who as a cardinal has written extensively on the liturgy and as pope has made important pronouncements on the subject, especially in the Post-Synodal Apostolic Exhortation *Sacramentum Caritatis* of February 22, 2007, and in the Motu Proprio *Summorum Pontificum* of July 7, 2007. The latter document, which came into force on September 14, 2007, lifted previous restrictions for the celebration of Mass and of the other sacraments according to the liturgical books used until the reform following the Second Vatican Council.

The Pope declares in his explanatory letter to the bishops accompanying the Motu Proprio that the older form of Mass according to the *Missale Romanum* of 1962 "was never juridically abrogated and, consequently, in principle, was always permitted."[2] This statement is highly significant, because for many years it was widely believed that the post-conciliar liturgical reform had effectively abolished the older form the rite. To be sure, Pope John Paul II in his Motu Proprio *Ecclesia Dei Adflicta* of 1988 demanded that "respect must everywhere be shown for the feelings of all those who are attached to the Latin liturgical tradition, by a wide and generous application of the directives already issued some time ago by the Apostolic See for the use of the Roman Missal according to the typical edition of 1962."[3] Nevertheless, priests have had great difficulties in obtaining the permission to celebrate this Mass, and the lawful aspirations of the laity who asked their bishops for celebrations

---

M. Lang (ed.), *Ever Directed Towards the Lord: The Love of God in the Liturgy Past, Present, and Hoped For. Proceedings of the Society of St Catherine of Siena Conference held in Oxford on 29 October 2005* (London: T&T Clark, 2007), 49–61.

2. Benedict XVI, *Letter to the Bishops that accompanies the Motu Proprio Summorum Pontificum* (July 7, 2007); cf. Motu Proprio *Summorum Pontificum* (July 7, 2007), Art. 1: *"Missae Sacrificium, iuxta editionem typicam Missalis Romani a B. Ioanne XXIII anno 1962 promulgatam et numquam abrogatam."*

3. John Paul II, Motu Proprio *Ecclesia Dei Adflicta* (July 2, 1988), 6c.

of it have often been frustrated and seldom genuinely fostered. With his new norms Pope Benedict implicitly acknowledges that the "wide and generous" access to the older form that John Paul II had encouraged has not been available to the faithful. The present Holy Father cites Saint Paul's words, "Our mouth is open to you, Corinthians; our heart is wide. You are not restricted by us, but you are restricted in your own affections. In return . . . widen your hearts also!" (2 Corinthians 6:11–13), and then exhorts all bishops, and indeed the whole Church: "Let us generously open our hearts and make room for everything that the faith itself allows."[4]

But Pope Benedict goes beyond exhortation, by establishing the rights of the faithful in terms of canon law, the law of the Church.[5] This is not another indult, or special permission, it is much more than that: each Catholic priest of the Latin rite has the right to celebrate Mass according to the *Missale Romanum* of 1962, and the lay faithful, for their part, have the right to request such a celebration. The Holy Father recognizes that those who are drawn to the older form of Mass are not only people who grew up with it. Today, more than forty years after Vatican II, many younger people have come to know and appreciate it. This is not just nostalgia or aestheticism; it is a real love for the Church's liturgical tradition, which nourishes and sustains their Christian lives.

The Motu Proprio *Summorum Pontificum* is a defining moment in the pontificate of Benedict XVI. And the main theme of this document and the explanatory letter is reconciliation: in the first place, reconciliation of the Church with her own tradition. For years, it was insinuated that those who were attached to the older liturgy were disobedient. Even from a merely psychological point of view, such a rejection of one's own past must have disastrous effects. The Bishop of Eichstätt in Germany in his statement welcoming this papal document says that we must overcome the "liturgical Oedipus complex"[6] from which the life of the Church has suffered for decades, that

---

4. Benedict XVI, *Letter.*

5. For a canonical commentary, see N. Lüdecke, "Kanonistische Anmerkungen zum Motu Proprio Summorum Pontificum," in *Liturgisches Jahrbuch* 58 (2008), 3–34.

6. *Stellungnahme des Bischofs von Eichstätt Dr. Gregor Maria Hanke OSB zu dem am 7. Juli 2007 veröffentlichten Motu Proprio "Summorum Pontificum"* (http://www.bistum-eichstaett.de/bischof/wortlaut/motu-proprio.htm).

is, the rejection, even amounting to hatred, of that which our ancestors considered most holy. The Pope also sees this problem clearly: "In the history of the liturgy there is growth and progress, but no rupture. What earlier generations held as sacred, remains sacred and great for us too, and it cannot be all of a sudden entirely forbidden or even considered harmful. It behooves all of us to preserve the riches which have developed in the Church's faith and prayer, and to give them their proper place."[7] Thus *Summorum Pontificum* should also be seen as an important application of the hermeneutic of continuity in interpreting the Second Vatican Council—the Pope acting on the principle he proposed in his momentous discourse to the Roman Curia on December 22, 2005.[8]

Vatican II reaffirmed traditional teaching, when it proclaimed that the liturgy is "the summit of all the Church's activities, and the source from which all her power flows."[9] In it, "the work of our redemption is accomplished," most of all in the Sacrifice of the Mass, and it manifests both to the faithful and to all others "the mystery of Christ and the real nature of the true Church."[10] In his writings on the liturgy, Joseph Ratzinger has recalled that our form of public worship must be a reflection of the glory of God. This holds good especially for the celebration of Holy Mass, where the paschal mystery of Christ's Passion, death, and Resurrection is made present ever anew in sacramental form. It is in the celebration of this sacrament that we are immersed into communion with the Lord, who blesses us with the gift of his love—the gift of himself under the appearances of bread and wine. This sacramental participation in the life of Christ has a specific form, given in the rite of Mass. In his preface to the book *The Organic Development of the Liturgy* by Alcuin Reid, then-Cardinal Ratzinger wrote: "The 'rite,' that form of celebration and prayer which has ripened in the faith and the life of the Church, is a condensed form of living Tradition . . . and thus at the same time the fellowship of generations one with another becomes something we can experience, fellowship with the people who pray before us and after us. Thus

---

7. Benedict XVI, *Letter*.

8. Benedict XVI, Address to the Roman Curia (December 22, 2005); cf. also Post-Synodal Apostolic Exhortation *Sacramentum Caritatis* (February 22, 2007), 3.

9. *SC*, 10.

10. *SC*, 2.

the rite is something of benefit which is given to the Church, a living form of *paradosis*—the handing-on of Tradition."[11]

For years now, the rite as the "condensed form of living Tradition" has been a controversial topic in the Catholic Church. The post-conciliar reform of the Roman rite of Mass was implemented with great haste, and in its wake liturgical abuses have become widespread. This situation has generated skepticism even among those whose loyalty to the Second Vatican Council cannot be doubted; they wonder whether the principles according to which the celebration of Mass was changed do justice to the traditional understanding and practice of the faith, or whether they are, at least in part, alien to them.

It is a fact that the Catholic liturgy is not in good shape today—not everywhere, not in every parish, but on balance and in every corner of the world. The Pope is very frank about this, when he speaks of "deformations of the liturgy which were hard to bear," and then adds on a personal note: "I am speaking from experience, since I too lived through that period with all its hopes and its confusion. And I have seen how arbitrary deformations of the liturgy caused deep pain to individuals totally rooted in the faith of the Church."[12] These words reflect the pastoral care of the Successor of Peter and need to be taken seriously. They also echo what Joseph Ratzinger said about the present crisis of the liturgy before his election to the Apostolic See. He repeatedly called for a wider use of the old liturgy and for a "reform of the reform". The Motu Proprio *Summorum Pontificum* is already achieving the former, and I am convinced it has also initiated the latter. The difficulty with the "reform of the reform" project is that the liturgy is never "made" or "fabricated." It develops and grows organically. As much as a "reform of the reform" is necessary, it cannot be "made" or "fabricated" either. There is the danger that a "reform of the reform," however conscientiously executed, would make similar mistakes to those made by the reformers of the sixties and seventies.

A liturgical rite is not owned by a generation and can therefore not be altered in an arbitrary fashion. As Ratzinger wrote shortly

---

11. J. Ratzinger, "Preface," in A. Reid, *The Organic Development of the Liturgy* (San Francisco: Ignatius Press, 2nd edn, 2005), 9–13, at 11.

12. Benedict XVI, *Letter*.

before the conclave of April 2005, liturgy is not "made," not even
by a pope: "With respect to the Liturgy, [the pope] has the task
of a gardener, not that of a technician who builds new machines and
throws the old ones on the junk-pile."[13] With this Motu Proprio,
Benedict XVI has shown himself a prudent and gentle gardener. The
1962 Missal has been brought back into the center of the Church's
life, as the "extraordinary form" of the Roman rite, while the Missal
of Paul VI will remain the "ordinary form" of the same rite. The Holy
Father notes that "the two forms of the usage of the Roman rite can
be mutually enriching." He suggests that new prefaces, and celebrations for some new saints, can and should be added to the 1962
Missal. Then he adds: "The Ecclesia Dei Commission, in contact
with various bodies devoted to the *usus antiquior*, will study the
practical possibilities in this regard." In fact, in the four centuries
between St Pius V and Blessed John XXII, several prefaces were
added to the Missal and the saints' calendar was changed many times;
hence such a development as envisaged by Benedict XVI would be
another step towards normality.

The Holy Father goes on to say that through the coexistence
of the two forms the "celebration of the Mass according to the Missal
of Paul VI will be able to demonstrate, more powerfully than has
been the case hitherto, the sacrality which attracts many people
to the former usage."[14] This is very significant: if indeed the celebration of the "ordinary form" of the Roman rite is more and more
inspired by the sacred and stable character of the "extraordinary form",
then the "reform of the reform" will be well on its way. In this sense,
Summorum Pontificum marks a new stage in the implementation of the
Council's Constitution on the Sacred Liturgy *Sacrosanctum Concilium*,
in accordance with the hermeneutic of continuity and the mind of
Pope Benedict.

---

13. Ratzinger, *Preface*, 11.
14. Benedict XVI, *Letter*.

Abbreviations

CCL   *Corpus Christianorum. Series Latina* (Turnhout: Brepols, 1953ff.)

CCM   *Corpus Christianorum. Continuatio Medievalis* (Turnhout: Brepols, 1966 ff.)

DS   *Enchiridion symbolorum, defnitionum et declarationum de rebus fidei et morum*, ed. H. Denzinger–A. Schönmetzer (Barcinone et al.: Herder, editio XXXVI emendata, 1976)

PG   *Patrologiae Cursus Completus, accurante J.-P. Migne. Series Graeca*, 166 vols (Paris: Petit-Montrouge, 1857–1883)

PL   *Patrologiae Cursus Completus, accurante J.-P. Migne. Series Latina*, 221 vols (Paris: J.-P. Migne, 1844–1865)

SC   Second Vatican Council, Constitution on the Sacred Liturgy *Sacrosanctum Concilium* (December 4, 1963), in *Sacrosanctum Oecumenicum Concilium Vaticanum II: Constitutiones; Decreta; Declarationes* (Città del Vaticano: Libreria Editrice Vaticana, 1993), 3–60

SCh   *Sources Chrétiennes*, Paris: Cerf, 1941 ff.

Chapter 1

Benedict XVI and the Liturgy

Eamon Duffy

The election of Joseph Ratzinger as Benedict XVI in April 2005 put a professional theologian at the helm of the Catholic Church for the first time in centuries. The theologian in question is a controversial figure, whose election was greeted with ecstasy in some quarters, and with alarm and dismay in others. The delight and dismay had a common cause in the reputation which this shy Bavarian Professor had acquired for himself during his 24-year tenure of the most influential post in the Vatican, as prefect of the Congregation for the Doctrine of the Faith. At least in his early years at the CDF he was a prolific writer and, most unusually for high-ranking curial officials, he gave a series of very high-profile book-length interviews to favored journalists, in which he made clear his unease with many developments in the post-conciliar Church.

   High among these unwelcome developments is his view of the general character of the post-conciliar Roman liturgy, repeatedly expressing his concern at the direction of liturgical change. That unease is often perceived as part of a general rejection on his part of the conciliar reforms, or, to put it more crudely, as part of a more general reactionary repudiation of the Council. But behind his criticisms of the modern liturgy lies a considered and coherent theology and ecclesiology which, even if he were not Pope, would merit a proper hearing: since he now occupies the chair of Peter, his views on these issues are a matter of the keenest interest.

   The first thing to register is the extent to which Joseph Ratzinger's views on the liturgy are shaped by his pre-war experience of growing up in small-town Bavaria, and the worship of his parish

church. He was the pious son of a pious family. His father, a police-
man, was a devout Mass-goer, and the child Ratzinger was given a
series of bi-lingual Missals by his parents, to help him to understand
what was going on at the altar. Pope Benedict has left a vivid account
of his own awakening with the help of these books to the beauty and
immemorial antiquity of the Mass:

> It was a riveting adventure to move by degrees into the mysterious world
> of the liturgy, which was being enacted before us at the altar. It was
> becoming more and more clear to me that here I was encountering a real-
> ity that no one had simply thought up, a reality that no official authority
> or great individual had created. This mysterious fabric of texts and actions
> had grown from the faith of the church over the centuries. It bore the
> whole weight of history within itself, and yet, at the same time, it was
> much more than the product of human history.[1]

For him, the "whole weight of history" meant both the history
of Christianity over two thousand years and in many cultures, of
course, but also, in a very concrete way, the liturgical culture of his
own Bavaria. He is a man very much at ease with, even gratefully
uncritical of, the communal religion which formed him, because
he believes it to have been a healthy and an authentic historical and
cultural expression of Catholic Christianity, everything from the
musical glory of a Haydn Mass in the gold and white splendor of a
southern Baroque church, to the folk-customs of the Bavarian coun-
tryside. Here he is, in a characteristic essay on "What Corpus Christi
means to me," recalling the Corpus Christi processions of his youth.
He has been reflecting on Saint Thomas' aphorism about the service
of God, *Quantum potes, tantum aude*—"are to do all that you are
able to," and he goes on.

> I can still smell those carpets of flowers and the freshness of the birch
> trees: I can see all the houses decorated, the banners, the singing; I can still
> hear the village band which, indeed, sometimes dared to do more, on this
> occasion, than it was able to! I remember the *joie de vivre* of the local lads,
> firing their gun salutes . . . .[2]

---

1. J. Ratzinger, *Milestones: Memoirs 1927–1977*, trans. E. Leiva-Merikakis (San Francisco:
Ignatius Press, 1998), 19–20.

2. J. Ratzinger, *The Feast of Faith: Approaches to a Theology of the Liturgy*, trans. G. Harrison
(San Francisco: Ignatius Press, 1986) 127 ff.

There is certainly a strong element of nostalgia in all this, and one may legitimately raise an eyebrow at the apparent lack of distance in this nostalgia directed so uncritically to the thought of young men processing with guns in 1930s Bavaria. Yet Ratzinger's gut knowledge that all this had made him what he was joined with his intellectual conviction that this was authentic Catholic Christianity at its best. Together, they make him suspicious of those professional liturgists who, during and after the Council, rejected such celebrations as evidence of a decadent or defective theology of the Eucharist, one which had forgotten that the Eucharist had been instituted to be eaten, not carried about on carpets of flowers or shot into the air over by lads with guns. By contrast, these processions for Ratzinger represented deep tradition, the authentic transmission of Catholic belief in and love for the Eucharist, within a culture shaped by and saturated in loyalty to Catholicism. If such celebrations did not square with the fashionable theology, then it was just too bad for that theology. So he comments that

> . . . when we walk our streets with the Lord on Corpus Christi, we do not need to look anxiously over our shoulders at our theological theories to see if everything is in order and can be accounted for, but we can open ourselves wide to the joy of the redeemed.[3]

Love and gratitude for his own Catholic upbringing was however only one dimension in the formation of his attitudes towards liturgy. Like most theologically engaged Catholics of his generation, Ratzinger was profoundly influenced by the liturgical movement which had become one of the major sources of theological excitement between the wars, and especially by the writings of the Munich-based theologian Romano Guardini, Karl Rahner's predecessor in the chair of Theology and Catholic *Weltanschauung* (or worldview) at Munich. In 1918, Guardini published a series of lectures under the title *The Spirit of the Liturgy*. This little book, which had no scholarly bibliography or learned footnotes, became almost at once one of the foundational texts behind the twentieth-century liturgical movement. In it, Guardini argued that the liturgy was the main vehicle for and expression of the Church's inner essence. Into its words and actions was

---

3. Ratzinger, *Feast of Faith*, 135.

distilled the deepest convictions and aspirations of the Christian community, so an appreciation of the meaning and methods of the liturgy was the best means of penetrating to the heart of the Church's Gospel. The liturgy was not just the sum total of rules governing the performance of the obligatory worship of God, it was the very heart of what it meant to be a Catholic, a school of wisdom and understanding, in which all the resources of human culture, in words, visual art, architecture and music were deployed into "the supreme example of an objectively established rule of spiritual life."[4]

Guardini laid great emphasis on the communal aspects of the liturgy, "the Liturgy does not say 'I,' but 'we,'"[5] and on its transcendence of the merely local or any particular congregation. In the liturgy, the Christian "sees himself face to face with God not as an entity, but as a member of the unity" of the Church. The liturgy was the immemorial distillation of Christian experience, so just as it discouraged individualism or the merely local, it also discouraged strong and immediate emotion in favor of restraint. Yet it was never frigid, its texts full of longing, hope, and love for God—"emotion flows in its depths . . . like the fiery heart of the volcano. The liturgy *is* emotion, but it is emotion under the strictest control." This universalizing restraint, the "style of the liturgy," in the words of another of Guardini's chapter titles, trained and liberated Christians into wider and deeper feelings than their own, drew them into the universal aspirations of the whole of redeemed humanity, identified them with the Christ whose prayer the liturgy was.

Joseph Ratzinger revered and reveres Guardini. He first read *The Spirit of the Liturgy* shortly after he began his theological training in 1946, and the book was a milestone in his intellectual and religious development. Reflecting on its importance in 2000, he wrote that

> It helped us to rediscover the liturgy in all its hidden beauty, hidden wealth, and time-transcending grandeur, to see it as the animating centre of the Church, the very centre of Christian life. It led to a striving for a celebration of the liturgy that would be 'more substantial' [that is, which would reveal the fundamental substance or structure]. We were now willing to see the liturgy—in its inner demands and form—as the prayer of

---

4. R. Guardini, *The Spirit of the Liturgy*, trans. A. Lane (London: Sheed & Ward, 1935), 121.
5. Guardini, *Spirit of the Liturgy*, 141.

the Church, a prayer moved and guided by the Holy Spirit himself, in which Christ unceasingly becomes contemporary with us, enters our lives."[6]

The Liturgical Movement was of course a movement for reform. Driven by a passionate belief that the liturgy preserved the deepest insights and the most fundamental longings of Christianity, Guardini and many of his colleagues and disciples were also driven by the conviction that in practice the liturgy was often cluttered by the accumulated rubbish of centuries, bogged down in excessive legalism and so no longer able to communicate with modern people. Guardini himself celebrated so-called "dialogue Masses" at an altar in a white-washed chapel facing the people, and using vernacular hymns, in a desire to let the liturgy speak clearly once again. And like many of the brightest minds of his generation, the young Joseph Ratzinger shared this reforming impatience. As a *peritus* at the Council, he was to deploy a rhetoric of impatience and disparagement which stressed the problems of a Latin liturgy rather than its glories, designed to speed along liturgical reform. So, before the Council the same Ratzinger who had written time and again of his deep and nostalgic love of the liturgy of his childhood, could deplore the communal dynamic of the old Mass, "a lonely hierarchy facing a group of laymen each one of whom is shut off in his own missal or devotional book." During the Council he would declare that the Latin Mass of his youth was "archaeological," and presented a picture "so encrusted that the original image could hardly be seen": it was therefore "a closed book to the faithful," which was why the liturgy had been marginal to many of the greatest Catholics, why the great mystics, like Saint John of the Cross and Saint Teresa of Avilla, in his opinion, had drawn little or nothing of their spiritual nourishment from the Mass.[7]

The actual outcome of the liturgical movement, its drift away from a rediscovery of sources to a search for modernity, a departure, as Ratzinger understood it, from the lines laid out by Guardini and others, however, was to change his mind about all this. From a bastion of daunting antiquarianism inaccessible to ordinary Catholics,

6. J. Ratzinger, *The Spirit of the Liturgy,* trans. J. Saward (San Francisco: Ignatius Press, 2000), 7.

7. J. L Allen, *Cardinal Ratzinger: The Vatican's Enforcer of the Faith* (New York–London: Continuum, 2000), 73–75.

the Latin liturgy came to seem to him a precious protection against a rootless *aggiornamento*, reform understood as the adoption merely of modern intellectual and cultural fads and fashions. In common with many of the fathers of the liturgical movement, he had hoped for a reform which would clarify and make more intelligible the beauty and wisdom of the ancient worship of the Church: he was not looking for fundamental change, but careful conservation and restoration. What he thought he saw in the wake of Vatican II was a liturgical revolution which jettisoned Latin, and with it a thousand years of liturgical music, from the Gregorian chant which Pius X had tried to revive after centuries of neglect, to the great polyphonic Masses from Palestrina to Haydn. Along with the loss of Latin went other changes which Ratzinger was convinced represented fundamental misunderstandings of the nature of liturgy: these included the introduction of improvised prayer-formulae, and the universal adoption of the westward-facing position of the priest at Mass.

For Ratzinger all this represented a disastrous break in the Church's tradition, the "magnificent work" of Guardini and others "thrown into the wastepaper basket,"[8] the introduction into the Church's worship of a restless modern obsession with change and innovation for their own sakes, and a preoccupation with human community which excluded or hindered true openness to God. All this came for him to be summed-up for him in the new Mass, introduced by Paul VI in the wake of the Council. Here is what Cardinal Ratzinger had to say about these issues, in his memoir, *Milestones*, published in 1998. The extract, which is an extended one, comes from his discussion of the early 1970s, when he was professor of dogmatic theology at Regensburg.

> The second great event at the beginning of my years at Regensburg was the publication of the Missal of Paul VI, which was accompanied by the almost total prohibition, after a transitional phase of only half a year, of using the missal we had had till then. I welcomed the fact that now we had a binding liturgical text after a period of exploration that had often deformed the liturgy. But I was dismayed by the prohibition of the old missal, since nothing of the sort had ever happened in the entire history of the liturgy. . . . The prohibition of the missal that was now decreed,

---

8. Ratzinger, *Feast of Faith*, 70–71.

a missal that had known continuous growth over the centuries . . . introduced a breach into the history of the liturgy whose consequences could only be tragic. It was reasonable and right of the Council to order a revision of the missal such as had taken place before and which this time was to be more thorough than before, above all because of the introduction of the vernacular. But more than this now happened. The old building was now demolished, and another was built, to be sure largely using the old building plans.

He concedes that the new missal had many marvelous things in it, but

. . . setting it as a new construction over against what had grown historically, forbidding the results of that historical growth, thereby makes the liturgy appear to be no longer a living development, but the product of erudite work and juridical authority. This has caused us enormous harm.

This matters because, Ratzinger believed,

. . . when liturgy is self-made . . . it can no longer give us what its proper gift should be, the encounter with the mystery that is not our own product, but rather our origin and the source of our life.

Declaring his conviction that "the crisis in the Church that we are experiencing today is to a large extent due to the disintegration of the liturgy," he called for a new liturgical movement, a movement of liturgical reconciliation which would recognize "the unity of the history of the liturgy, and that understands Vatican II not as a break but as a stage of development."[9]

In recent years, he has returned again and again in his writings and speeches to his conviction that the imposition of the Missal of Paul VI as the sole legitimate liturgical norm for Roman Catholics, was nothing short of a catastrophe. For Ratzinger the theologian, following Guardini, the power of the Tradition to mediate to us the Divine is derived from the fact that we experience that tradition as a *given*, something which is in the first-place the self giving of God, a participation in the worship of the Incarnate Logos, directed to the Father in the Spirit, and, secondarily, the distillation of the Church's age-old encounter with that Lord. On both counts, it is emphatically not something we make up or improvise for ourselves.

9. Ratzinger, *Milestones*, 146–48.

Liturgical change and revision is a constant of the Church's life, whose necessity and value he accepts, but that revision must always happen, and, till Vatican II , historically he believes only ever happened, as a process of refinement and purification of what went before, never as a fresh start. It is of the essence of our encounter of God within the liturgy that we experience the liturgy precisely as the gift of God, an entry into the *obsequium rationabile*, the rational worship of the Logos, and therefore as an inheritance, a space we inhabit as others have inhabited it before us, never as an instrument we design or manipulate. He considers that we in the West have much to learn from the orthodox description of the liturgy as "Divine liturgy," for this reminds us that we receive it, not invent it. Self-made liturgy is for him an abomination, and indeed a contradiction in terms, and so he distrusts and resists liturgies which emphasize spontaneity, self-expression and local inculturation at the expense of the tried and tested forms. In 2000, he published a major study of the liturgy called, in tribute to Guardini, *The Spirit of the Liturgy*. In it, at the end of a somewhat pedestrian exploration of the Exodus story as a theological paradigm for understanding the liturgy, he comes up with the follow-ing revealing—and really rather savage—passage on the Golden Calf, behind which can be discerned his low opinion of much modern Catholic liturgy.

> The worship of the Golden Calf is a self-generated cult. When Moses stays away for too long, and God himself becomes inaccessible, the people just fetch him back. Worship becomes a feast that the community gives itself, a festival of self-affirmation. Instead of being worship of God, it becomes a circle closed in on itself: eating, drinking and making merry. It is a kind of banal self-gratification. The narrative of the Golden Calf is a warning about any kind of self-initiated and self-seeking worship. Ultimately it is no longer concerned with God but with giving oneself a nice little alternative world, manufactured from one's own resources.[10]

Ratzinger's fundamental objections to what I may call the spirit of the new liturgy lie in what he sees as its human-centered frenetic business, which instead of opening us out to God closes us in on ourselves. He believes that behind this phenomenon lies a whole raft of disastrous cultural, sociological and aesthetic convergences

---

10. Ratzinger, *Spirit of the Liturgy*, 23.

linked to the time in which the liturgical reforms were carried out, but also, and perhaps more importantly, a catastrophic theological mistake. Twentieth-century theologies of the Eucharist, he believes, have placed excessive emphasis on the paradigmatic character of the Last Supper, and hence have constructed liturgical practice round the mistaken notion that the fundamental form of the Eucharist as that of a meal, in the process underplaying the cosmic, redemptive, and sacrificial character of the Mass. Calvary and the empty tomb, rather than the Upper Room, are the symbolic locations of Christian liturgy. This takes us to the heart of Ratzinger's theological reflection on the meaning of the Mass, and the roots of his unease with much in modern eucharistic celebration, and so it is worth teasing out rather carefully.

His most extended discussion of this question comes in a paper he published in 1977 on "Form and Content in the Eucharistic Celebration," reissued, in a slightly amplified form in 1981, in the remarkably rich little collection *The Feast of Faith*.[11] Ratzinger considers in this paper the attempt by Guardini and the other fathers of the liturgical movement to discern underneath all the rites and complexities of the Mass the master "form" which *informs* it, which is "as such, the key to what takes place in the Eucharist," and which would provide the key to its *reform*. Once discerned, this "form" could be used "to determine whether particular aspects were to be heightened or lightened. Thus the concept of form or structure, *Gestalt*, a hitherto unknown category entered the theological dialogue, clearly recognizable as a power for reform."[12]

Few had then doubted that the obvious key to this form was the fact that it had been instituted at the Last Supper, and took the form of a meal. "It seemed therefore that the Eucharist's basic structure was unequivocally that of a meal," and this was the position adopted by Guardini and most other theorists of liturgical reform from the 1930s onward. Immediately, however, the dogmatic theologians detected a problem. Was not this precisely the position Luther had adopted in renaming the Mass the Lord's Supper, and hence, was not this the view condemned at Trent? Did not an account of the Mass as in essence a meal reduce or obliterate its sacrificial character?

---

11. Ratzinger, *Feast of Faith*, 33–60, originally published as "Gestalt und Gehalt der eucharistischen Feier," *Internationale Katholische Zeitschrift Communio* 6 (1977), 385–96.

12. Ratzinger, *Feast of Faith*, 34.

According to Ratzinger, the response of German liturgists like Joseph
Pascher was to argue that we were dealing here with two different
levels of discourse. To call the Mass a sacrifice was "a dogmatic
statement referring to the hidden theological essence of what takes
place in it; to speak of the meal structure, on the other hand, was
to direct attention to the visible liturgical performance, in no way
denying the theological content defined by Trent. What was presented
liturgically in the structure of the meal could without difficulty
mediate what, dogmatically speaking, was a sacrifice."

In Ratzinger's judgment, this was a fudge, concealing a sort
of theological schizophrenia: if the structure of the liturgy was not
a mere ceremonial form, but "at its core an indispensable manifestation of its essential content," then the sacrificial character of the
Eucharist had to be more evident in its celebration than this account
permitted. The lack of clarity caused by this apparent separation
of dogmatic content and liturgical structure, even during the Council
itself, seemed to him "the central problem of the liturgical reform."
He suspected that thorough-going proponents of the "meal" view
did not in fact give any real meaning to the Church's teaching that
the Mass was a sacrifice, and he took a low view of attempts to meet
this difficulty by discerning symbols of sacrifice within the meal
structure itself, such as Pascher's suggestion that "the separation of
the bread and wine" represented, symbolically, "the fatal spilling
of Jesus' blood."

For Ratzinger the draconian solution to this problem was to
jettison the notion that the fundamental form of the Eucharist is in
fact that of a meal. He was building here on suggestions from the
liturgist Josef Andreas Jungmann, first, that the fundamental form of
the Eucharist after the Apostolic age (that is, when we first begin to
be able to say anything positive about its celebration), is not that of
meal, but of *eucharistia*, the prayer of thanksgiving. *Eucharistia* is what
the celebration is called from the earliest post-biblical sources, and
at all times in Christian history till the reformation, the prayer of
thanksgiving has been a more prominent feature of the external celebration than the meal aspect. Secondly, Ratzinger cited Jungmann in
support of the view that an examination of the patristic and medieval
literature on Eucharist reveals that, apart from 1 Corinthians 11
and direct discussions of it, the Eucharist is seldom or never referred

to in the tradition as a *supper* until the sixteenth-century reformers did so: after the Apostolic age, when the Eucharist was as a matter of fact embedded in a community meal, "the designation of the Eucharist as a meal," Ratzinger writes, "does not occur again until the sixteenth century."

I suspect in the semantic shift from "supper" to "meal" Ratzinger overstates his case: to look no further, the Corpus Christi antiphon *O Sacrum Convivium*, certainly describes the Eucharist as a meal, for that is one of the principal meanings of the word *convivium*, and can hardly be considered marginal to the tradition of Eucharistic reflection in the medieval Church. Be that as it may, he insists that "the *Eucharistic* thesis is able to put the dogmatic and liturgical levels in touch with each other," for the eucharistic thanksgiving is the form in which Jesus at his Last Supper attached sacrificial meaning to his death, and identified the elements of bread and wine with his flesh and blood given for the forgiveness of sins. Hence, the Eucharistic prayer is the fundamental form of the Eucharistic sacrifice, the *oblatio rationabilis* of which the Mass itself speaks. The notion of a verbal sacrifice is derived from pagan antiquity as well as from the Old Testament concept of the spiritual sacrifice, so the Eucharist is first and foremost, a prayer. The prayer of Jesus over the bread and wine at the Last Supper transforms the Passover Haggadah by applying it to his death: the eucharistic words of Jesus are the transformation of existence—and of death—into thanksgiving, and the words "this is my body, this is my blood, given for you" are derived both from the Temple sacrifices and from the sacrificial suffering of the Servant in Second Isaiah. Hence, the Canon of the Mass, derived from the Haggadah of Jesus, is "the true sacrifice, the word of the Word: in it speaks the one who, as Word, is life."[13] So, "the Eucharistic prayer is an entering into to prayer of Jesus himself, and provides a profoundly Trinitarian understanding of the nature of the Eucharistic sacrifice: it is the Church's entering in to the Logos, the Father's Word, into the Logos' self-surrender to the Father, which in the Cross, has also become the surrender of mankind to him." Moreover, on this privileging of the Eucharistic prayer as the essential form of the Mass, the meal

---

13. J. Ratzinger, *God is Near Us: The Eucharist the Heart of Life*, trans. H. Taylor (San Francisco: Ignatius Press, 2003) 42–55, quote at 51.

element is preserved, since the form of the eucharistic prayer is also "but not solely," the grace said before the sacred meal.

Ratzinger of course recognizes and emphasizes the centrality of the theme of nourishment in the Eucharist, and in his preaching and devotional writing is happy to emphasize it: so, in representative eucharistic homilies he can describe the Eucharist as the "Feast of Faith," "the Banquet of the Reconciled," and declare that "it is the royal privilege of the Christian to share in paschal fellowship with the Lord, in the Paschal Mystery. The Lord has made the first day of the week his own day, on which he comes to us, on which he spreads the table for us and invites us to share with him."[14] But he is equally concerned to limit the use of this meal symbolism as the theological key to the Eucharistic mystery as a whole: "the meal," he insists, "is subordinated to a larger whole and integrated into it."[15] Indeed, in employing the phrase "the Banquet of the Reconciled" Ratzinger seeks to limit the associations of the Eucharist with meals: because the Eucharist is the banquet of the reconciled—holy things for the Holy, the family meal of those who have "let themselves be reconciled by God, who have become members of his family and put themselves into his hands."[16] So the Eucharist is to be sharply distinguished from Jesus' table-fellowship with sinners during his life: those meals are *not* forerunners of the Eucharist. The Passover dimension of the Last Supper was crucial to Christian understanding of the meaning of the death of Jesus, and hence of the Eucharist, but the Passover meal, a once-a-year event, was not what Jesus commanded to be continued in the Church's breaking of bread, any more than was the Apostolic *agape*, to which the Eucharist at Corinth in the first Christian generation was attached.[17] So, with considerable daring, he asserts "The real mistake of those who attempt uncritically to deduce the Christian liturgy from the Last Supper lies in their failing to see this fundamental point: the Last Supper of Jesus is certainly the basis of all Christian liturgy, but in itself it is not yet Christian." We may therefore take the earlier suggestions of the liturgical movement and turn them on

---

14. Ratzinger, *God Is Near Us*, 103.

15. Ratzinger, *Feast of Faith*, 38–39.

16. Ratzinger, *God is Near Us*, 61.

17. Although he acknowledges in *Deus Caritas Est*, 14 the validity of calling the Eucharist "Agape."

their head: "the last Supper is the foundation of the dogmatic content of the Christian Eucharist, not of its liturgical form. The latter does not yet exist."[18]

He has returned to this theme in later writings, seeing in the evolution of the Mass away from the Supper and from the Apostolic *agape* not a falling away from primitive purity and simplicity, but the right and natural freeing of the Christian rite, with its immense Trinitarian significance and its sacrificial heart, from the historical contingencies which surrounded its origins. The emergence of the Mass rite, combining liturgy of the word and liturgy of sacrifice was thus the fulfillment of the whole of Israelite religion, both teaching and cult. "This new and all-encompassing form of worship could not be derived from the meal, but had to be defined through the interconnection of Temple and Synagogue, Word and sacrament, Cosmos and Liturgy."[19]

There is behind all this a characteristic insistence on the integrity of the tradition as a whole, a rejection of the idea of any rift between the Church and the Apostles or Christ. The actual shape of the unfolding tradition is the legitimate and right expression of Christ's will for his Church, hence his growing resistance to the idea of Vatican II as a drastic purification of the decadent forms of Christianity. And it will be evident that this specific questioning of one of the building blocks of modern liturgical reform places Ratzinger at right angles to a good deal of the most characteristic features of the post-conciliar liturgy. Once reject the paradigm of the meal as the interpretative key to the Mass, and the inner logic of many of the post-conciliar changes, from the reorientation of sanctuaries to the deliberate cultivation of community spirit in such institutions as the sign of peace, collapses. Ratzinger, incidentally, though insistent on the communal dimensions of Eucharistic union with Christ, nevertheless thinks "community," *Gemeinde*, as a theological category is a Protestant rather than a Catholic, concept, pointing out that it is a term barely used by the Council, and then without any consistency in what the term denotes.[20] In a word, he finds himself at odds with a good deal that

---

18. Ratzinger, *Feast of Faith*, 41.

19. Ratzinger, *Spirit of the Liturgy*, 78.

20. See the remarks in J. Ratzinger, *Principles of Catholic Theology: Building Stones for a Fundamental Theology*, trans. M. F. McCarthy (San Francisco: Ignatius Press, 1987), 288–89.

has been taken to be most characteristic of post-Conciliar liturgical practice. We now have a Pope profoundly unhappy about much of what goes on in our parish churches Sunday by Sunday.[21] I think I can best convey the essence of his position by considering three related issues: the notion of the "active participation" of everyone present at Mass, the role of silence in the Mass, and the position of the priest at the altar.

ACTIVE PARTICIPATION

Perhaps the most crucial single utterance in the whole of the documents of the Second Vatican Council occurs at paragraph 14 of the Council's constitution on the liturgy, *Sacrosanctum Concilium*. It runs like this:

> Mother Church earnestly desires that all the faithful should be led to that full, conscious and active participation in liturgical celebrations which is demanded by the very nature of the liturgy, and to which the Christian people . . . have a right and obligation by reason of their baptism.
>
> In the restoration and promotion of the sacred liturgy the full and active participation by all the people is the aim to be considered before all else . . . . Therefore, in all their apostolic activity, pastors of souls should energetically set about achieving it through the required pedagogy.[22]

Later in the document, in paragraph 30, this *participatio actuosa* is characterized and described in the following terms. "To promote active participation, the people should be encouraged to take part by means of acclamations, responses, psalms, antiphons, hymns, as well as by actions, gestures and bodily attitudes. And at the proper time a reverent silence should be observed."

"Full, conscious and active participation," pastoral energy and liturgical pedagogy: these were momentous notions. As anyone who has lived through the two generations of change which flowed from these paragraphs knows, they were to have revolutionary implications for the character and celebration of Catholic liturgy and sacraments,

---

21. See Benedict XVI, *Letter to the Bishops that accompanies the Motu Proprio Summorum Pontificum (7 July 2007):* "in many places celebrations were not faithful to the prescriptions of the new Missal, but the latter actually was understood as authorizing or even requiring creativity, which frequently led to deformations of the liturgy which were hard to bear."

22. SC, 14.

for in accordance with them both rites and texts were revised and simplified so that the people "should be able to understand them with ease and take part in them fully, actively, and as a community," and the Mass itself became an altogether more vocal and activity centered event.

We are only now, I think, beginning to be in a position to draw up a balance sheet of loss and gain from these changes, which were based on the assumption that the mysteries celebrated in the sacraments could or should be "understood with ease," that the liturgy was an activity concerned primarily with pedagogy, that liturgical rites should be "short, clear and free from useless repetitions," or that "full, conscious and active participation" in worship and sacraments inevitably involved ritual regimentation, with everybody doing or saying or listening to the same things, at the same moment, all the time.

Pope Benedict believes that all this is destructive of true worship. The liturgy is meant to still and calm human activity, to allow God to be God, to quiet our chatter in favor of attention to the Word of God, in reflection on the scripture, in which Christ too is present, and in our sacramental encounter, in adoration and communion, with the great self-gift of the Word incarnate in the Blessed Sacrament. So excessive business, and too much talk, even holy talk, subvert the essence of the Mass. The call for instant accessibility is a mistake and a misunderstanding, which has dumbed-down the mystery we celebrate, and left us with a banal, thin and inadequate language of prayer. He deplores the "theatricalization" of liturgy by the introduction of too many actions, too many people, too much business. He rejects especially the value of improvisation and spontaneity, as contradicting the universal character of liturgy, and as subjecting congregations to the often lamentably deficient talents of those doing the improvising. As he has said, "Only respect for the liturgy's fundamental un-spontaneity and pre-existing identity can give us what we hope for: the feast in which the great reality comes to us which we ourselves do not manufacture but receive as a gift."[23] He doubts the value of offertory processions, the kiss of peace (which disrupts the adoring silence of communion) and even the desirability

---

23. Ratzinger, *Spirit of the Liturgy*, 168.

of the invariable recitation of the Eucharistic Prayers aloud. He considers that it would deepen our awareness that the Mass was more than a meal celebrating and consolidating community if we more often abstained from communion—maybe by discontinuing the communion of the faithful on Good Friday. He deplores the disappearance of the magnificent repertoire of European liturgical music and its replacement with vulgar and trivialized "utility music," often derived from a profane and secularizing culture which he believes is incompatible with the Gospel. In part, his objection here is unashamedly elitist—he thinks most modern liturgical music is banal, and that we have wantonly thrown away the highest fruits of European culture in favor of what is cheapest and most ephemeral. He has commented sarcastically that "It is strange, that in their legitimate delight in the new openness to other cultures, many people seem to have forgotten that the countries of Europe also have a musical inheritance which . . . has sprung from the very heart of the Church and her faith."[24]

ROLE OF SILENCE

Hence he offers an explanation of "active participation," which while hardly plausible as an account of the intentions of the drafters of *Sacrosanctum Concilium*, goes to the heart of his own liturgical convictions. The phrase *actuosa participatio*, he argues, emphatically does not mean participation in many acts. Rather, it means a deeper entry by everyone present into the one great action of the liturgy, its only real action, which is Christ's self-giving on the cross. For Ratzinger, Article 30 of *Sacrosanctum Concilium* does not mean we should all be active at Mass all the time. Quite the contrary. With its mention of bodily gesture and of silence as well as words and activity as modes of participation, the Council suggests, he maintains, that we can best enter into the action of the Mass by a recollected silence, and by traditional gestures of self-offering and adoration—the sign of the cross, folded hands, reverent kneeling. And above all silence, silence by the people *and* silence by the priest: he has repeatedly argued that it would be a good thing if the Eucharistic prayer were not always

---

24. Ratzinger, *Feast of Faith*, 125.

recited aloud. Instead, the priest might simply recite aloud the opening words of each paragraph, so that the laity are able to identify
the point in the prayer he has reached. They can then follow in their
missals and in their hearts, reverently internalizing in silence the
meaning of the prayer, in a way impossible when they have to listen to
the priest reciting aloud words which in any case threaten to lose their
impact from over-familiarity and boredom.

POSITION OF PRIEST AT THE ALTAR

Pope Benedict's views on the position of the priest at the altar are in
line with all this, and above all here we can see one of the practical
workings-out of his privileging of the Eucharistic prayer over the
sharing of food in the Mass. For twenty years, he has argued that the
spread of the celebration of Mass *versus populum*, facing the people,
is an unfortunate error. Derived from the currency of the meal paradigm, it was not in fact ordered by the Council, and rests, he believes,
on bad historical scholarship, bad theology, and bad social anthropology. As we have seen, Guardini had pioneered this form of celebration
as a means of restoring among his students a sense of the reality
and immediacy of their involvement in the liturgy, but no one antici-
pated its universal adoption in the wake of the Council, and the
reconstruction and reordering of most Catholic churches to make any
other form of celebration impossible. The rationale for this development will be familiar to all of you. Here is how Cardinal Ratzinger
described it in 2000.

> The Eucharist, so it was said, had to be celebrated *versus populum*. The altar,
> as can be seen in the normative model of St. Peter's, had to be positioned
> in such a way that the priest and people looked at each other and formed
> together the circle of the celebrating community. This alone, so it was
> said, was compatible with the meaning of the Christian liturgy, with the
> requirement of active participation. This alone conformed to the primor-
> dial model of the Last Supper.

All of this, he believes, is founded in misunderstanding. As
we have seen, he does not consider that the Mass is properly understood primarily as a meal, and hence, the physical dispositions for a
meal can have no normative function in the liturgy. In any case, meals

in antiquity did not resemble, or mandate, celebration *versus populum*. At the last supper, Jesus did not face the apostles, but in the classical manner must have lain to one side of the loop of a u-shaped table. The Pope at the altar of St Peter's does indeed stand facing the people, but this is because St. Peter's, unlike the majority of ancient churches, is orientated West East, not East West, and so the Pope in standing behind the altar, faces East, the universal position for both priest and people during the Eucharistic Prayer in the early church. This eastward facing position for the priest is not a matter of standing back to the people, but of everyone, including the priest, facing the same way, towards the rising Sun which symbolizes the risen Christ, the Second Coming, and the eschatological dimension of the Eucharist. In this gesture, the Church expresses the true form of the Mass, the *eucharistia*, confesses the sovereignty of God, and expresses her hope and conviction that the Eucharist opens outwards towards eternity. She acknowledges the incompleteness of our salvation here, and displays her yearning for the return of our Savior. By contrast, the closed circle of the community when priest and people face each other across the altar is in his view a closing down against the transcendent God, a centeredness on ourselves and our self-created community which represents a break with the eschatological openness symbolized by the orientation of two millennia of Christian celebration. So he says is reordering, he insists "not only signifies a new external arrangement of the places dedicated to the liturgy, but also brings with it a new idea of the essence of the liturgy, the liturgy as a communal meal."[25]

> The turning of the priest to the people has turned the community into a self-enclosed circle. In its outward form it no longer opens out towards what is ahead and above, but is closed in on itself. . . . [Whereas in the past, by facing east at Mass] They did not close themselves into a circle; they did not gaze at one another; but as the pilgrim people of God they set off for the *Oriens*, for the Christ who comes to meet us.[26]

In the light of these strong opinions of Cardinal Ratzinger, what is Pope Benedict XVI likely to do to remedy what he perceives as this great breach in the Catholic memory? We have a Pope who has made clear his strong and controversial views on many contested

---

25. Ratzinger, *Spirit of the Liturgy*, 77.
26. Ratzinger, *Spirit of the Liturgy*, 80.

aspects of Catholic worship, and these include a decisive rejection
of types of music, art, and language which in his view are Trojan
horses, smuggling into Christian worship values deeply inimical to it.
If the Eucharist is the Church's entrance into the rational worship
of the Logos, everything in the liturgy must reflect the coherence and
enhancement of meaning which the Logos brings. Hence, his rejection of rock music–and many kinds of ethnic music—in Catholic
worship, for they represent the chaotic and elemental triumph of the
Dionysian over the harmony of Apollo/Christ. He believes that the
Tridentine Mass, whatever the difficulties of comprehension and
participation it presented, embodied fundamental Christian percep-
tions undervalued or ignored in modern Catholic worship: and
he wishes to see the return of a Eucharistic Prayer recited silently in
whole or in part, and the celebration of Mass with both priest and
people facing east.

Not much of this, it seems, is likely to become papal policy:
after the sometimes hectic energy of his predecessor, Benedict XVI
has proved gratifyingly inert as a Pope. He has more than once
indicated his sensitivity to the dangers of liturgical fatigue among the
laity, and he has said that constant change, even change back toward
the traditional ways of doing things, can be very destructive. The
liturgy is about stability and openness towards eternity, not about
restless innovation or the restoration of the past. Certainly, he believes
that there is an urgent need to correct abuses in Catholic worship: at
his inauguration Mass, loudspeakers issued warnings against non-
Catholics in St. Peter's square taking communion, and lectured
Catholics on the proper posture and frame of mind for devout and
fruitful reception. The encyclical *Ecclesia in Eucharistia* which he
helped John Paul II draft speaks rather ominously of "juridical
interventions" to correct liturgical abuse, and in his inaugural address
to the cardinals he called on Catholics everywhere to demonstrate
their Eucharistic faith in the "solemnity and correctness" of their
eucharistic celebrations. But the interventions of *Vox Clara* over the
translations of the Sacramentary suggest the limited nature of what
may have been in mind here. With his Motu Proprio *Summorum
Pontificum*, Benedict has now lifted the restrictions on the celebration
of the Tridentine liturgy, restrictions which, as we have seen, for him

embody a deep and disastrous rupture in the continuity of Catholic tradition, and a scarring of the Church's memory.

You may recall that among the disastrous consequences which Ratzinger the theologian saw flowing from the imposition of the new liturgy was the fact that it rested not on immemorial tradition, on the liturgy as the received product of two millennia of the Church's lived experience, but instead, derived its binding force from a juridical act of the Pope: in the imposition of the Missal of Paul VI, Ratzinger saw the tradition set aside in the name of a liturgy invented by scholars and imposed by arbitrary and irresponsible papal command, or as he says, living development set aside in favor of "erudite work and juridical authority." It is a paradox that a man universally seen as the chief defender of and apologist for a strongly centralizing papal authority should feel so deeply that that the exercise of that authority under Paul VI had created a disastrous hiatus in the continuity of the tradition, from the evil consequences of which the Church is still suffering. Ratzinger the theologian understands the nature of tradition as an organic cumulative growth, a plant unfolding, not a machine constructed, and possessing an inherent authority and identity deeper than and prior to the exercise of any hierarchical jurisdiction, however much the instincts of Ratzinger the curial official might be thought to be at odds with that perception. In his book on the *Spirit of the Liturgy*, in 2000, he even spelled out the limits on the Pope's right to change the liturgy. In the history of the Western Church, he remarked that

. . . the Pope more and more clearly took over responsibility for liturgical legislation, thus providing a juridical authority for the continuing formation of the liturgy. The more vigorously the primacy was displayed, the more the question came up about the limits and extent of this authority . . . . After the Second Vatican Council, the impression arose that the Pope really could do anything in liturgical matters, especially if he were acting on the mandate of an ecumenical council. Eventually the idea of the given-ness of the liturgy, the fact that one cannot do with it what one will, faded from the public consciousness of the West. In fact, the First Vatican Council had in no way defined the Pope as an absolute monarch. On the contrary, it presented him as the guarantee of obedience to the revealed Word. The Pope's authority is bound to the tradition of faith, and that also applies to the liturgy. It is not manufactured by the authorities. Even the

Pope can only be the humble servant of its lawful development and abiding integrity and identity.[27]

We are accustomed to think of Joseph Ratzinger as an apologist for central authority and papal power. It is salutary, and ironic, to reflect that here, in the central prayer and sacramental life of the Church, he recognizes a more fundamental dimension of Catholicism, which takes precedence over mere authority, and demands our deeper loyalty.

---

27. Ratzinger, *Spirit of the Liturgy*, 165–166.

Chapter 2

Rhetoric of Salvation: The Origins of Latin as the Language of the Roman Liturgy

Uwe Michael Lang

Liturgical Language

Language is more than just a means of communication; it is also a medium of expression. Human speech is not just a utilitarian instrument that serves to communicate facts, and should do so in the most simple and efficient manner. It is also the means of expressing the workings of our mind in a way that involves our whole personality.[1]

Language is also the medium in which we express religious thoughts and experiences. We are conscious of the transcendence of the divine and, at the same time, of its presence—a presence that is both real and incomprehensible. There are extreme forms of expressing this experience: "speaking in tongues" and "mystical silence." Speaking in tongues, or *glossolalia* a phenomenon familiar to us from Saint Paul's *First Letter to the Corinthians* and has had an astonishing revival for the last hundred years in the charismatic movements; it also known also in other religion traditions, for example, the Oracle of Delphi. *Glossolalia* makes human communication impossible; the person who speaks "in tongues" can only be understood with the help of an interpreter. Saint Paul clearly has reservations about *glossolia* and prefers "prophecy," because this is in the service of charity and builds

---

1. Thus C. Mohrmann, *Liturgical Latin: Its Origins and Character. Three Lectures* (London: Burns & Oates, 1959), 1-26, with reference to Ferdinand de Saussure and the Geneva school of linguistics.

up the church (1 Corinthians 14). In "mystical silence," human communication is excluded as well, as in the experience Saint Augustine and his mother Saint Monica shared at Ostia, described in book nine of the *Confessions*.[2]

"Sacred language" does not go as far *glossolalia* and mystical silence in excluding human communication completely, or at least attempting to do so. However, it reduces the element of comprehensibility in favor of other elements, notably that of expression. Christine Mohrmann proposes to see in sacred language, and in particular in its vocabulary, a specific way of organizing religious experience. She also argues that every form of belief in the supernatural, in the existence of a transcendent being, leads necessarily to adopting a form of sacred language in worship—just as a consistent secularism leads to rejecting any form of it.

Languages do not exist in a vacuum, but in the context of a structured system that is determined by a variety of factors (social, cultural, psychological etc.). Modern linguistics speaks of "contexts," "situations," "registers," "language games," "special languages," or "group languages." Sacred language is the medium of expression not just of individuals, but of a community living according to certain traditions. Its linguistic forms are handed down from generation to generation; they are often deliberately "stylized" and removed from contemporary language. We find a similar phenomenon in the field of literature, with the *Homerische Kunstsprache*, the stylized language of the Homeric epos with its consciously archaic and colorful word forms. The language of the *Iliad* and the *Odyssey*, which is also found in Hesiod and in later poetic inscriptions, was never a spoken language used in everyday life.[3]

With Mohrmann, we can name three characteristics of sacred or, as she also says, "hieratic" language:

1.   Sacred language is conservative; it shows tenacity in holding on to archaic linguistic forms. In the pagan Roman tradition, this characteristic was so pronounced that that for centuries prayers

---

2. Augustine, *Confessions*, IX,10,25: ed. J. J. O'Donnell, *Augustine, Confessions. Introduction, Text, and Commentary*, 3 vols. (Oxford: Clarendon Press, 1992), *ad loc.*

3. See Mohrmann, *Liturgical Latin*, 10–11. Cf. the seminal work by K. Meister, *Die Homerische Kunstsprache* (Leipzig: Jablonowski, 1921).

were used, while their meaning was not even understood by the priests who recited them. In the early Middle Ages, command of Latin was sometimes so poor that even the most crucial sacramental formulas were badly understood by priests and basic mistakes were made. In the middle of the eighth century, Saint Boniface found that Bavarian children had been baptized *in nomine patria et filia et spiritus sancti* and considered it necessary to readminister the sacrament.[4]

2.   Foreign elements are introduced in order to associate with ancient religious tradition; a case in point is the Hebrew Biblical vocabulary in the Latin use of Christians. Augustine has interesting observations on this in his *De doctrina christiana*: "In some cases, although they could be translated, the original form is preserved for the sake of its solemn authority (*propter sanctiorem auctoritatem*)," such as "amen" and "alleluia." Other words "are said to be incapable of being translated into another language. . . . This is especially true of interjections, which signify emotion, rather than an element of clearly conceived meaning"; he provides the example "osanna."[5]

3.   Sacred language uses rhetorical figures that are typical of oral style, such as parallelism and antithesis, rhythmic clausulae, rhyme, and alliteration.[6]

It is generally agreed that the text of the Eucharistic Prayer was relatively fluid in the first three centuries. Its exact wording was not yet fixed, and the celebrant had some room to improvise. However, as Allan Bouley notes in his study *From Freedom to Formula*, "Conventions governing the structure and content of improvised anaphoras are ascertainable in the second century and indicate that extempore prayer was not left merely to the whim of the minister. In the third century, and possibly even before, some anaphoral texts already existed in writing." Bouley speaks of an "atmosphere of

---

4. Cf. the letter of Pope Zacharias to Boniface, *Ep. 68*: Monumenta Germania Historica, Epistulae Selectae I, 141 (dated 1 July 746).

5. Augustine, *De doctrina christiana* II,34–35 (xi,16): ed. and trans. R.P.H. Green, Oxford Early Christian Texts (Oxford: Clarendon Press, 1995), 73.

6. See C. Mohrmann, "The Ever-Recurring Problem of Language in the Church," in *Études sur le latin des chrétiens*, 4 vols., Storia e letteratura 65, 87, 103, 143 (Roma: Edizioni di Storia e Letteratura, 1961–1977), vol. IV, 143–59, at 151–52.

controlled freedom,"[7] because concerns for orthodoxy limited the
celebrant's liberty to vary the texts of the prayer. This need became
particularly pressing during the doctrinal struggles of the fourth
century; hence this era saw the emergence of fixed Eucharistic
Prayers, such as the Roman Canon, the Anaphora of Saint John
Chrysostom and others. There is another important aspect of
this development, which is noted by Mohrmann: "notably in the
West, where free composition remained in vogue for a very long time
in certain liturgical prayers, it is precisely this system which leads
to a marked traditional prayer style."[8] The freedom to improvise
existed only in a framework of fixed elements of content and style,
which was, above all, biblically inspired. A similar phenomenon can
be observed in the earliest Greek epos: the freedom of individual
singers to improvise on the given material led to a stylized language.
In the liturgy, the early tradition of oral improvisation in prayer
helped to create a sacred style.

Mohrmann introduces a useful distinction between sacred
languages of a "primary" and a "secondary" kind. "Primary" sacred
languages were formed as such from the beginning, for example, the
language of the Greek oracles that was close to the *Kunstsprache* of the
Homeric epos. "Secondary" sacred languages have come to be experi-
enced as such only in the course of time. The languages used in
Christian worship would seem to fall under this category: Greek in
the Byzantine tradition; Syriac in the Patriarchate of Antioch and the
"Nestorian" Church of the East with its missions reaching to India
and China; Old Armenian; Old Georgian; Coptic; Old Ethiopian
(*Ge'ez*); Church Slavonic; not to forget the Elizabethan English of the
Book of Common Prayer and the German used in the Lutheran books
of worship (from the *Brandenburgisch-Nürnbergische Kirchenordnung* of
1533 to the *Lutherische Agende I* of 1955); and, of course, the Latin of
the Roman Rite and other Western liturgical traditions.

---

7. A. Bouley, *From Freedom to Formula: The Evolution of the Eucharistic Prayer from Oral
Improvisation to Written Texts*, Studies in Christian Antiquity 21 (Washington: Catholic
University of America Press, 1981), xv.

8. Mohrmann, *Liturgical Latin*, 24.

There are stylistic features in all these liturgical languages that separate them from the ordinary languages of the people.[9] This distance was often the result of linguistic developments in the common language that were not adopted in the liturgical language because of its conservative nature. However, in the case of Latin as the language of the Roman liturgy, a certain distance existed right from the beginning: the Romans did not speak in the style of the Canon or of the collects of the Mass. As soon as Greek was replaced by Latin in the Roman liturgy, a highly stylized medium of worship was created.

FROM GREEK TO LATIN: THE LANGUAGE OF THE ROMAN LITURGY

The prevailing language of the first Christian communities in Rome was Greek. This is evident from Saint Paul's letter to the Romans, and from the earliest Christian literary works that originated in Rome, for instance, the *First Letter of Clement*, the *Shepherd of Hermas* and the writings of Justin Martyr. In the first two centuries, there were several popes with Greek names, and Christian tomb inscriptions were written in Greek.[10] It would be reasonable to assume that, during this period, Greek was also the common language of the Roman liturgy. The situation was probably similar in other parts of the Western Empire; for instance, Irenaeus, Bishop of Lyon, who died around the year 200, wrote in Greek. The shift towards Latin began not in Rome, but in North Africa, where the "earliest known converts were Latin-speaking natives of the province rather than Greek-speaking immigrants."[11] By the middle of the third century, however,

---

9. *Pace* the comments made by Donald Trautman, Bishop of Erie and then-Chairman of the *United States Bishops' Conference Committee on Liturgy*, at a liturgical conference that "scholars have pointed out that the celebration of the Eucharist always followed the language of the people. There was no such thing in East or West as a sacred language." D. Trautman, "A Pastoral Deficit," in *The Tablet* of February 3, 2007, 8–9, at 8.

10. M. K. Lafferty, "Translating Faith from Greek to Latin: Romanitas and Christianitas in Late Fourth-Century Rome and Milan," in *Journal of Early Christian Studies* 11 (2003), 21–62, at 29, notes that epitaphs continued to be in Greek even for popes with Latin names, Urbanus, Pontianus, Fabianus, and Lucius. The exception is Pope Cornelius (d. 253), whose epitaph is in Latin. On the presence of Greek-speaking Christians in Rome, see C. P. Caspari, *Ungedruckte, unbeachtete und wenig beachtete Quellen zur Geschichte des Taufsymbols und der Glaubensregel*, 3 vols. (Christiania: Malling, 1866–1875), vol. III, 303–466, esp. 456–57.

11. Lafferty, *Translating Faith*, 29, n. 27, with reference to J. Rives, *Religion and Authority in Roman Carthage from Augustus to Constantine* (Oxford: Clarendon, 1995), 223–226.

a transition towards Latin can be noticed in the Roman Church as
well: members of the Roman clergy wrote to Cyprian of Carthage in
Latin; Latin was also the language in which Novatian composed his
De trinitate and other works, quoting from an existing Latin version
of the Bible.[12] In addition, the stream of immigrants from East to
Rome seems to have diminished in the second half of the third
century. This demographic change meant that the life of the Roman
church began to be increasingly shaped by native Latin speakers.

There is a passage from Marius Victorinus' *Adversus Arium*,
book II, written around 360, which is usually taken to indicate
that Greek continued to be used in the Roman liturgy until the
second half of the fourth century. Victorinus, writing in Rome in
Latin, quotes from a Eucharistic Prayer (*oratio oblationis*): σῶσον
περιούσιον λαόν, ζηλωτὴν καλῶν ἔργων "save the people of thine
own, zealous for good works," a phrase taken from Titus 2:14.[13]
However, this evidence should not be taken at face value. The context
for this quotation is Victorinus' defense of the Nicene ὁμοούσιος
against those who argue that the word οὐσία/*substantia* is not found
in Holy Scripture. He points to a similar use of language, that is,
compound adjectives ending on −ούσιος: first, the petition from the
Lord's Prayer, "Give us this day our daily bread (ἐπιούσιος ἄρτος;
then, Titus 2:14, where the redeemed are called λαὸς περιούσιος,
"a people for his own possession"; and, finally, the *oratio oblationis* as
quoted above.[14] In book I of *Adversus Arium*, Victorinus makes the
same argument and adduces the same texts, but here his quotation
from the Eucharistic prayer is in Latin: *munda tibi populum circumvi-
talem, aemulatorem bonorum operum*. Since the Latin word *circumvi-
talem* obviously does not help him to make his point, he adds the
explanation *circa tuam substantiam venientem*.[15] It does not seem clear

---

12. No mention is made here of the so-called *Traditio Apostolica*, attributed to Hippolytus
of Rome, because of uncertainties about its date, origin and authorship. The text can hardly
be used as a source for the early Roman liturgical tradition, see B. Steimer, *Vertex traditionis: Die
Gattung der altchristlichen Kirchenordnungen*, Beihefte zur Zeitschrift für die neutestamentliche
Wissenschaft 63 (Berlin/New York: de Gruyter, 1992), and P. F. Bradshaw, M. E. Johnson,
L. E. Philips, *The Apostolic Tradition: A Commentary*, Hermeneia (Minneapolis, MN: Fortress
Press, 2002).

13. Marius Victorinus, *Adversus Arium* II,8: CSEL 83,182–83.

14. This is a good example of the principle *ut legem credendi lex statuat supplicandi* later
formulated by Prosper of Aquitaine (+ 455); see DS 246.

15. Marius Victorinus, *Adversus Arium* I,30: CSEL 83,64.

to me whether the prayer cited by Marius Victorinus was actually said in Greek or in Latin, or perhaps in either language, in the various churches of Rome. The skilled rhetorician might have chosen to refer to a version of the prayer that had already fallen out of use by his time, in order to reinforce his argument in favor of the ὁμοούσιος. Moreover, it should be noted that the petition "save the people of thine own, zealous for good works" is echoed in the Prayers of the Faithful of the East Syrian rite,[16] but not in the later Roman rite.

Whatever we make of the complex evidence from Marius Victorinus, by the middle of the fourth century, the Latin language was widely used in the Roman liturgy. This emerges from an otherwise unknown author writing between 374 and 382. In his discussion of various exegetical questions, this author tells us that the Eucharistic prayer in Rome refers to Melchisedek as *summus sacerdos* — a title that is familiar to us from the Roman Canon of the Mass.[17] The intriguing remarks on the use of language in worship in Ambrosiaster's commentary on 1 Corinthians 14, which can be placed in the pontificate of Damasus (366–384), are also indicative of the transition from Greek to Latin.[18]

The most important source for the Roman Eucharistic Prayer in the late fourth century is Saint Ambrose of Milan. In his *De*

---

16. F. E. Brightman, *Liturgies Eastern and Western*, vol. I (Oxford: Clarendon Press, 1896), 264, l. 3.

17. Ps.-Augustine, *Quaestiones veteris ac novi testamenti*, 109,21: CSEL 50,268. A. Baumstark, "Ein Übersetzungsfehler im Meßkanon," in *Studia catholica* 5 (1928), 378–82, and *Missale Romanum: Seine Entwicklung, ihre wichtigsten Urkunden und Probleme* (Eindhoven–Nijmegen: van Eupen, 1929), 13, argues that this is an erroneous translation from the original Greek text of the Canon, which would have followed the Septuagint text of Genesis 14:18, ἦν δὲ ἱερεὺς τοῦ θεοῦ τοῦ ὑψίστου, "he was priest of God the Most High." Baumstark conjectures that the Greek Canon would have read something like τὴν προσφορὰν Μελχισεδὲκ τοῦ δὲ ἱερέως τοῦ θεοῦ τοῦ ὑψίστου. The Latin translator would have mistaken the reference to Melchisedek as "the most high priest of God," hence the translation *quod tibi obtulit summus sacerdos tuus Melchisedech*. Baumstark's argument is ingenious, but there is evidence against it: the late fourth-century *Apostolic Constitutions*, VIII,12,23: SCh 336,188, also refer to Melchisedek as "high priest" (τὸν Μελχισεδὲκ ἀρχιερέα). This is indicated by B. Botte, *Le Canon de la messes romaine*, Textes et études liturgiques 2 (Louvain: Abbaye du Mont César, 1935), 42.

18. Ambrosiaster, *In Epistulas ad Corinthios* I,14: CSEL 81/2,149–63. This text would merit a detailed analysis, which cannot be done here; cf. the observations of Mohrmann, *Liturgical Latin*, 50: "Ambrosiaster has touched on the essential problem of the phenomenon of a foreign traditional liturgical language, which really turns on the conflict between religious expression and communication. . . . We have here a man who indeed advocates the use of Latin, but not without having deeply considered the problems attached to the use of a liturgical language nor without having put in a plea for the rights of a foreign sacral language."

sacramentis, a series of catecheses for the newly baptized that was held around 390, Ambrose quotes extensively from the Eucharistic Prayer employed at that time in his city. The passages quoted are earlier forms of the prayers *Quam oblationem, Qui pridie, Unde et memores, Supra quae,* and *Supplices te rogamus.* Elsewhere in *De sacramentis,* the Bishop of Milan emphasizes that he desires to follow the use of the Roman Church in everything; for this reason, we can safely assume that the same Eucharistic Prayer he quotes was also used in Rome.[19] There also is evidence for the Roman Canon in the sermons of Zeno, Bishop of Verona from 362 to 372, which would testify to the geographical spread of this Eucharistic Prayer.[20]

The wording of the prayers cited by Ambrose is different from the Canon that was settled by Saint Gregory the Great in the late sixth century and has come down to us, with only a few minor changes, in the oldest extant liturgical books, especially the Old Gelasian Sacramentary, dating from the middle of the eighth century, but believed to reflect the liturgical use of the middle of the seventh century. The differences between Ambrose's Eucharistic Prayer and the Gregorian Canon are far less remarkable than their similarities, given that the almost three hundred years lying between the two texts were a period of intense liturgical development.[21]

---

19. Ambrose, *De sacramentis* III,1,5: CSEL 73,40: *ecclesia Romana . . . cuius typum in omnibus sequimur et formam . . . . In omnibus cupio sequi ecclesiam Romanam.* Explaining the baptismal ceremonies in Milan, Ambrose pays particular attention to the main point where he differs from Roman usage, that is, in the washing of the feet of the candidates. Liturgical scholars tended to emphasise the disparate nature of the Roman Canon and have used the methods of higher criticism to explain the origin and development of its prayers. With a view to such hypothetical reconstructions (including his own), Anton Baumstark published a remarkable retraction: "Das 'Problem' des römischen Messkanons, eine Retractatio auf geistesgeschichtlichem Hintergrund," in *Ephemerides liturgicae* 53 (1939), 204–43. Baumstark even considers it possible that the Latin text of the Canon, possibly the translation of a Greek original, was introduced in Rome not long after the pontificate of Cornelius, the first pope whose epitaph was composed in Latin and the last pope whose name was included among the saints invoked in the *Communicantes* section of the Canon. However, it would seem very unlikely that a Latin Eucharistic prayer was introduced into the Roman liturgy as early as the middle of the third century, as observed by C. Mohrmann, "Quelques observations sur l'évolution stylistique du Canon de la Messe romain," *Études sur le latin des chrétiens,* vol. III, 227–44, at 230–31. Mohrmann agrees with Baumstark and Callewaert that the Canon, in its definitive form, is distinctively Roman.

20. G. Jeanes, "Early Latin Parallels to the Roman Canon? Possible References to a Eucharistic Prayer in Zeno of Verona," in *Journal of Theological Studies* 37 (1986), 427–31.

21. Ambrose, *De sacramentis* IV,5,21–22; 6,26–27: CSEL 73,55 and 57; see J. Beumer, „Die ältesten Zeugnisse für die römische Eucharistiefeier bei Ambrosius von Mailand," in *Zeitschrift*

According to Optatus of Milevis, writing in the 360s, there were more than forty churches in Rome already before the Constantinian settlement.[22] Hence it would be reasonable to assume that there were Latin-speaking communities in the third century, if not before. Parts of the liturgy were already in Latin before the second half of the fourth century, notably the readings from scripture. By the late fourth century, the ancient version of the psalms used in the liturgy had acquired such a sacrosanct status that Saint Jerome only revised it with caution. Later he translated the Psalter from the Hebrew, as he said, not for liturgical purposes, but to provide a text for scholarship and controversy.[23] It is also likely that the baptismal liturgy was celebrated in Latin at an early stage.

Mohrmann introduces a useful distinction between, first, "purely prayer texts," where language is, above all, a medium of expression, secondly, texts that are "destined to be read, the Epistle and Gospel," and, thirdly, "confessional texts," such as the creed. In "prayer texts we are concerned with expressional form; in the others, primarily with forms of communication."[24] Recent research on language and ritual, such as the work of Catherine Bell, confirms Mohrmann's insight that language has different functions in different parts of the liturgy, which go beyond mere communication or information.[25] These theoretical reflections help us to understand the development of the early Roman liturgy: those parts where the element of communication was prevalent, such the Scripture readings, were translated earlier, whereas the Eucharistic prayer continued to be said in Greek for a much longer period.

---

für katholische Theologie 95 (1973), 311–24; Bouley, *From Freedom to Formula*, 200–15. The term „canon" seems to have been used first in the sixth century; the oldest known reference to „*prex canonica*" is Pope Vigilius, *Ep. ad Profuturum*, 5: PL 69,18; see Bouley, *From Freedom to Formula*, 208–209.

22. Optatus, *Contra Parmenidem*, II,4: CSEL 26,39.

23. See Jerome's two prefaces to the Psalter in *Biblia sacra iuxta Vulgatam versionem*, ed. R. Weber and R. Gryson (Stuttgart: Deutsche Bibelgesellschaft, fourth edition, 1994), 767–69; cf. C. Mohrmann, "The New Latin Psalter: Its Diction and Style," in *Études sur le latin des chrétiens*, vol. II, 109–31, at 110–11.

24. Mohrmann, *Liturgical Latin*, 75, detects this distinction already in Christian antiquity.

25. C. Bell, *Ritual: Perspectives and Dimensions* (New York: Oxford University Press, 1997).

To sum up, the transition from Greek to Latin in the Roman liturgy happened slowly and gradually.[26] This development took more than a hundred years and that it was completed in the pontificate of Damasus, who died in 384. From then on, the liturgy in Rome was mostly celebrated in Latin, with the exception of a few reminders of the older use, such as the Greek readings in the Papal Mass. As for the intriguing question why the move toward a Latin liturgy in Rome occurred rather late, various answers have been given, and there is something to be said for all of them. The German liturgist Theodor Klauser attributed this to the general conservatism of Romans and their tenacity in keeping religious traditions. This is certainly true for the Roman Church as well. According to the American Benedictine Allan Bouley, the need for a carefully formulated orthodox language, especially during the Arian crisis of the fourth century, provided the leaven for creating an official Latin form of the prayers of the Mass. Bouley's thesis that it was the need for orthodox prayers that advanced the creation of Latin rites is certainly borne out by the efforts of Saint Ambrose to formulate the Catholic faith in liturgical hymns and prayers against the current Arianism of the barbarian tribes. Christine Mohrmann argues that the formation of liturgical Latin became possible only after the Peace of the Church, established by the Emperor Constantine. There was no longer such a strong need for Christian communities to define themselves in opposition to the surrounding pagan culture. Their new secure status gave the local churches in the West greater freedom to draw, at least for purposes of style, not for contents, on the religious heritage of Rome for the development of their liturgies.

Peter Burke, a major contributor to the relatively new academic discipline of "sociolinguistics" or "social history of language," has alerted us to the fact that "the choice of one language over

---

26. Mohrmann, *Liturgical Latin*, 50–53; J. A. Jungmann, *Missarum Sollemnia: Eine genetische Erklärung der römischen Messe*, 2 vols. (Wien: Herder, 5th edn, 1962), vol. I, 65–66; Bouley, *From Freedom to Formula*, 203–07; *pace* T. Klauser, „Der Übergang der römischen Kirche von der griechischen zur lateinischen Liturgiesprache," in *Miscellanea Giovanni Mercati: 1. Bibbia, letteratura cristiana antica*, Studi e testi 121 (Città del Vaticano: Biblioteca Apostolica Vaticana, 1946), 467–82. Against Klauser's hypothesis that the Latin Canon of the Mass came from Milan, see C. Mohrmann, "*Rationabilis–λογικός*," *Études sur le latin des chrétiens*, vol. I, 179–87.

another is never a neutral or transparent one."[27] Hence, it is important to consider the transition from Greek to Latin in the Roman liturgy in its historical, social and cultural context. The formation of a Latin liturgical language should be seen as part of a wide-ranging effort to Christianize Roman culture. The pontificate of Damasus was a milestone on the way toward a Christian *Latinitas*, and it is significant that the shift towards a Latin liturgy in Rome was completed during his reign. The importance of Damasus' own contribution is disputed by scholars; Klauser credits him with the initiative to determine Latin as the "new" liturgical language, whereas Bernard Botte and Charles Pietri argue more convincingly that Damasus' pontificate saw the conclusion of a development that had been underway for a considerable time.[28] In the second half of the fourth century, the leading bishops in Italy, above all Damasus in Rome and Ambrose in Milan, were striving to Christianize the culture of their day. In the city of Rome, there was a strong pagan presence, and especially the aristocracy continued to adhere to pagan customs, even if they had become nominal Christians.[29] Rome was no longer the center of political power, but its culture continued to have an hold on the thought-world of its elite; In fact the fourth century is now considered a period of literary renaissance, with a renewed interest in the "classics" of Roman poetry and prose. There was even a revival of Latin in the Eastern half of the Empire. The Emperors of the fourth century certainly cultivated this *Latinitas*.[30] With characteristic tenacity, Rome kept its ancient traditions.

---

27. Lafferty, *Translating Faith from Greek to Latin*, 24, referring to P. Burke, *The Art of Conversation* (Ithaca: Cornell University Press, 1993).

28. A decisive role in the introduction of the Latin liturgy is attributed to Pope Damasus by Klauser, *Der Übergang der römischen Kirche*, and M. H. Shepherd, "The Liturgical Reform of Damasus I," in P. Granfield–J. A. Jungmann (ed.), *Kyriakon: Festschrift Johannes Quasten*, 2 vols. (Münster: Aschendorff, 1970), vol. II, 847–63. For a different analysis with less emphasis on Damasus' contribution, see B. Botte, "Histoire des prières de l'ordinaire de la messe," in B. Botte–C. Mohrmann (ed.), *L'ordinaire de la messe*, Études liturgiques 2 (Paris: Cerf, 1953), 17, and C. Pietri, "Damase évêque de Rome," in *Saecularia Damasiana: Atti del convegno internazionale per il XVI centenario della morte di Papa Damaso I (11–12-384–10/12–12-1984)*, Studi di antichità cristiana 39 (Città del Vaticano: Pontificio Istituto di Archeologia Cristiana, 1986), 29–58, at 50.

29. On the difficulty of defining Christian identity in the late Roman Empire, see R. Marcus, *The End of Ancient Christianity* (Cambridge: Cambridge University Press, 1990), 19–83.

30. See Lafferty, *Translating Faith from Greek to Latin*, 26–28, with references to A. Cameron, "Latin Revival of the Fourth Century," in W. Treadgold (ed.), *Renaissances before the Renaissance: Cultural Revivals of Late Antiquity and the Middle Ages* (Stanford: Stanford

The popes of the late fourth century, above all Damasus, made a conscious and comprehensive attempt to appropriate the symbols of Roman civilization for the Christian faith. Part of this attempt was the appropriation of public space through extensive building projects. After the Emperors of the Constantinian dynasty had taken the lead with the monumental basilicas of the Lateran and St. Peter's, as well as the cemetery basilicas outside the city walls, the popes continued this building program that was to make Rome into a city dominated by churches. Perhaps the most prestigious project was the construction of a new basilica dedicated to Saint Paul's on the *Via Ostiensis*, replacing the small Constantinian edifice by a new church that would match the size of St. Peter's.[31] Another important aspect was the appropriation of public time with a cycle of Christian feasts throughout the year replacing pagan celebrations, as with the Philocalian calendar of the year 354. The formation of liturgical Latin was part of this effort to evangelize Roman culture and attract the influential elites of the Empire to the Christian faith. It would not be accurate to describe this process as an adoption of the "vernacular" language in the liturgy. The Latin of the Roman Canon, of the collects and prefaces of the Mass was removed from idiom of the ordinary people. It was a highly stylized language that would have been difficult to understand by the average Roman Christian of the fifth century or later, given especially that the rate of literacy was very low compared to our times.[32] And we should also remember that the adoption of *Latinitas* in the West made the liturgy more accessible to the people of Milan or Rome, but not necessarily to those whose native language was Celtic or Gothic.

It was by no means a foregone conclusion that the whole Western church would adopt Latin as its liturgical language. There were native languages in the Western Empire, such as Gothic, Celtic,

University Press, 1984), 42–58, and C. W. Hedrick, *History and Silence: Purge and Rehabilitation of Memory in Late Antiquity* (Austin: University of Texas Press, 2000).

31. See now the beautifully illustrated volume of H. Brandenburg, *Die frühchristlichen Kirchen in Rom* (Regensburg: Schnell und Steiner, 2nd edn, 2005).

32. Mohrmann, *Liturgical Latin*, 53-54; see also M. Klöckener, "Zeitgemäßes Beten. Meßorationen als Zeugnisse einer sich wandelnden Kultur und Spiritualität," in R. Meßner–E. Nagel–R. Pacik (ed.), *Bewahren und Erneuern. Studien zur Meßliturgie. Festschrift für Hans Bernhard Meyer SJ zum 70. Geburtstag*, Innsbrucker theologische Studien 42 (Innsbruck–Wien: Tyrolia, 1995), 114–142, at 126–127.

Iberic, or Punic. It is possible to imagine a Western Church with
local languages in its liturgy, as in the East, where, in addition to
Greek, Syriac, Coptic, Armenian, Georgian, and Ethiopic was used.
However, the situation in the West was fundamentally different;
the centralizing force of the Roman church was such that Latin
became the only liturgical language. This was an important factor in
furthering ecclesiastical, cultural, and political unity. *Latinitas* became
one of the defining characteristics of Western Europe.[33]

Characteristics of Liturgical Latin

In the third part of this paper, I shall discuss a number of characteristics of liturgical Latin, taking my examples from the Canon of the
Mass and from one collect, which I have chosen for its antiquity.

The stylistic features of the Roman Canon can be seen best if
we compare the earlier form attested in Ambrose's *De sacramentis* with
the established text from the Old Gelasian Sacramentary (see Table
2.1).[34] One notable development in the Gelasian Canon is the replacement of paratactic constructions by a relative clause or an ablative
absolute. In Ambrose, the individual sections of the Eucharistic prayer
are not grammatically connected with the preceding one. In the later
revision, however, these sections were connected with relative clauses.
For instance, *Fac nobis hanc oblationem scriptam, rationabilem, acceptabilem* was changed to *Quam oblationem tu, Deus, in omnibus, quaesu-
mus, benedictam, adscriptam, ratam, rationabilem acceptabilemque facere
digneris* ("Vouchsafe, O God, we beseech thee, in all things to make
this oblation blessed, approved and accepted, a perfect and worthy
offering").[35] *Tu, Deus* and *in omnibus* are embellishments on stylistic

---

33. As Mohrmann, *The Ever The Ever-Recurring Problem of Language in the Church*, 152,
notes, "liturgical Latin was not brought to these people as an isolated linguistic phenomenon.
At the same time, Latin was introduced as the language of higher civilisation, of the schools, and
of ecclesiastical and governmental administration. Thus all through the Middle Ages, Latin as the
language of the sacred liturgy was supported by Latin as the second language of the cultural élite.
The first real opposition to liturgical Latin coincided with the end of medieval Latin as a 'living
second language,' which was replaced by a truly 'dead' language, the Latin of the humanists."

34. This analysis is based on Mohrmann, *Liturgical Latin*, 58-62, and G. G. Willis (†), *A
History of Early Roman Liturgy to the Death of Pope Gregory the Great*, Henry Bradshaw Society,
Subsidia 1 (London: Boydell Press, 1994), 23–32.

35. The English version of the Roman Canon used here is the one found in the Anglican Use
Book of Divine Worship, which is approved for use in a number of Catholic parishes in the United
States: *The Book of Divine Worship* (Mt. Pocono, PA: Newman House Press, 2003).

grounds, which make the form of the prayer appear more rounded and graceful. The verb *dignare* is taken from curial style and often found in papal correspondence.[36]

Table 2.1

Ambrose of Milan, De sacramentis[37]	*Canon Romanus*[38]
Fac nobis hanc oblationem scriptam, rationabilem, acceptabilem, quod est figura corporis et sanguinis Domini nostri Iesu Christi.	Quam oblationem tu, Deus, in omnibus, quaesumus, benedictam, adscriptam, ratam, rationabilem acceptabilemque facere digneris, ut nobis corpus et sanguis fiat dilectissimi Filii tui Domini Dei nostri Iesu Christi.
Qui pridie quam pateretur, in sanctis manibus suis accepit panem, respexit ad caelum, ad te, sancte Pater omnipotens aeterne Deus, gratias agens benedixit, fregit, fractumque apostolis et discipulis suis tradidit dicens: Accipite et edite ex hoc omnes; hoc est enim corpus meum, quod pro multis confringetur. Similiter etiam calicem, postquam cenatum est, pridie quam pateretur, accepit, respexit ad caelum, ad te, sancte Pater omnipotens aeterne Deus, gratias agens benedixit, apostolis et discipulis suis tradidit dicens: Accipite et bibite ex hoc omnes ; hic est enim sanguis meus. quotienscumque hoc feceritis, totiens commemorationem mei facietis, donec iterum adveniam.	Qui pridie quam pateretur accepit panem in sanctas ac venerabiles manus suas elevatis oculis in caelum ad te Deum Patrem suum omnipotentem tibi gratias agens benedixit, fregit, dedit discipulis suis dicens: Accipite et manducate ex hoc omnes. Hoc est enim corpus meum. Simili modo, posteaquam cenatum est, accipiens et hunc praeclarum calicem in sanctas ac venerabiles manus suas, item tibi gratias agens benedixit, dedit discipulis suis dicens: Accipite et bibite ex eo omnes. Hic est enim calix sanguinis mei, novi et aeterni testamenti, mysterium fidei, qui pro vobis et pro multis effundetur in remissionem peccatorum. Haec quotiescumque feceritis, in mei memoriam facietis.

---

36. It has been translated here as "vouchsafe" here; etymologically, it is related to "deign," a word that was rejected in the new (much improved!) ICEL version of the Roman Canon; see A. Roche, "Search for Truth and Poetry," in *The Tablet* of August 5, 2006, 10–11, at 11: "Early in the process, we proposed that the priest should say: 'To us sinners also . . . deign to grant some share and fellowship with your holy apostles and martyrs.' 'Deign' was greeted with howls of derision from all sides: it was thought to belong to too formal a register for the liturgy. So we tried a much more colloquial version, 'please grant some share and fellowship.' This was judged too informal. So we finally settled on 'be pleased to grant,' which seems to fall between the two."

37. A. Hänggi–I. Pahl, *Prex eucharistica. Volumen I: Textus e variis liturgiis antiquioribus selecti*, Spicilegium Friburgense 12 (Freiburg/Schweiz: Universitätsverlag, third edition, 1998), 421–422.

38. Hänggi–Pahl, *Prex Eucharistia*, 433–435.

Ergo memores gloriosissimae eius passionis et ab inferis resurrectionis et in caelum ascensionis offerimus tibi hanc immaculatam hostiam, rationabilem hostiam, incruentam hostiam, hunc panem sanctum et calicem vitae aeternae.

Unde et memores sumus, Domine, nos tui servi sed et plebs tua sancta Christi Filii tui Domini Dei nostri tam beatae passionis nec non et ab inferis resurrectionis sed et in caelos gloriosae ascensionis offerimus praeclarae maiestati tuae de tuis donis ac datis hostiam puram, hostiam sanctam, hostiam immaculatam, panem sanctum vitae aeterna et calicem salutis perpetuae.

Et petimus et precamur, uti hanc oblationem suscipias in sublime altare tuum per manus angelorum tuorum, sicut suscipere dignatus es munera pueri tui iusti Abel et sacrificium patriarchae nostri Abrahae et quod tibi obtulit summus sacerdos Melchisedech.

Supra quae propitio ac sereno vultu respicere digneris et accepta habere, sicuti accepta habere dignatus es munera pueri tui iusti Abel et sacrificium patriarchae nostri Abrahae et quod tibi obtulit summus sacerdos tuus Melchisedech, sanctum sacrificium, immaculatam hostiam. Supplices te rogamus, omnipotens Deus, iube haec perferri per manus angeli tui in sublime altare tuum in conspectu divinae maiestatis tuae, ut quotquot ex hac altaris participatione sacrosanctum Filii tui corpus et sanguinem sumpserimus, omni benedictione caelesti et gratia repleamur. Per Christum Dominum nostrum.

There is another example for a simpler and more "popular" paratactic construction being exchanged for a more "formal" relative clause: where Ambrose has *Et petimus et precamur, uti hanc oblationem suscipias,* the received text of the Canon reads *Supra quae propitio ac sereno vultu respicere digneris et accepta habere* ("Vouchsafe to look upon them with a merciful and pleasant countenance; and to accept them"). The parataxis can also be replaced by an ablative absolute; thus *respexit in caelum* in Ambrose's Institution Narrative becomes *elevatis oculis in caelum* ("with eyes lifted up to heaven").

In the *Quam oblationem* prayer, we also can observe series of consecutive synonyms or near-synonyms. This is a characteristic of Roman euchological style that is already employed in Ambrose's earlier form of the Canon, for instance, *et petimus et precamur* ("we both ask and pray"). The doubling of the verb and the alliteration are typical of pagan prayers, where formulae such as *do dedicoque* ("I give and devote") occur frequently. The formula in Ambrose in fact an elegant one if compared with the common *precor quaesoque* ("I pray and beseech"), which is well attested in Livy, because it introduces some variation in meaning between the two verbs.[39] There are several examples of this stylistic feature in other parts of the Canon, for instance, in the section *Te igitur: supplices rogamus ac petimus; haec dona, haec munera, haec sancta sacrificia illibata; quam pacificare, custodire et regere digneris.*

A striking example for the use of adjectives with a similar meaning is found in Ambrose, where there are three epithets governing the substantive *oblationem: scriptam, rationabilem, acceptabilem.* In the later form of the prayer *Quam oblationem*, their number is increased to five: *benedictam, adscriptam, ratam, rationabilem, acceptabilemque.* This accumulation of adjectives that are virtually synonymous helps to make the language of the prayer more solemn and rhetorically effective. Note also the use of legal terms, such as *ratam* ("approved").[40] For further patterns of juridical style, Mohrmann points to the conjunctions *nec non et* and *sed et.* However, these are found in classical authors like Cicero, Virgil, Suetonius and Juvenal, and it would seem that they are simply a feature of later Latin rather than a borrowing from Roman legal language.

Another chain of adjectives is used in the anamnesis prayer after the consecration, which reads in Ambrose: *offerimus tibi hanc immaculatum hostiam, rationabilem hostiam, incruentam hostiam, hunc panem sanctum et calicem vitae aeternae.* The sequence of adjectives and the use of asyndeton are reminiscent of pagan Roman prayers.[41] In the Gelasian Canon, this phrase is modified to *offerimus praeclarae maiestati tuae de tuis donis ac datis hostiam puram, hostiam sanctam,*

---

39. On *precor quaesoque*, see F. Hickson, *Roman Prayer Language: Livy and the Aeneid of Virgil* (Stuttgart: Teubner, 1993), 49 and 77.

40. Mohrmann, *Liturgical Latin*, 60, observes: "This monumental verbosity coupled with juridical precision . . . was the typical form of expression of the old Roman prayer."

41. Lafferty, *Translating Faith from Greek to Latin*, 48–49, cites a prayer attributed by Livy to Scipio as he sets out to invade Africa: "make them come back home with me healthy and safe victors, having conquered the enemy, decorated with spoils, laden with booty, and making their triumph; give them the opportunity of taking vengeance on their enemies and foes (*salvos incolumesque victis perduellibus victores, spoliis decoratos, praeda onustos triumphantesque mecum domum reduces sistatis; inimicorum hostiumque ulciscendorum copiam faxitis*)"; Livy, *Ab Urbe Condita* 29, 27, 2–4.

hostiam immaculatam, panem sanctum vitae aeternae et calicem salutis perpetuae ("we offer unto thine excellent majesty of thine own gifts and bounty, the pure victim, the holy victim, the immaculate victim, the holy Bread of eternal life, and the Chalice of everlasting salvation"). There are several other interesting features in this revision: for instance, the simple *tibi* is replaced with *maiestati tuae* ("thy majesty"), derived from curial style. The phrase *de tuis donis ac datis*[42] has a parallel in the Anaphora of Saint John Chrysostom, in the anamnesis prayer after the Institution Narrative, "thine own of thine own (τὰ σὰ ἐκ τῶν σῶν) we offer unto thee on behalf of all and for all."[43] The older formula *hunc panem sanctum et calicem vitae aeternae* is replaced with the more balanced parallelism *panem sanctum vitae aeternae et calicem salutis perpetuae*.

A significant feature in the fully developed Roman Canon is its prose rhythm or *cursus*. According to the classical tradition of rhetoric, rhythm was an important factor in the structure and beauty of a prose text. Aristotle says that prose should not be metrical, but at the same time it should not be un-rhythmical either. What is without rhythm is "unlimited" and hence not pleasing to the classical ear; hence Aristotle stipulates that every part of the sentence should have a certain rhythm.[44] Cicero equally appreciates the function of rhythm in artistic prose, but he confines it to the most important parts of the colon, that is, the beginning and the end of a clause. In the Latin rhetorical tradition shaped by Cicero and Quintilian, the ending or *clausula*, became the most important part of a sentence to be constructed according to rhythmical principles.[45]

Most Church Fathers were trained in classical rhetoric and made use of its rules in their writings. Therefore, it is not surprising to find the use of rhythmic clausulae in the sermons and treatise of authors like Augustine or Leo the Great. Augustine also discusses the

---

42. The phrase appears to be inspired by 1 Chronicles 29:14: *tua sunt omnia et quae de manu tua accepimus dedimus tibi* (Vulgate).

43. Cf. Mohrmann, *Liturgical Latin*, 59.

44. Aristotle, *Rhetoric*, III,8: 1408b21–1409a24.

45. Cicero, *De oratore*, III,50,192; Quintilian, *Institutio oratoria*, IX,4,60–66.

use of *clausulae* in the fourth book of his *De doctrina christiana*, which is concerned with the way a preacher should make use of rhetoric.[46]

It was quite natural that the use of the *clausulae*, or *cursus* in the terminology of the Middle Ages, is found in the public prayer of the Church too. *Clausulae* are a stock feature of Roman liturgical composition from the late fourth century to the middle of the seventh, especially in the collects dating from this time.[47] Geoffrey Willis identified 22 rhythmical endings in the Gelasian Canon (see Table 2.2). The list shows that the forming of *clausulae* was characteristic of the stylistic development of the Canon: there are seven in the central parts of the Gelasian version, compared to only one in the corresponding text cited by Ambrose. At the same time, the number of *clausulae* in the Gelasian Canon, a prayer of considerable length, is low compared with their frequency in the collects. Hence, the conclusion can be drawn that the Canon was revised not long after its first appearance around the year 390 and before the formative period of the collects, which would seem to commence in the middle of the fifth century.[48]

This discussion of rhythmic clausulae is somewhat simplified, because it does not consider the quantity of syllables, on which classical meter is based. For the purposes of this paper, the ictus of a line is taken to coincide with the stressed accent of a word. By the end of the fourth century, the quantitative distinction was no longer present in spoken language; the accent, which used to indicate a raising of pitch in the voice, became tonal, that is, it became a forceful stress of the accentuated syllable, as in modern languages. Thus, a new sort of rhythmical versification based on the number of syllables and the placing of accents began to appear; an early example is Augustine's so-called *Psalmus contra partem Donati*.[49]

In the Roman Canon, there are examples various types of *clausulae*:

- *cursus planus* ("even"), with the accent on the second and the fifth syllables from the end: *órbe terrárum*, *placátus accípias*, *páce dispónas*;

---

46. Augustine, *De doctrina christiana* IV,115-117 and 147 (xx, 41 and xxvi,56): 250 and 274 Green.

47. M. G. Haessly, *Rhetoric in the Sunday Collects of the Roman Missal: with Introduction, Text, Commentary and Translation* (Cleveland: Ursuline College for Women, 1938), 7–9.

48. See Willis, *Early Roman Liturgy*, 61–67, on the variable prayers of the Mass.

49. Cf. H. B. Vroom, *Le Psaume abecedaire de Saint Augustin et la poesie latine rhythmique*, Latinitas Christianorum primaeva 4 (Nijmegen: Dekker and van de Vegt, 1993).

Table 2.2   Rhythmic Clausulae in the Roman Canon[50]

Te igitur	
rogámus et pétimus	*tardus*
régere dignéris	*trispondaicus*
órbe terrárum	*planus*
Memento, Domine	
nóta devótio	*tardus*
Communicantes	
sanctórum tuórum	*planus*
precibúsque concédas	*planus*
muniámur auxílio	*tardus*
Hanc igitur	
familíae túae	*planus*
placátus accípias	*planus*
páce dispónas	*planus*
damnatióne nos éripi	*tardus*
grége numerári	*trispondaicus*
Quam oblationem	
Déus in ómnibus	*tardus*
fácere dignéris	*trispondaicus*
Qui pridie	
—none—	
Unde et memores	
plébs tua sáncta	*planus*
gloriósae ascensiónis	*velox*
salútis perpétuae	*tardus*
Supra quae	
respícere dignéris	*trispondiacus*
Supplices te rogamus	
[sánguinem sumpserímus	*velox]*
grátia repleámur	*velox*
Memento etiam, domine	
indúlgeas deprecámur	*uelox*
Nobis quoque peccatoribus	
donáre dignéris	*planus*
largítor admítte	*planus*

- *cursus tardus* ("slow"), with the accent on the third and the sixth syllables from the end: *damnatióne nos éripi, salútis perpétuae*;
- *cursus velox* ("fast"), with the accent is on the second and seventh syllables from the end: *gloriósae ascénsionis, grátia repleámur*;
- *cursus trispondiacus*, consisting of three spondees, that is, three metrical feet with long or stressed syllables: *grége numerári, respícere dignéris*.

In the prayer *Supplices te rogamus*, I have added the *clausula sánguinem sumpserímus*, as suggested by the Hungarian classicist Zoltán Rihmer, who argues that, according to late ancient grammarians, the stress would have been on the second syllable from the end, not on the third, according to the Renaissance humanists that formed our understanding of Latin.[51] The two *clausulae sánguinem sumpserímus* and *grátia repleámur* would then form a neat parallelism at the end of the prayer, emphasizing the petition to enjoy the supernatural fruits of sacramental communion:

> . . . that all we who at this partaking of the altar shall receive the most sacred Body and Blood of thy Son (*ut quotquot ex hac altaris participatione sacrosanctum Filii tui corpus et sánguinem sumpserímus*),
> may be fulfilled with all heavenly benediction and grace (*omni benedictione caelesti grátia repleámur*).

Note that there are no *clausulae* in the Institution Narrative. This suggests that this part of the prayer did not undergo the same revision according to the rules of rhetoric as the other parts. The sacrosanct character of the Narrative with the Lord's own words would seem to account for this reticence.

The collect chosen for this brief discussion is contained in the Veronese or Leonine Sacramentary under the title *In ieiunio quarti mensis*, "for the fast of the fourth month," that is, for the Ember week after Pentecost.[52] In the Gelasian Sacramentary, it is used for the Vigil of Pentecost and the Wednesday of the fast of the fourth month.[53] In the *Missale Romanum* of 1570, it is the final prayer in the rite

---

51.I owe this point to a discussion with Dr Zoltán Rihmer in Oxford in September of 2006.

52. *Sacramentarium Leonianum*, ed. C. L. Feltoe (Cambridge: University Press, 1896), 25.

53. *The Gelasian Sacramentary: Liber sacramentorum romanae ecclesiae*, ed. H. A. Wilson (Oxford: Clarendon Press, 1894), 125.

of blessing and imposition of ashes on Ash Wednesday, and in the
Missale Romanum of 1970, it is the opening collect of the Ash
Wednesday Mass:

Concéde nóbis, Dómine,	Grant us, O Lord,
praesídia milítiae christiánae sánctis	to lay the foundation of the protec-
inchoáre ieiúniis [cursus tardus];	tions of Christian warfare with holy
ut cóntra spirituáles nequítias pug-	fasts;
natúri [cursus velox],	that, against the spiritual wickedness
continéntiae muniámur auxíliis	we are about to fight,
[cursus tardus].	we may be strengthened by the aids
	of continence.

The prayer is particularly interesting from a historical point
of view, because there is a striking parallel with a passage from
Leo the Great's *Sermo* 78. The Leonine sacramentary, where this
prayer first appears, was probably not used in public worship in
the form it has come down to us, but should be taken as a private
compilation of Roman formularies of different age and authority.
The Veronese manuscript dates from the first quarter of the seventh
century, but the prayers in it are dated variously from 400 to 560.[54]
The obvious literary parallels between various prayers in the Leonine
Sacramentary and passages in Leo's sermons have been explained
in different ways. While Camille Callewaert sees in Leo the author
of these prayers,[55] Frank Leslie Cross argues that Leo in his preaching quotes phrases from liturgical texts already in use. This would
mean that some of the prayers of the Leonine Sacramentary are older
than Leo. Cross certainly makes a good case for the collect under
discussion here, which is quoted almost in its entirety in Leo's *Sermo*
78; hence it is likely that this prayer dates from the early decades of
the fifth century.

The collect begins straightaway with the petition, which
includes the simple address "Lord." The prayer is centered on the idea
of *militia christiana*, "Christian warfare" or "campaign" against spiritual wickedness and, as a whole, has strong military connotations:

---

54. See C. Vogel, *Medieveal Liturgy: an Introduction to the Sources*, trans. W. Storey–N.
Rasmussen (Washington, D.C.: The Pastoral Press, 1981), 38–45.

55. C. Callewaert, *S. Léon le Grand et les textes du Léonien*, Extrait de *Sacris Erudiri* I, 1948
(Bruges–La Haye: Beyart–Nijhoff, 1948), esp. 56–59.

we ask God to enable us to "to lay the foundation of the protections of Christian warfare with holy fasts." *Praesidia* can be translated as "defenses," "protections," "posts," or "fortifications"; *inchoare* means "to lay the foundations" of something or "to begin." The means by which we lay these foundations are "holy fasts," which is a reference to the Embertide fast (the "fast of the fourth month"), during which time this prayer was made.

The petition of the prayer is amplified in the form of a purpose clause: we ask that we who are about to "engage with" (*pugnare*) spiritual evils may be "strengthened" (*muniare*—another term with military connotations, "to build a wall around," "to defend," "to secure") by "aids of continence." These "aids" (*auxilia* also evoking "auxiliary troops") are the "holy fasts" of the season. The parallel between the conclusion of the prayer and the main petition is highlighted not only by the rhyme *auxiliis—ieiuniis*, but also through the *cursus tardus* found at the end of both cola: *inchoáre ieiúniis— muniámur auxíliis.*

CONCLUSION

To sum up this cursory analysis, the many rhetorical features of the Roman Canon and the collects of the Mass mark these texts as belonging to the world of antiquity, where any literary text was formed according to technical rules of composition.[56] These rhetorical features help to create a distinctive prayer-style that is both Roman and Christian. The Canon draws on the style of pagan prayer, including its juridical elements, but its vocabulary and contents is distinctively Christian, indeed Biblical. Its diction has Roman *gravitas* and avoids the exuberance of the Eastern Christian prayer style, which is also found in the Gallican tradition. Mohrmann sees in these early Roman prayers the fortuitous combination of a renewal of language, inspired

---

56. Cf. E. Norden, *Die antike Kunstprosa vom VI. Jahrhundert v. Chr. bis in die Zeit der Renaissance*, 2 vols. (Leipzig: Teubner, 2nd edn, 1909), vol. II, 457: "Es findet sich . . . in der ganzen antiken Literatur (abgesehen von einzelnen fachwissenschaftlichen Schriften), kein stilistisches ἄτεχνον, was sich eben aus ihrem dem gemeinen Leben abgewandten, aristokratischen Grundcharakter erklärt." See also C. Mohrmann," Problèmes stylistiques dans la littérature latine chrétienne," *Études sur le latin des chrétiens*, vol. I, 147–170, at 147–148.

by the newness of Christian revelation, and a stylistic traditionalism that was firmly imbedded in the Roman world. The formation of this sacred language was part of a comprehensive effort to evangelize classical culture, which formed the basis of Christian civilization and has survived and will continue to flourish even in the present day.

Chapter 3

Poetry in the Latin Liturgy

Gabriel Díaz Patri[*]

While the Christian liturgy originally consisted of biblical texts, with time poetic compositions were incorporated into it. Although these poetic texts did not gain the importance and complexity in the West that they enjoy in the Byzantine liturgy, they constitute a genre in which there was much productivity over a long time, making it deserving of special study.

The type of liturgical poetry that has lasted to this day in the Latin liturgy is the hymn, which, with the exception of its rather limited use in the Missal,[1] ordinarily has its place within the Divine Office. Another poetic genre categorized under the general term "trope" (this includes the genre of the "sequence") was widely circulated in the Middle Ages, both in the Divine Office and in the Missal, but has practically disappeared from the liturgy after the Middle Ages—for instance, only four sequences are preserved in the Missal of Saint Pius V.[2]

THE "HYMN" IN CLASSICAL ANTIQUITY, THE BIBLE, AND CHRISTIANITY

The term *hymnus* rarely appears in pagan Latin literature, where *carmen* was the common word, but it was the preferred term in

---

[*] Translated by Alexander Morrison.

1. These are to be found in the Holy Week ceremonies (*Ubi caritas, Crux fidelis, Vexilla Regis*).

2. *Victimae paschali laudes, Veni Sancte Spiritus, Lauda Sion, Dies irae,* to which the *Stabat Mater* was added in the eighteenth century.

Christian Latin.[3] It is taken from the Greek ὕμνος,[4] which in secular
literature denoted a festive song in praise of a god, or of a hero,
(that is, in the strictest sense of that word, of a deified man) with a
specifically religious character,[5] as distinguished from ἐγκώμιον
ἔπος, which was an ode in honor of a mere human, probably sung
in the context of a banquet or a solemn ceremony. These were
originally written in epic meter (such as the ancient *Delphic Hymn to
Apollo*), but later they were written in distichs or in the refined meters
of Alcaeus, Anacreon, and Pindar, of which some of the melodies
are still preserved.[6]

The Septuagint uses the term ὕμνος with the meaning "song
of praise," translating with it various Hebrew words (Psalm 39:4,
64:2, 99:4, 118:171); the verb ὑμνέω is frequently used, meaning "to

---

3. In his famous consultation to Trajan, Pliny the Younger said that the Christians gathered
together to sing *carmina* to Christ as God (*Ep.* X, 97).

4. This term, while of uncertain etymology, is found in Homer, who only uses it in the
expression ἀοιδῆς ὕμνος which is probably meant to signify something like the "melody of the
song" (*Odyssey* 8, 429); Pindar (*Olympian Odes* 2,1) and Aeschylus (*Agamemnon* 1191, *The
Eumenides* 306, 332, 344; *The Persians* 625) use it to mean "song." Herodotus (IV,35,3 and
elsewhere) uses ὕμνον ποιέω ("to compose a hymn") referring to text and melody. Euripides uses
the expression "to appease, to move" by means of *songs* (*Alcestis* 359), and in the proper sense of a
religious song, he speaks of "giving honor with hymns" (*Hippolytus* 55–56). The same meaning is
found in an expression of Aristophanes, ἱεροὶ ὕμνοι ("sacred hymns" *Birds*, 210), while Herodotus
(IV,35,2–3) for his part emphasises the importance of the invocation of the names of the gods in
the hymn. Plato in *Laws* III (700B,D) insists that the ancient distinction between different forms
of song be maintained and renewed: hymns (ὕμνοι), which are "prayers to the gods" (εὐχαὶ πρὸς
θεοὺς), lamentations (θρῆνοι), paeans (παίωνες) and dithyrambs (διθύραμβοι). The singing of
"hymns to the gods and hymns of praise" (ὕμνοι θεῶν καὶ ἐγκώμια) is associated with prayers
(*Laws* VII, 801E). In fact, he readmits poetry into his ideal state, including Homer's and
Hesiod's, but only "hymns to the gods and praises of virtuous men" (ὕμνους θεοῖς καὶ ἐγκώμια
τοῖς ἀγαθοῖς, *Republic* X, 607A; cf. Aristotle, *Poetics* 1448b27). But he who would introduce in
the state "ὕμνοι different from those established would be prosecuted for ἀσέβεια" (*Laws*
VII,799B), and ultimately the living should not be honoured by encomiums and hymns (802A).
Epictetus for his part says that while digging, ploughing and eating the hymn Μέγας ὁ θεός
("God is great") ought to be sung, in gratitude to him who has granted us tools and given us
hands, a throat and a stomach (Epictetus, *Discourses* I, 16, 16–20; cf. 3, 26, 30). On the other
hand, the word ὑμνέω means "to sing a hymn of praise" and then "to honour the gods with
choral singing"; but it can also simply mean "to honor," "to praise," "to exalt" generally.

5. Callisthenes reminded Alexander, who, claiming hymns for himself, or at least allowed
them to be addressed to him, that "hymns are composed in honor of the gods, and eulogies for
men"; Arrian, *Anabasis Alexandri* IV, 11).

6. For the melodies, cf. C. Del Grande, "Cenni sulla musica greca," in *Enciclopedia Classica*,
ed. G. B. Pighi, C. Del Grande, P. E. Arias, vol. V (Torino: SEI, 1960), s.v.

celebrate," "to exalt," often implying worship, meanings which are also used by other Hexaplaric translators.[7]

The historian Josephus speaks of the Old Testament's ὕμνοι, to emphasize that Judaism offered a genre parallel to that of the ancient Greek hymns. For Philo of Alexandria, on the other hand, this is a definite reference to the psalms, even used to introduce quotations: for example, he says, ἐν ὕμνοις λέγεται and the textual quotation follows.

In the New Testament, the term appears only twice, in two letters of Saint Paul (Colossians 3:16 and Ephesians 5:19). It always occurs in the plural, accompanied by ψαλμόι and ὠδαὶ πνευματικαί. The verb ὑμνέω carries the meaning "to praise" in Hebrews 2:12 and Acts 16:25 and "to sing psalms" in Matthew 26:30 and Mark 14:26. The term is not used in the works of the Apostolic Fathers, and the apologists (with one exception in Justin Martyr, *Apology* 13, 2) only use it in quotations, both biblical and classical, as in the case of the quotation from Aeschylus used by Athenagoras.[8]

With the gradual crumbling of the distinction between human and divine that marked the decline of Greece and Rome, and with the usurping of divine honors on the part of men, ὕμνος came to be applied more often to men; this did not, however, pass unnoticed and unchallenged.[9] When the word was assumed into the language of the Church, this essential distinction clung to it still.

Among the Fathers of the Latin Church, it appears once in Tertullian.[10] The later Fathers have fairly complete definitions of the term *hymnus*. St Ambrose says: "a hymn is addressed specifically to God" (*hymnus specialiter Deo dicitur*);[11] St Augustine, however,

---

7. In this sense, Psalms 135, 117, 145 and 148 can truly be considered Old Testament hymns, as can the canticle in Dan 3:52–90 and 1 Chronicles 16:8–36. In 2 Chronicles 7:6, the term ὕμνοι appears, referring strictly speaking to the Psalms, and in 4 Maccabees 18:15, David is called ὑμνόγραφος.

8. Athenagoras, *Legatio pro christianis*, 21,5. For more on this theme, cf. G. Delling, "ὕμνος, ὑμνέω, ψάλλω, ψαλμός," in *Theologisches Wörterbuch zum Neuen Testament*, ed. G. Kittel–G. Friedrich, 10 vols. (Stuttgart: Kohlhammer, 1933–1979), vol. VIII, 492–506; the entry Ψαλμός, ὕμνος, ὡδή, in R. C. Trench, *Synonyms of the New Testament* (London: Kegan Paul, Trench, Trübner & Co, 1890), 295-301 (§ LXXVIII); and the comprehensive study of M. Lattke, *Hymnus: Materialien zu einer Geschichte der antiken Hymnologie*, Novum Testamentum et orbis antiquus 19 (Freiburg/Schweiz–Göttingen: Universitätsverlag–Vandenhoeck und Ruprecht, 1991).

9. Trench, *Synonyms of the New Testament*, 297.

10. Tertullian, *Ad uxorem*, 2, 8.

11. Ambrose, *De officiis*, I,45.

explains more: "Do you know what a hymn is? It is a song with praise of God. If you praise God and do not sing, you do not utter a hymn. If you sing and do not praise God, you do not utter a hymn. If you praise anything else, which does not belong to the praise of God, even though you sing and praise, you do not utter a hymn. A hymn, then, contains these three things: song, and praise, and that of God. Hence praise of God in song is called a hymn."[12]

Development of the Genre: Primitive Hymnody in Prose

Originally, *hymnus* took on a wide range of meanings; on the one hand it covered the psalms and canticles of the Old Testament and even those of the New (Amalarius of Metz in the ninth century continued to called the *Magnificat* the "hymn" of the Blessed Virgin), since the Greek term was used for these; and on the other hand, it covered the hymns of praise—probably improvisatory[13]—of the early Church.[14]

In studying some the most ancient Christian hymns, attempts have been made to identify the influence of Hebrew biblical versification by looking at its three fundamental characteristics, namely, verse, melody and parallelism. The first two are only visible in the original language, but any stylistic recourse to parallelism (the use of the same or similar structure in each phrase, so that between phrases there is a direct correspondence of thoughts and words) would be just as visible in a translation, and could easily be imitated in another language. The first Christian hymns would have used this sort of linking of ideas which elsewhere was already found to be present in the ancient Latin poetic tradition.[15]

---

12. Augustine, *Enarrationes in Psalmos*, 148,14; cf. also 72, 1: "Hymns are praises of God in song: hymns are songs that contain praises of God. If there is praise, and it is not of God, there is no hymn; if there is praise, and it is of God, and it is not sung, there is no hymn. Therefore a hymn must have these three elements; praise, which is of God, and which is sung."

13. Cf. Acts 4:24 and Tertullian, *Apologeticum*, 39,18.

14. Cf. H. Leclercq, "Hymnes," in *Dictionnaire d'archéologie chrétienne et de liturgie*, vol. VI, pt. 2 (Paris: Letouzey et Ané, 1925), 2826–2929, at 2827.

15. Cf. C. Mohrmann, "La langue et le style de la poésie latine chrétienne," in *Études sur le latin des chrétiens. Tome I: Études sur le latin des chrétiens*, Storia e letteratura 65 (Roma: Edizioni di Storia e Letteratura, 2nd edn, 1961; ristampa anastatica, 1994), 151–168, at 163.

We are left today with just a few examples from this early period. Four hymns are transcribed in the *Apostolic Constitutions*: the very ancient φῶς ἱλαρόν (second or third century) which is still used today in the Byzantine Liturgy, a hymn written as a grace before meals, and the twin hymns Αἰνεῖτε παῖδες Κύριον and Δόξα ἐν ὑψίστοις θεῶ, that start with Biblical passages, Psalm 112:1 and Luke 2:14 respectively, and then develop into songs of praise. The *Te Deum*, while probably set in its present form by Nicetas of Ramesiana (end of the fourth century),[16] dates at least in its essential parts from these early times, and follows a pattern similar to the two hymns just mentioned, without the introductory biblical verse.[17]

Other characteristics of hymns from this primitive period include both an absence of meter and division into verses or strophes, and the unrestricted use of the Christian idiom.

LATIN POETRY WITH A CHRISTIAN CONTENT

We must first of all remember that the poetic system of ancient languages was completely different from modern poetic systems; it was in fact based on the distinction between short and long vowel sounds (long being double the value of short) that was made naturally when speaking these languages. For instance, "people" was *pŏpulus*, but *pōpulus* (with a long "o," while spelt the same) meant "poplar." Similarly, *mălus* was used to mean "evil," but *mālus* meant "apple tree." For a Roman of the classical period distinguishing between these words would have seemed just as natural as the distinction between "feel" and "fill," or "lead" and "lid" for an Englishman. The other fundamental element is the musical emphatic accent, called the ictus. The regular combination of short and long syllables with various ictus became known as "feet." Each foot, according to the different

---

16. G. Morin, "Nouvelles recherches sur l'auteur du Te Deum" in *Revue Bénédictine* 11 (1894), 49–77, 377–345. See also the list of other articles in the same periodical by G. Morin, *Études, Textes, Découvertes, Contributions à la littérature et à l'histoire des douze premiers siècles*, Anecdota Maredsolana II/1 (Maredsous/Paris: Abbaye de Maredsous/Picard, 1913), 16, and A. E. Burn, *The Hymn Te Deum and its Author* (London: The Faith Press, 1926).

17. In some manuscripts it is found preceded by the first verse of Psalm 112, *Laudate pueri Dominum, laudate nomen Domini*, for example, in the Antiphonary of Bangor (seventh century). For more details about the *Te Deum*, see A. E. Burn, *An introduction to the creeds and to the Te Deum*, (London: Methuen & Co., 1899).

combinations of short and long syllables and the placing of the
ictus, has a proper name, the most common being: the trochee
(long-short, with the ictus on the first, as in *pán-ge*), the iamb (short-
long, with the ictus on the last, as in *di-és*), the dactyl (long-short-
short, with the ictus at the beginning, as in *scán-de-re*), and the
spondee (long-long, with the ictus on the first of these, as in *cás-to*).[18]
The feet, alone or in pairs, in turn form a meter, which is the unit
of measurement for verse.[19]

In this way, classical poetry had a noticeably musical feel,
to the extent that a poet could even exploit meter so that it reflected
rhythmically what he was saying. This can be seen in the following
verse of Virgil's *Aeneid*, where the dactylic rhythm of the line seems to
imitate the gallop of horses described in it: *Quādrŭpĕdāntĕ pūtrēm, //
sŏnĭtū quătĭt ūngŭlā cāmpum* (*Aeneid* 8, 596). We note, however,
that the ictus does not always coincide with the accent of the word, as
in this example taken from Horace: *Rec-tiús vi-vés Li-ci-ní ne-qu'áltum*. In prose, it would be: *Réctius víves Lícini, neque áltum* (Horace,
Odes II, 10).

In the West, Latin Christian poetry that was stylistically
related to the classical tradition developed only after prose writing
had conformed itself for some time with the same ancient tradition.
Leaving aside Commodianus, upon whose dates the specialists cannot
agree (some proposing dates two whole centuries after others), the
first poet and poetry that we can date with any certainty are the
Spanish priest Juvencus (writing around 330) and his work *Historia
Evangelica*, a retelling of the life of Christ in Virgilian hexameter,
mimicking not only the meter of the great classical poet but also the
vocabulary, often carefully avoiding Christian terminology.[20] To give

---

18. It is not necessary that the foot coincide with a word, a foot can contain more than one word and, vice versa, a word can contain more than one foot.

19. For this topic cf. J. Luque Moreno, *Arsis, Thesis, Ictus, Las marcas del ritmo en la música y en la métrica antiguas* (Granada: Universidad de Granada, 1994). In this book there is a presentation of the current situation of studies referring to this question with an extensive and updated bibliography.

20. It is important not to forget that, as Christine Mohrmann points out, this early Christian poetry of classical meter has its origin, more than in an authentic poetic inspiration directed to the expression of religious sentiments or experiences, but instead in considerations of a practical order: it has to serve as a complement to the education of Christian who otherwise would have remained completely pagan. Given that the foundation of the latter was the great poets, especially Virgil, the principal source of human knowledge, a poetry that had preserved its

just a few examples, the classical word *nuntius* is used instead of *angelus,* the verb *rogare* appears instead of *orare,* the word *ara* is preferred to *altare, vates* replaces *propheta,* and instead of *martyr,* the word *testis* is used. This genre continued to flourish for a while, although it was restricted to works on the Old Testament (the historical books were more suited to poetic elaboration and did not conflict with the expressive form of epic poetry). Only Sedulius continued in Juvencus's footsteps by putting the Gospels into verse, in his *Carmen Pascale,* which is made up of 1737 hexameters over five cantos. The success of this work, which was widely read through to the Renaissance, earned him the title *Poeta Christianissimus.* Two lines (63-64) from the second book of this work were adopted as the Introit to the Mass of the Nativity of Our Lady, and were later incorporated into the Common of the Blessed Virgin. It is curious that this Introit (a text, usually reserved for scriptural quotations) takes from Virgil (*Aeneid* V, 80) the line which has made it famous—*Salve, sancta parens*—just adapting the vocative case as necessary.

  This imitation of the classics became almost grotesque in the genre named "cento,"[21] which consisted of the direct copying of entire lines, half lines or still smaller parts of lines taken from classical works and incorporating them into a new work.[22] The first Christian example of this genre is the retelling of the Bible story written by a lady named Proba around the year 350. Since the form of the cento did not allow for biblical names or direct quotations from the sacred text to be included, it was only possible to make veiled allusions or forced transformations. In this way, the words of God the Father in Mark 1:11: *Tu es Filius meus dilectus, in te complacui* ("Thou art my beloved Son, in thee I am well pleased") become, in Proba's work, Venus's words to Cupid in Book I of Virgil's Aeneid: *Nate meae vires, mea magna potentia, solus* ("Oh Son, my strength, my mighty power alone"; *Aeneid* I, 664).

---

same poetic structure, style and language but which transmitted Sacred History, avoiding all the expressions that could have pagan overtones, could appear to be the adequate complement. See C. Mohrmann, *La langue et style de la poésie Chrétienne,* 154.

  21. *Cento, -onis* ; from the Greek κέντρον: a piece of patched-up fabric, a garment made from all sorts of pieces sewn together, hence the meaning of a literary "pot-pourri," a poem composed of verses taken from here and there.

  22. D. V. Meconi, "The Christian Cento and the Evangelization of Christian Culture," in *Logos* 7 (2004), 109–32.

But along with this genre of classicized poetry and erudite pretension we find examples of another poetic genre, one which did not respect the classical meter (based on the quantity of syllables) but which made the ictus of the line coincide with the stressed accent of a word. At the end of the fourth century the quantitative distinction was no longer present in the spoken language, and while the accentuated syllables were perhaps kept in certain regions for one or two centuries longer, people began to notice the accent less; previously it was an raising of pitch in the voice, but it became tonal, that is to say, it became a forceful stress of the accentuated syllable, such as appears in modern languages. The system of classical meter was thus transformed into an artifice only visible to the learned.

In this way, a new sort of rhythmical versification based on the number of syllables and the placing of accents began to appear. The most ancient example we have is the so-called *Psalmus contra partem Donati* or *Psalmus abecedarius* of Saint Augustine.[23] In it we find a constant number of syllables per line with an accent, or stress, in a fixed place, so that it is impossible to identify it as being in classical meter. Furthermore, as its title indicates, it is alphabetical; each of its 20 verses begins with one of the letters of the alphabet, following a pattern found in biblical poetry. Each verse is also preceded by a *ritornello* that Augustine calls *hypopsalma*, and sometimes the second half of the line rhymes with the first, both of which are characteristics displaying a link with Eastern hymnology. The same author indicates that he had composed it without submitting to any particular poetic genre, in order to avoid being forced by the meter into using words that were not ordinarily used.[24]

Another ancient example of versification that departs from the classical model (even though the true nature of his verse is much debated) is that of Commodianus, whose dates, as we have already seen, are not yet definitely fixed. He was probably a Syrian resident in Carthage, a convert to Christianity from Judaism, not formed by reading the Latin classics. He is the author of the *Instructiones adversus gentium deos per litteras versuum primas*, a collection of

---

23. Cf. H. B. Vroom, *Le Psaume abécédaire de Saint Augustin et la poésie latine rhythmique*, Latinitas Christianorum primaeva 4 (Nijmegen: Dekker & van de Vegt, 1933).

24. Cf. Augustine, *Retractationes* I, 20: CCL 57, 61.

80 poems of acrostic structure[25] (two of which are alphabetical), which is a style drawn from Syriac poetry and is totally absent in classical art. According to some authors, these curious hexameters are founded more on accentuation (keeping to six *ictus*) and on the number of syllables than on their length.[26] Others claim that he had the intention of writing straight hexameters, but failed in this endeavor.[27]

In the *Carmen apologeticum* (the other work of his which is preserved), only 26 out of 1066 lines are quantitatively correct, and in general he maintains the qualitative distinction of accentuated syllables, only sometimes missing and using unaccented words.[28] On the other hand the work incorporates rhyme, albeit in a rudimentary fashion. These works can be seen to illustrate either the evolution of the primitive psalmodic genre into the profane forms adapted for contemporary language (if we date the author from the middle of the third century), or on the contrary, the crumbling of the classical literary forms (if we date him from the fifth century). Strangely for learned Romans, his works remained a misfit; Saint Jerome does not mention him, and only at the end of the fifth century is he recalled by Gennadius of Marseilles, who judges him somewhat severely,[29] and by the Pseudo-Gelasius who prohibits the reading of his books.[30]

HISTORICAL DEVELOPMENT OF HYMNOLOGY

Clearly, none of that poetry was written for the liturgy. The religious hymn properly speaking appeared in the Church during the fourth century. A time before, the leaders of various heretical movements (such as Marcion and Valentinus, the Syrian Bardesanes [Bar Daisan], his son Harmonius, and the Arians) had started using attractive poetic and musical media in order to spread their doctrines. This provoked opposition in the third century against the use of

---

25. The initials of the last poem (n. 80), read backward, give *Commodianus Mendicus Christi.*

26. Cf. A. Michel, *In hymnis et canticis. Culture et beauté dans l'hymnique chrétienne latine,* Philosophes médiévaux 20 (Louvain: Publications Universitaires, 1978), 55.

27. Cf. P. Lejay, "Commodianus," in *The Catholic Encyclopedia,* 15 vols. (New York: Appleton, 1913), vol. IV, s.v.

28. Cf. J. Oroz Reta, M. Marcos Casquero, *Lirica latina medieval* (Madrid: Biblioteca de Autores Cristianos, 1995), 5.

29. Gennadius of Marseilles, *De viris illustribus,* 15: PL 58, 1068–1069.

30. Ps.-Gelasius, *De Libris recipiendis et non recipiendis*: PL 59, 163.

non-scriptural hymns in the Christian liturgy, which grew to such an extent that the Council of Laodicea in the fourth century (c. 364) forbade their use.[31] Perhaps this was the reason for the disappearance of the primitive hymnody of the Church, of which only small fragments remain. The orthodox writers, warning of the success and wide diffusion of such heterodox materials among the people, began composing hymns that conformed to sound doctrine of the Councils. The first of these was the deacon Saint Ephraem (fourth century), named the "harp of the Spirit," who composed acrostic hymns (*madrashe*), where the first letters of each line are in alphabetic sequence together or spell a key word. These were designed to be sung by a choir, to which the people would respond with a refrain. The Syriac poetic technique was characterized by a fixed number of syllables in the line and a regular accentuation, as well as by other qualities only noticeable to one who has studied the original language: antithesis, alliteration, word play and rhyme which lend to the poetry an unmatched richness, variety, sonority and harmony that compliment the simple structure of its parallelism. Many of these hymns were adopted by the Syriac liturgy and are still in use today.

These Eastern initiatives were promptly imitated in the West. The first Latin writer to follow the example of Saint Ephraem, whose hymns he had perhaps known during his exile in Phrygia, was Saint Hilary of Poitiers (+ 366). His works were probably written in order to combat Arianism, of which he was such a strong enemy in the West. It is difficult to judge his hymns, because we only have fragments of three or four (the *Liber Hymnorum* attributed to him by St Jerome has been lost), and none of them were incorporated into the liturgy.

Half a century later, the true master-craftsman of Latin Christian hymnody appeared: Saint Ambrose of Milan (+ 397). While being locked inside his Church with the faithful in order to stop the Arians from using it, this great bishop organized vigils and composed hymns to be sung along with the psalms:

---

31. Canon 15: "No others shall sing in church, save only the canonical singers, who go up into the ambo and sing from a book." Canon 59: "No psalms composed by private individuals nor any uncanonical books may be read in the church, but only the canonical Books of the Old and New Testaments." J. D. Mansi, *Sacrorum Conciliorum nova et amplissima collectio*, 54 vols. (Graz: Akademische Druck–und Verlagsanstalt, 1960–1961), vol. II, 568 and 573.

The church of Milan had only recently begun to employ this mode
of consolation and exaltation with all the brethren singing together with
great earnestness of voice and heart. For it was only about a year—not
much more—since Justina, the mother of the boy-emperor Valentinian,
had persecuted thy servant Ambrose on behalf of her heresy, in which
she had been seduced by the Arians. The devoted people kept guard in the
church, prepared to die with their bishop, thy servant. Among them my
mother, thy handmaid, taking a leading part in those anxieties and vigils,
lived there in prayer. And even though we were still not wholly melted
by the heat of thy Spirit, we were nevertheless excited by the alarmed and
disturbed city. This was the time that the custom began, after the manner
of the Eastern Church, that hymns and psalms should be sung, so that
the people would not be worn out with the tedium of lamentation.
This custom, retained from then till now, has been imitated by many,
indeed, by almost all thy congregations throughout the rest of the world.[32]

The holy Bishop of Milan was gifted with the most refined
literary taste, and he knew exactly how to strike the perfect balance
between the essential elements of Christian poetry and the traditional
elements of the Roman Latin heritage in which he had been educated;
he chose iambic diameter grouped in strophes of four verses, which
he combined with an element of accentuated rhythm and the parallelism
of ancient Christian hymns; meanwhile he used a vocabulary that
in general respected the classical forms, but which he enriched by
including words and idioms proper to Christian Latin, thereby creating
a Christian poetic language. The "Ambrosian" form became a model
for later hymns, and after the gradual incorporation of the genre into
the liturgy, the hymns of the Milanese bishop secured forever the
place of honor they still occupy. It was thus that the genre of the
hymn, strictly speaking, was born, with its characteristics of identical
syllables and line lengths, enabling it to be sung to one tune. Attributed
to St Ambrose are: *Aeterne rerum conditor, Splendor paternae gloriae,
Deus creator omnium, Veni redemptor gentium (= Intende qui regis Israel),
Hic est dies verus Dei, Iam surgit hora tertia, Aeterna Christi munera,
Apostolorum passio, Agnes beatae virginis,* and others with less certainty.[33]

---

32. Augustine, *Confessions*, IX, 7, 15: J. J. O' Donnell, *Augustine, Confessions. Introduction, Text,
and Commentary*, 3 vols. (Oxford: Clarendon Press, 1992) *ad loc.*

33. On the poetry of St Ambrose, the fundamental reference is: *Ambroise de Milan: Hymnes*,
ed. and trans. J. Fontaine (Paris: Cerf, 1992). Also worth reading, particularly for the musical

Hereafter, numerous hymns were composed in the same style initiated by Saint Ambrose, although the authors of many of these hymns, labeled collectively by the generic term "Ambrosian," are unknown, as is the case with outstanding compositions such as *Ad coenam Agni providi*, *Tristes erant Apostoli*, *Vox clara ecce intonat*, etc.

Furthermore, poetic passages were adapted into hymns from far larger works. For example, liturgical hymns were made by lifting verses out of the lyrical works of the Spaniard Aurelius Prudentius (+ 405),[34] *Cathemerinon* (*Ales diei nuntius*, *Nox et tenebrae et nubila*) and *Peristephanon*, which had been composed using the iambic diameter of Saint Ambrose, from which they were also inspired. These featured in the Offices of various dioceses and were especially used in the Visigoth Mozarabic rite as well as in the Roman rite. Prudentius managed to create such an excellent genre of Christian poetry that he is considered to be the greatest Christian poet of the West. After a somewhat dissipate youth training for the forum, he took on important administrative jobs as prefect in important cities. When he came to the end of his life, he felt like he had still not done anything of merit before God, and so consecrated his poet's pen to Him: "The devout man," he said, "presents God with the offering of his conscience; another gives money to relieve the poor; we, however, lacking both sanctity and alms for the poor, consecrate our light iambs and our rolling trochees."[35] A comparison could be made between the poetic works of Prudentius and that which Saint Augustine had at that time achieved in the order of philosophical and theological science; both solved the problem of the relation of faith and reason in similar ways, Augustine by Christianizing Platonic wisdom and Prudentius by doing the same with the lyrical poems of Horace. It must be noted, however, that Prudentius, who perfectly mastered the more complex classical meters and was capable of using them with a versatility reminiscent of Horace, did not have any trouble in using the simple and innovative Ambrosian meter which afterwards rose to become the meter *par excellence* of Christian hymnody.

---

references: L. Migliavacca, *Gli inni ambrosiani. Poesia e musica al servizio del culto divino* (Milano: Rugginenti, 1997).

34. Cf. *Obras completas de Aurelio Prudencio*, ed. and trans. I. Rodríguez. (Madrid: Biblioteca de Autores Cristianos, 1981).

35. Cf. Prudentius, *Epilogus*.

An alphabetic-acrostic poem by Coelius Sedulius (+ c. 450) in the style of St Ephraem was also cut and used, of which two fragments are still to be found in the Breviary for Christmastide: *A solis ortus cardine* and *Hostis Herodes impie*.

As the centuries passed, many more hymns were composed, some of which were later incorporated into the liturgy. The authors of some of these are known with certainty, while others are more or less confidently attributed to various authors. Many remain anonymous.

In antiquity the series of six Vespers hymns celebrating the successive works of God on the six days of creation,[36] was attributed to Pope St Gregory the Great (+ 604). Also attributed to him are the two hymns for Sundays in Lent: *Audi benigne conditor* and *Ex more docti mystico*.

Venantius Fortunatus (+ 600), the most outstanding poet of the Merovingian period, was the author of numerous poems for special occasions and hymns for liturgical processions, two of which are particularly outstanding; they were composed for the solemn reception of special relic of the Holy Cross sent by the Eastern Roman Emperor Justin II to Saint Radegund for a convent of nuns she had founded near Poitiers, and they are now used in the liturgy for Passiontide: *Vexilla Regis prodeunt* (Vespers) and *Pange lingua gloriosi / proelium certaminis*.[37]

The Carolingian literary renaissance brought with it a return to other forms of classical poetry, and among the great leaders of this movement were Alcuin of York, Paulinus of Aquileia, and Theodulf of Orléans. The elaborate Sapphic verses of the famous hymn *Ut queant laxis*, attributed to Paulus Diaconus, and the well known *Veni Creator Spiritus* (which was believed to have been the work of Rabanus Maurus) are examples from this period.

In this way, the rich treasures of Latin hymnody were being created. The monastic Hymnarium in the eleventh century was constructed as follows:[38] there was an invariable hymn for each of the

---

36. *Lucis creator optime, Immense caeli conditor, Telluris ingens conditor, Caeli Deus sanctissime, Magnae Deus potentiae, Plasmator hominis Deus.*

37. This hymn, inspired by Prudentius' "Hymn for all hours" (*Cathemerinon* 9, 82), served as a model for an enormous quantity of hymns throughout the Middle Ages. The *Analecta Hymnica* contains some 75 hymns beginning with the words *Pange lingua*, of which the most famous is undoubtedly the Corpus Christi hymn attributed to Saint Thomas Aquinas.

38. Cf. P. Batiffol, *Histoire du Bréviaire Romain* (Paris: Picard, 3rd edn, 1911), 211–212.

small canonical hours: *Iam lucis orto sidere* for Prime; *Nunc Sancte nobis Spiritus* for Terce; *Rector potens verax Deus* for Sext; *Rerum Deus tenax vigor* for None; and either *Te lucis ante terminum* or *Christus qui lux es et dies* for Compline. These were all anonymous "Ambrosian" hymns written before the sixth century.

The hymns contained in the ferial hymnody are also Ambrosian except two of them that belong to Prudentius:

SUNDAY	(Noct.)	*Primo dierum omnium*
	(Laud.)	*Aeterne rerum conditor*
	(Vesp.)	*Lucis creator optime*
MONDAY	(Noct.)	*Somno refectis artubus*
	(Laud.)	*Splendor paternae gloriae*
	(Vesp.)	*Immense caeli conditor*
TUESDAY	(Noct.)	*Consors paterni luminis*
	(Laud.)	[*Ales diei nuntius*] (Prudentius)
	(Vesp.)	*Telluris ingens conditor*
WEDNESDAY	(Noct.)	*Rerum creator optime*
	(Laud.)	[*Nox et tenebrae et nubila*] (Prudentius)
	(Vesp.)	*Caeli Deus sanctissime*
THURSDAY	(Noct.)	*Nox atra rerum contegit*
	(Laud.)	*Lux ecce surgit aurea*
	(Vesp.)	*Magnae Deus potentiae*
FRIDAY	(Noct.)	*Tu Trinitatis unitas*
	(Laud.)	*Aeterna caeli gloria*
	(Vesp.)	*Plasmator hominis Deus*
SATURDAY	(Noct.)	*Summae Deus clementiae*
	(Laud.)	*Aurora iam spargit polum*
	(Vesp.)	*O lux beata trinitas*

The hymns of the Proper of the Time were, for the most part, also Ambrosian hymns:

ADVENT	(Vesp.)	*Conditor alme siderum*
	(Noct.)	*Verbum supernum prodiens*
	(Laud.)	*Vox clara ecce intonat*
CHRISTMAS	(Vesp.)	*Veni redemptor gentium*
	(Noct.)	*Christe redemptor omnium*
	(Laud.)	[*A solis ortus cardine*] (Sedulius)

EPIPHANY	(Vesp.)	*Iesus refulsit omnium*
	(Noct.)	*[Hostis Herodes impie]* (Sedulius)
	(Laud.)	*Illuminans altissimus*
LENT	(Vesp.)	*Audi benigne conditor*
	(Noct.)	*Ex more docti mystico*
	(Laud.)	*Iam Christe sol iustitiae*
EASTER	(Vesp.)	*Ad coenam agni providi*
	(Noct.)	*Hic est dies verus Dei*
	(Laud.)	*Aurora lucis rutilat*
ASCENSION	(Vesp.)	*[Festum nunc celebre]* Rabanus Maurus(?)
	(Noct.)	*Optatus votis omnium*
	(Laud.)	*Iam Christus ascendit polum*

After the Carolingian era, hymn-writing poets stopped using the artificial technique of classical meter, and gradually became attached to rhythmic, accented verse which allowed for a greater liberty of poetic expression, with clearly visible stylistic qualities. From the tenth to the thirteenth centuries, the most famous monastic communities in Germany (Fulda, Prüm, Reichenau), Switzerland (St Gall), France (Cluny, Saint Victor) and Italy (Montecassino) each had their own poetic schools which produced vast quantities of material, not just hymns but also a new genre that appeared in the mid eleventh century, that of the "tropes"; the function of this new genre was to comment on the liturgical context, either as a prelude and frame to it, or as a text inserted into it.[39]

The sequence originally came from the *jubilus* of the Alleluia, which was a passage of melismas on the final "a" of the word. Notker Balbulus wrote of the difficulties of committing such extremely long melodies to memory, and of his great delight when a refugee priest from Jumièges near Rouen (which had just been destroyed by the Normans) arrived at the Abbey of Saint Gall with an Antiphonary containing versicles set to the music of the *jubilus*. Although these versicles did not seem to him to be of any great value in themselves, he nevertheless liked the idea and was prompted to imitate this practice. Notker himself began to write similar texts to accompany the

---

39. For more on this topic, cf. E. Costa, *Tropes et sequences dans le cadre de la vie liturgique au Moyen Age*, Bibliotheca Ephemerides liturgicae. Subsidia 17 (Roma: C.L.V. Edizioni Liturgiche, 1979).

melodies and was congratulated by his master Iso, who did however suggest some corrections—in particular he taught him that "each note of the melody should be given a separate syllable of text."[40] The new texts, written according to this criterion, were immediately accepted and the genre gained increased popularity. After six centuries of existence, hundreds of sequences were written. From their original prosaic form, where their function was just to fill-in under the melody of the *jubilus*, they developed into a sort of rhyming prose, still closely linked to the melody. Finally, in particular with Adam of Saint Victor, they became poetic works that were increasingly similar to the hymn in terms of versification.[41]

To return to the production of hymnody, it was a devotion to the humanity of Christ, so much a part of the Cistercian spirituality of Saint Bernard, that gave rise to the famous fifty verse hymn *Jubilus de nomine Jesu*, two excerpts from which form the hymns *Dulcis Jesu memoria* and *Jesu Auctor clementiae*.[42]

The high point of all hymnody written out of Eucharistic devotion, which was also very widespread in these times, is in the hymns of Saint Thomas Aquinas for the Office of Corpus Christi which are known throughout the world. Among other outstanding work of this period we also find the *Stabat Mater*, undoubtedly a work of Bonaventurian influence, long attributed to Jacopone da Todi (+ 1306).

After the promulgation of the Tridentine Breviary, new hymns were created for the feasts which, in time, had been introduced into the liturgical year. In general, these new hymns follow the classical model, avoiding grammatical and metrical characteristics of Christian Latin, but although technically beyond reproach, they suffered from a rather stilted and recherché style, which meant they lost popularity.

Writers of this period include: Cardinal Silvio Antoniano (+ 1603), secretary to Saint Charles Borromeo and a scholar who,

---

40. *Notkeri Poetae–Balbuli–Liber Hymnorum: Notker des Dichters (des Stammlers) Hymnenbuch*, ed. W. von den Steinen (Bern: Francke, 1960). Cf. W. von den Steinen, *Notker der Dichter und seine geistige Welt* (Bern: Francke, 1948).

41. *OEuvres poétiques d'Adam de Saint-Victor*, ed. L. Gautier (Paris: Picard, 3rd edn, 1894). The same edition with English translation: D. S. Wrangham, *The Liturgical Poetry of Adam of St. Victor* (London: Kegan Paul, Trench & Co, 1881).

42. A. Wilmart, *Le "jubilus" dit de Saint Bernard: Étude avec textes*, Storia e letteratura 2 (Roma: Edizioni di Storia e Letteratura, 1944).

when he spoke in "La Sapienza" College in Rome on Cicero's speeches, had an audience that comprised of no less than 25 cardinals. The Vespers hymn from the Common of Holy Women (*non Virginum*) is his, *Fortem virili pectore*. Cardinal Borromeo for his part wrote the hymn *Pater superni luminis* for the feast of Saint Mary Magdalen in Ambrosian meter. Both hymns were included in Pope Clement VIII's edition of the Breviary (1602). Pope Urban VIII (1568–1644) composed works such as the asclepiads in honor of Saint Hermenegild (April 13), hymns to Saint Martina (January 30) and Saint Teresa (October 15). The asclepiads of the Carmelite John of Saint Joseph (Juan Blanch Mur: 1642–1718) entitled *Te Joseph celebrent* were adopted for the feast of Saint Joseph (March 19), which proved a very popular song. For the same feast, *Iste quem laeti* and *Caelitum Joseph* written by Cardinal Jeronimo Casante, OP (+ 1700), were also adopted. The iambic diameter verses of the Piarist Father Filippo Bruni (+ 1771), *Auctor beate seculi, Eu tu superba* and *Cor arca legem continens* were adopted for the feast of the Sacred Heart, decreed by Pope Clement XIII in 1765. The hymns for the feast of Our Lady of the Rosary, *Caelestis aulae Nuntius, In monte olivis consito, Jam morte, victor, obruta* and *Te gestientem gaudiis*, were written in 1757 by the Dominican Thomas Richini (+ 1779) and first appeared in the Dominican Breviary. In 1888, when this feast was approved for the Universal Church by Pope Leo XIII, these four hymns were added to the Roman Breviary. We owe the hymns for the feast of the Holy Family to Pope Leo XIII (1810–1903). In the twentieth century we find Pietro Piacenza (+ 1919) and Biagio Verghetti (+ 1945), hymnographers of the Sacred Congregation of Rites, and the Redemptorist Francesco Saverio Reuss (+ 1924) whose ability for the composition of Latin poetry was outstanding. In the early twentieth century these men composed the hymns included in the Offices of the *Commune pro aliquibus locis*. The writers of the reign of Pius XI were Vittorio Genovesi, SJ (1887–1967), who was author of the hymns for the feasts of Christ the King and Saint John Chrysostom as well as the hymn for the Office of the Assumption of Our Lady, and Evaristo D'Anversa (+ 1968), who wrote the hymns for the feast of St Joseph the Worker, *Te pater Joseph* and *Aurora solis nuntia*. Both of these men were also hymnographers at the Sacred Congregation of Rites.

The Introduction of Hymns into the Divine Office

In the West, hymns were introduced without resistance into the monastic Office; Saint Benedict prescribed hymns for each hour in his *Rule*, a practice which seems to have been in use in other monasteries (like that of Lerins). Cassian, Saint Caesarius and Saint Aurelianus of Arles (sixth century) also prescribed in their rules the singing of a hymn at each hour of the Office. In Cathedral Offices, however, the acceptance was not universal; the synod of Agde in France permitted them in the year 506 (canon 30) and the Council of Tours (567) ensured that at least the Ambrosian hymns were incorporated into the canon of the Office, and also permitted those of other notable authors.[43]

Throughout the Spanish peninsula, however, the Synod of Braga (563) firmly excluded hymns from the Offices: "Other than the Psalms and canonical scriptures of the Old and New Testaments, let no piece composed in verse be sung in Church; for this is as the holy canons prescribe."[44] Nevertheless, some years later the Fourth Council of Toledo (633), declaring laws for the whole of Spain and the province of Narbonne (Gaul) said:

> As for the singing of hymns, we have the example of the Savior and of the Apostles; for we are told that the Lord Himself said the hymn . . . . And we know that hymns were composed by man for the praise of God and in order to celebrate the triumphs of the martyrs and of the Apostles, such as the Blessed Doctors Ambrose and Hilary have written (*hymni humano studio in laudem Dei atque apostolorum et martyrum triumphos compositi esse noscuntur, sicut hi quos beatissimi doctores Ilarius atque Ambrosius ediderunt*). Some, however, condemn these songs, on the pretext that they are not to be found in the scriptures recognized by the holy canons or in the apostolic tradition; in that case, let them also reject that hymn written by men that we say each day in the public and private Office at the end of ever psalm: *Gloria et honor Patri, et Filio, et Spiritui Sancto in saecula saeculorum. Amen.* And let them reject also that hymn which the Angels sung to Christ Incarnate: *Gloria in excelsis Deo et in terra pax hominibus bonae voluntatis*: All that follows was written by the doctors of the Church.

---

43. "Although we have the Ambrosian hymns in the canon, still, since there are also others that deserve to be sung, we wish that those ones as well are generously included. The names of their authors have been noted at the end"; Mansi, *Sacrorum Conciliorum*, vol. IX, 803.

44. Mansi, *Sacrorum Conciliorum*, vol. IX, 778.

So these hymns should not be sung in Churches, because they are not to be found in sacred scripture. Hymns are composed just as Masses, prayers, collects, orations of recommendation, the imposition of hands; if we cannot sing any of that in Churches, all ecclesiastical Offices are empty . . . . No less than with the collects, henceforth let none of you condemn hymns, but let them be sung both in Gaul and in Spain: and let those who dare reject hymns be excommunicated (*excommunicatione plectendi qui hymnos reicere fuerint ausi*).[45]

In this way, the hymn was increasingly accepted throughout the Latin West, except in Rome, or more specifically in the Roman basilicas, since in the numerous monasteries of the city hymns were sung as the Benedictine Rule prescribed. Without condemning the customs already established elsewhere, the conservative spirit of the Roman liturgy resisted their introduction for centuries. But that was not all. At one point, thanks to the prestige and exemplarity of the Roman liturgy, attempts were made to adapt all the churches of the empire to the Roman use and to suppress hymns. Agobard, Archbishop of Lyon in the ninth century reminded his clerics: "The reverend councils of the Fathers decreed that common songs should not be sung in church at all, and that nothing composed in a poetic style should be used in divine praises."[46] Nevertheless, the use of hymns had already taken root in Gaul and had already acquired a stable place in the Romano-Gallican liturgy; as well as this, when the Romano-Gallican liturgy had "conquered" Rome, hymns began to be heard in St. Peter's and in St. John Lateran. Like a trace of the old Roman tradition, the Breviary of Saint Pius V does not contain any Office hymns for the Sacred Triduum of Holy Week or the octave of Easter, nor for Matins of the feast of Epiphany. It is curious that this process in the West was the exact opposite of what was happening in the East, where it was the monks who refused to accept the hymns that were sung in the Cathedral Offices.

The nucleus of the hymnody that passed into the Roman Breviary was made up of an Irish collection from the eighth century containing 38 hymns. Since it was believed that these were the work

---

45. Mansi, *Sacrorum Conciliorum*, vol. X, 626.

46. *Reverenda concilia Patrum decernunt nequaquam plebeios psalmos in Ecclesia decantandos, et nihil poetice compositum in divinis laudibus usurpandum*; Agobard, *Liber de divina psalmodia*: PL 104,327A; cf. *Liber de correctione antiphonarii*, 17: PL 104,337C.

of Saint Gregory the Great who had sent them to Saint Columba, they gained great prestige and were consequently distributed throughout Gaul in the ninth and tenth centuries and from there to Rome, where they were later incorporated into the Roman Breviary.

THE HYMN: ITS LITERARY CHARACTERISTICS AND LITURGICAL FUNCTION

In the light of this historical description, we are able to test a definition of the genre in its most perfect form. We can say that the hymn is a lyric poem of equal strophes, of Christian inspiration and language, which sings the praises of God, of the mysteries of redemption, or of the saints.

This means, in the first place, that it belongs to the poetic genre, and more specifically the "lyrical" poetic genre, to distinguish it from other forms such as the epic or didactic genres. Moreover, it is written to be sung, as were the hymns of antiquity (both pagan and Old Testament hymns), since having equal verses allows for a single melody, whether the verse be rhythmical or metrical. It is also Christian in language and content, distinguishing itself from profane lyrical poetry as well as its imitation with Christian content. We can also say that it has a latreutic character, that is to say, not a theological, historical or didactical one. This praise is first and foremost that of God, be it directly or in his works or in his Saints; for God is truly praised in his saints and in all of his works, since "praise of the saints" is also a "praise of God."

Let us detail here some more of the literary aspects. The language, which is Christian in the ancient hymns in prose, classical in those written after the Renaissance and a equal mixture of both in the Ambrosian hymns, favors a vocabulary that is easily pronounced. There are many nouns and verbs (primordial elements of movement and expression), whereas adjectives only appear when their use— be it determinative, comparative, qualifying, or discretely ornamental— is absolutely essential. Since the technique of parallelism was not exclusive to the Hebrew language but rather also to be found in the Latin tongue (particularly in archaic Latin), it has remained throughout the centuries one of the most characteristic traits of Christian hymnody, through all the metrical and rhythmical innovations that were introduced as time went by.

The genre has attracted the attention of great writers who took on the task of translating them. The poetic translations into French by Racine and Corneille are notable. We can mention that in Germany in the nineteenth century there was the work of Heinrich Bone (1813–1893), some of whose versions constitute a rare example of fidelity to the text in a translation in verse that preserves the metric of the original and the literary quality.[47] In the middle of the twentieth century 51 hymns of the Breviary were also translated into Spanish by Francisco Luis Bernárdez.[48] In England, the Oxford Movement marked a revival of Latin hymns in a translated form. One may highlight the translations of John Mason Neale (1818–1866),[49] and those of John Henry Cardinal Newman (1801–1890), who rendered forty-seven of the hymns in the Roman Breviary into English verse.[50]

As for versification, this began as quantitative, in continuity with classical Greco-Roman poetry and steered towards the rhythmo-syllabic form. It is based on two principles: "isostrophism," or the identical construction of strophes, and "isosyllabism," having the same number of syllables on each line. This enables the poetry to be set to a musical melody, one which can be applied to the different verses of a hymn, but also to other hymns; conversely, the same hymn can be sung to different melodies (according to the level of solemnity, for example).

Music has always accompanied the performance of hymns; there are some simple melodies that essentially date back to the time of Saint Ambrose. When singing these melodies, however, there remains a mystery: were they performed at an isochronous tempo as they are today, or did they maintain the short-long value of iambic feet that was already being lost in speech?

---

47. For this subject see R. Schmidt, *Gegen den Reiz der Neuheit: Katholische Restauration im 19. Jahrhundert—Heinrich Bone, Joseph Mohr und Guido Maria Drewes*, Mainzer hymnologische Studien 15 (Tübingen: Francke, 2005).

48. This Argentine poet, friend of Jorge Luis Borges, was one of the great exponents of the Spanish language in his generation.

49. R. E. Messenger, "John Mason Neale, Translator," in *The Hymn* 3 (1951), 5–24.

50. D. A. Withey, *John Henry Newman: the Liturgy and the Breviary: Their influence on his Life as an Anglican,* (London: Sheed & Ward, 1992), 124–136.

The meters in use were:
a) Iambic: can be diameter (grouped in strophes of four lines) or triameter.
b) Sapphic verse.
c) Trochaic: catalectic tetrameter in strophes of three lines, diameter, tripodic, senario.
d) Asclepiadic verse.

There are others that do not fall into any classical metrical pattern but rather combine the number of syllables with the placing of the accent. The most ancient hymns were composed in structures a) and c), while b) and d) were the latest; once into the Middle Ages, there was a definite fascination with the classical authors.

In general, elision is not used a lot, and hiatus is mostly avoided. Substitutions are also rare occurrences; we only find them in Saint Ambrose, Prudentius (who did not strictly speaking compose hymns), and in a few of the after Renaissance classicizing authors. Acrostic hymns were also used in various periods from Sedulius to Piacenza and Verghetti in the twentieth century.

The number of strophes in a hymn is not fixed, although it is usually between four and eight. The first usually contains a direct invocation to the Triune God or to one of the Three Persons, or a declaration of the mystery being celebrated, or of the hour of the day at which the hymn is sung. It thus serves as a *proemium* in which one is invited to the act of praise. These initial verses form an anthology of greatly inspired invocations to God, Christ and the saints, but also of metaphors and poetic descriptions of the dawn, the night, celestial phenomena, etc. These other aspects are characteristic of Latin hymnody and are quite absent from the Eastern tradition, which tends to focus on contemplation of the "mysteries" and of symbolism.

The dawn is blessed with some of the most beautiful descriptions and metaphors. By way of an illustration, let us take an example from Saint Ambrose, a model in this, who in his hymn *Aeterne rerum conditor* ("Eternal Creator of all things") stops to consider the dawn from its breaking until cockcrow. With beautiful metaphors he calls this time *praeco diei*, "herald of the day," *noctis profundae pervigil*, "the tireless watchman of the deepest night," *nocturna lux viantibus*, "the guiding light for nightly pilgrims," and he says that to sing it,

Hoc [sc. canente], excitatus lucifer	Roused at the note, the morning star
Soluit polum caligine;	Heaven's dusky veil uplifts afar:
Hoc omnis erronum chorus	Night's vagrant bands no longer
Vias nocendi deserit.	roam,
	But from their dark ways hie them
	home.
Hoc, nauta vires colligit	The encouraged sailor's fears are o'er,
Pontique mitescunt freta.	The foaming billows rage no more.
Hoc ipsa petra ecclesiae	Lo! e'en the very Church's Rock
Canente culpam diluit.	Melts at the crowing of the cock.

(translated by W. J. Copeland)

The cockcrow invites us to get up, because when the cockerel sings:

Gallus iacentes excitat	As they lie, the cock stirs them awake,
Et somnolentos increpat	Rebukes who will not dreams forsake,
gallus negantes arguit	He shames who yet their Lord denies
Gallo canente spes redit.	And, by his crowing, hope supplies.
Aegris salus refunditur	To feeble frames health is restored,
Mucro latronis conditur	The robber sheathes his lawless sword.
Fides lapsis revertitur	Faith to the falling now returns,
Iesu labentes respice.	Look in us, Jesu, when we fall.

(translated by O. P. Curry, after W. J. Copeland)

Prudentius picks up this theme but compares the cockerel with Christ:

Ales diei nuntius	The wingèd herald of the day
Lucem propinquam praecinit:	Proclaims the morn's approaching ray,
Nos excilator mentium	And Christ the Lord our soul excites,
Iam Christus ad uitam uocat.	And so to endless life invites.

(translated by J. M. Neale)

More is explained of the beneficial effects of this song:

Ferunt vagantes daemonas	'Tis said that baleful spirits roam
Laetos tenebris noctium,	Abroad beneath the dark's vast dome;
Gallo canente exterritos	But, when the cock crows, take their flight
Sparsim timere et cedere.	Sudden dispersed in sore affright.
Invisa nam vicinitas	For the foul votaries of the night
Lucis, salutis, numinis	Abhor the coming of the light,
Rupto tenebrarum situ	And shamed before salvation's grace
Noctis fugat satellites.	The hosts of darkness hide their face.

(translated by R. M. Pope)

It is notable that these very images, across the centuries, end up in the mouth of Shakespeare's Horacio when, after the ghost of Hamlet has vanished as the cock crew, he says:

I have heard
The Cock, that is the trumpet to the morn,
Doth with his lofty and shrill-sounding throat
Awake the God of day; and at his warning
Whether in sea or fire, in earth or air,
The extravagant and erring spirit hies
To his confine.
(*Hamlet*, Act I, sc. 1, vv 150–155)

This, then, is the purpose of the first introductory strophe. It is followed by the main body of the hymn, in which the theme of the mystery or the life of the saint being celebrated is more or less fleshed out. Finally, the last strophes are a petition for grace, pardon, intercession and help. The final strophe is always a doxology. In this way, the hymns with the antiphons, more than the other parts of the Office display a different character for each hour and each feast.[51]

Classicism and Christian Latin in Hymnography

One thing which draws the attention of one who is used to the Roman Breviary and is assisting at the Monastic Office or that of any religious

---

51. For what concerns the place occupied by the hymn and the Office, cf. L. Dobszay, "The Liturgical Position of the Hymn in the Medieval Office," in A. Haug–C. März–L. Welter (ed.), *Der lateinische Hymnus im Mittelalter: Überlieferung–Ästhetik–Ausstrahlung,* Monumenta monodica medii aevi. Subsidia 4 (Kassel: Bärenreiter, 2004), 9–22.

order is the realization that while the hymns of both Offices are
in general terms the same, there are often notable differences which
go beyond the usual variants of an ancient text. These differences
are due to the reform of Roman Hymnarium that took place in the
seventeenth century.

The disdain that the Renaissance generally had for the
Middle Ages, whose art was labeled "gothic" because compared with
classical art—the archetypical model for the humanists—it appeared
as barbarian and primitive, was without exception felt with regard to
Christian poetry. The humanists of the sixteenth and seventeenth
centuries, lovers of classical Latin and "elegant diction," considered
medieval meter to be barbarian and unauthentic, apt to provoke
derision from the learned.[52]

Pope Leo X charged Zaccaria Ferreri (1479–1524),[53] with the
creation of a new Breviary, the hymnody of which was all he managed
to complete. In the title of the printed text of 1525, it is written that
the text was compiled *iuxta veram metri et latinitatis normam* which
was a *sanctum et necessarium opus*. Clement VII had authorized "every
priest" to use them "in the Office and in the recitation of the
Breviary." The decided course of action was to create a completely new
Hymnarium (with only a few feeble reminders of the traditional one)
according to the norms of classical poetry, without retaining any
pagan expressions, allusions or references.[54]

---

52. "The Humanism of the Renaissance, which had its ardent champions even in the
Church—such as Bembo, Sadoletus, etc., to say nothing of certain popes—caused the idea of a
special reform of the Breviary to be entertained in certain quarters, in the interests of greater
literary purity and perfection. Strange schemes were proposed, little in consonance with the spirit
of the Church. A Florentine canon, Marsiglio Ficino, and Peter Pomponatius, for instance,
suggested that the clergy should read the classical authors instead of the Breviary. Others, though
not going so far as this, thought the diction of the Breviary barbaric, and wanted to translate it
into Ciceronian Latin. The corrections suggested included such astounding phrases as the
following: the forgiveness of sins becomes 'superosque manesque placare'; the Begetting of the
Word was to be 'Minerva Jovis capite orta'; the Holy Ghost was 'Aura Zephyri coelestis,' etc."
F. Cabrol, "Breviary," in *The Catholic Encyclopedia*, vol. II, s.v.

53. A Benedictine of Montecassino, later to be Abbot of Subiaco, then went to the
Charterhouse and was finally named Bishop of Guardalfieri in the Kingdom of Naples.

54. The Trinity is called *Triforme Numen Olympi*, and the Blessed Virgin *dearum maxima* or
nympha candidissima.

The third strophe of the hymn *ad matutinum* for Lent gives us an idea of the style:

Bacchus abscedat, Venus ingemiscat.
Nec iocis ultra locus est, nec escis,
Nec maritali thalamo, nec ulli
Ebrietati!

However, Ferreri died and the project of the new Breviary was left unfinished.[55] Only after the Council of Trent reforms in the Roman Breviary began.[56] The Breviary of Saint Pius V (1568) left the hymns practically intact. Excepting some added pieces and some corrections of minor details, its hymnody was that of the old books of the Curia;[57] it is in fact more similar to that found in manuscripts from the thirteenth and fourteenth centuries than that of the breviaries printed from the early sixteenth century which were overloaded with Proper Offices that the Tridentine reform would put aside.[58]

Some years later, in the last quarter of the sixteenth century, Pope Sixtus V began preparing a revision of the Roman Breviary. The recently created Congregation of Rites took on the task, and its first prefect, Cardinal Gesualdo, wrote to the different Nuncios, asking them to consult devout and learned men in their respective countries on the reforms to be made to the Missal and the Breviary.[59] Among the replies transmitted by the Nuncios there were a few proposals of corrections to the hymns, principally corrupted readings, but also the odd suggestion of the elimination of the *cacometri* hymns, and even of their adaptation, in order to bring them *ad mensuram et latinitatem*.[60]

Finally, in 1602 under Clement VIII, the newly corrected edition of the Breviary was published, but the commission headed by

---

55. For more on the Ferreri's Hymnarium, cf. S. Bäumer, *Histoire du Bréviaire*, trans. R. Biron, 2 vols. (Paris: Letouzey et Ané, 1905), vol. II, 117–124.

56. For the following topic, see Y. Delaporte, "Les Hymnes du Bréviaire Romain de Pie V à Urbain VIII," in *Rassegna Gregoriana*, 6 (1907), 495-512 and 7 (1908), 231–250.

57. Delaporte, *Les Hymnes du Bréviaire Romain*, 496–499.

58. The 1522 edition from Venice, for example, contains almost 250 hymns, with many proper Offices, many of them to be freely chosen. Cf. Delaporte, *Les Hymnes du Bréviaire Romain*, 496.

59. The approximate text of this circular letter can be found in Bäumer, *Histoire du Bréviaire*, vol. II, 255.

60. A summary of these replies, kept in the *Bibliotheca Vallicelliana* in Rome among the papers of Cardinal Baronius (Mss. G.79 and G 83), can be seen in Delaporte, *Les Hymnes du Bréviaire Romain*, 500–506.

Cardinal Baronius only allowed minimum corrections to the hymns (the change of a letter or syllable),[61] besides the correction of copyists' errors[62] and the addition of two new hymns.[63] A few years later (1606–1608), Paul V made another edition of the Breviary, with numerous modifications, but the text of the hymns was only slightly altered.[64]

Thirty years later, the Pope Urban VIII, whose opinions differed from the criteria hitherto followed, decided upon the correction of the hymns of the Roman Breviary according to classical norms. The Pope, a poet himself, personally took on the responsibility for this work of revision with the help of four Jesuits who were considered to be *eruditi et sapientes viri*: Mathias Casimir Sarbiewski, Famiano Strada, Tarquinio Galuzzi, and Girolamo Petrucci.

In total, 952 corrections were made to 1,714 verses, affecting 81 of the total of 98 hymns which in that period formed the hymnody of the Breviary.[65] They were as follows: 58 corrections to the 23 hymns of the *Psalterium feriatum per hebdomadam*, 359 in the 17 hymns of the *Proprium de tempore*, 283 in the almost 40 hymns of the *Proprium Sanctorum*, and 252 in the twenty odd hymns that form the *Commune Sanctorum*. The correctors showed a particular lack of mercy for the rhythmical hymns. The new Breviary thus amended was

---

61. Cardinal Antoniano, in analyzing each hymn in turn, had proposed corrections for a huge quantity of metrical errors. Nevertheless, contrary to what is usually said (cf. Batiffol, *Histoire du Breviaire Romain*, vol. II, 324), he was personally against making metrical corrections to the Hymnarium, and Delaporte cites several examples of his thoughts to this effect. It was only obedience that made him undertake this work about which he was not at all enthusiastic. Cf. Delaporte, *Les Hymnes du Bréviaire Romain*, 507–512. A reconstruction of the works of the commission, the critics to the project of reform and the list of the corrections finally made, can be found in Delaporte, *Les Hymnes du Bréviaire Romain*, 231–244.

62. *Quae videbantur errata librariorum, vel quae poterant unius litterae vel syllabae mutatione restitui, ac prsesertim in hymnis Ambrosii el Prudentii, quos non est credibile cum erroribus ab initio fuisse compositos*; Vallicelliana, Ms. G. 83, fol. 110–111. See. Bäumer, *Histoire du Bréviaire*, vol. II, 273.

63. These hymns, about which we have spoken above, were composed by St Charles Borromeo and Cardinal Antoniano for the feast of Saint Mary Magdalen and from the Common of Holy Women (*non Virginum*), respectively.

64. About this reform, see Delaporte, *Les Hymnes du Bréviaire Romain*, 244–248, especially 245–246, where he provides a comparative scheme with the differences (more or less fifty) between the hymns in the breviaries of Saint Pius V (1568) and Paul V (1606–1608).

65. Among the seventeen hymns left intact are those of Thomas Aquinas for the Offices of Corpus Christi (*Pange lingua, Sacris solemniis, Verbum supernum*) which they thought were composed *etrusco rythmo* or the *Ave Maris Stella* because it was *soluta oratione comprehensum*; this shows their ignorance of rhythmic and accentual poetry.

published in 1632. The intention was to arrive at a situation of compromise: the correction of the form while respecting the ideas:

> With a few exceptions, the hymns that are not metrical but are in a free style (*soluta oratione*) or even rhythmical, have been returned to the laws of Latin poetry. Where possible, this has been done by using better edited sources or by making some other change, but where this was really not possible, they have been written afresh, although the sense has been kept the same as far as possible.[66]

Specifically, these were the criteria that were followed: 1) The search for more grammatical correctness in the use of cases and various constructions, avoiding tautology, anacoluthon, etc.; 2) the use of a purer language, eliminating vulgar forms, redundancies, etc. (which included many terms in Christian Latin); 3) above all, a greater adjustment to classical prosody and meter.

In general, these corrections, aside from the occasional success, frequently brought about the loss of the devout simplicity and even misunderstood boldness of the original. Furthermore, the new compilation frequently presupposed a private recitation rather than communal singing of the texts.[67]

The completed corrections range from small alterations, for example a word that changes case—*arte* (ablative) for *ars* (nominative)—to lines and even entire stanzas that are practically rewritten (the second verse of *Aeterne rerum Conditor*). On more than thirty occasions where the first line of the hymn is rearranged, the "incipit," that is, the name of the hymn, changes. Thus *Plasmator hominis Deus* becomes *Hominis superne Conditor*, with an uncomfortable substitution of the first long vowel by two short syllables; adding a syllable (a perfectly classical procedure but one which was generally avoided by Christian hymnographers) made the singing of this line rather difficult. The *Ad coenam agni providi* in turn became *Ad regias Agni dapes*. In the alphabetic hymn of Sedulius, the verse corresponding to the letter "H" began *Hostis Herodes* but became *Crudelis Herodes*, thus losing its alphabetic ordering. In two cases, hymns originally written

---

66. Urban VIII, *Divinam Psalmodiam*, January 25, 1631.

67. In fact, the correction does not seem to have taken into account the musical aspect of the hymns, to such an extent that often the corrected text forces important musical changes, to make it singable. Cf. Y. Delaporte, "Un mot a propos de l'hymnaire: La correction d'Urbain VIII et le chant liturgique," in *La Tribune de Saint-Gervais*, 10 (1904), 264–271.

in one meter (trochaic catalectic tetrameter) were directly transformed into another (iambic diameter), as happened to the hymn for the feast of Saint Michael, *Tíbi Chríste spléndor Pátris, víta vírtus cordiúm*, which was changed to *Te spléndor ét virtús Patrís*, and the hymn for the dedication of a church, *Úrbs beáta Jérusálem dícta pácis vísió*, which became *Caeléstis úrbs Jerúsalém*.

But not only was the form effected, but sometimes the ideas expressed in the original completely disappeared, to be replaced by generic equivalents. If we take, for instance, the start of the hymn for Vespers of the feast of Christmas:

Christe Redemptor omnium,	Christ the Redeemer of all,
Ex Patre Patris Unice	Thou Only [Son] of the Father,
Solus ante principium,	Alone before the beginning
Natus ineffabiliter.	Wert ineffably born of the Father.

Compare this with the corresponding verse in the Urbanian revision:

Jesu, redemptor omnium,	Jesus, Redeemer of all,
Quem lucis ante originem	Whom before the origin of light
Parem paternae gloriae	In equality with the paternal glory
Pater supremus edidit.	The Supreme Father begot.

Another example is the second strophe of Saint Ambrose's *Aeterne rerum Conditor*, upon which we have already commented, where the order has been completely changed and the achieved poetic expression—*noctis profundae pervigil* ("untiring watchman of the deep night")—has been lost:

Praeco diei iam sonat,	Already the herald of the day resounds,
Noctis profundae pervigil,	Untiring watchman of the deep night,
Nocturna lux viantibus,	A night-light to the traveler,
A nocte noctem segregans.	Separating night from night.
Nocturna lux viantibus,	Night-light to the traveler,
A nocte noctem segregans.	Separating night from night,
Præco diei iam sonat,	Already the herald of the day resounds,
Iubarque solis evocat	Reclaiming the sun's ray.

There is the beginning of the magnificent poem to the Cross by Venantius Fortunatus:

Pange lingua gloriosi praelium certaminis

Sing, O my tongue, of the combat of the glorious battle

This was changed to:

Pange lingua gloriosi lauream certaminis

Sing O my tongue, of the victory of the glorious battle.[68]

It is certain that the large part of the corrections make the meaning secondary to the expression, changing only the order of words:

Qui Paraclitus diceris
Donum Dei altissimi

You who are called Paraclete,
Gift of God most High

This became:

Qui diceris Paraclitus
Altissimi donum Dei

However, the motive behind some of the changes is difficult to understand, such as in the hymn *Splendor paternae gloriae*:

Votis vocemus et Patrem
Patrem perennis gloriae,
Patrem potentis gratiae,
Culpam releget lubricam.

Let us also call upon the Father with prayers,
The Father of eternal glory,
The Father of powerful grace,
So that he removes the dangerous fault.

This became:

Votis vocemus et Patrem
Patrem potentis gratiae,
Patrem perennis gloriae,
Culpam releget lubricam.

---

68. It is important to note that in the original version there is not a pleonasm: *proelium* refers to the battle, and *certamen* to the occasion or cause of it; thus, *proelium gloriosi certaminis* refers to the battle for the souls of men. The expression is found in Cyprian, *Ep. 55* (*ad Antonianum*), 4,1: CCL 3B, 259: *Praelium gloriosi certaminis in persecutione ferveret* ("the struggle of a glorious contest was raging in the persecution"). The Roman Martyrology for June 11, in the *Passio Sanctorum Felicis et Fortunati*, notes that the two saints, after suffering multiple tortures, *ad ultimum, cum in Christi confessione persisterent, gloriosi certaminis cursum, obtruncati capite, impleverunt* ("they completed the course of the glorious contest, being beheaded, since they persevered to the end in confessing Christ"). For this reason, *certamen* ("contest") reveals the importance and length of the fight and underlines the directive idea behind the entire poem. Cf. H. T. Henry "Pange lingua gloriosi," in *The Catholic Encyclopedia*, vol. XI, s.v.

The text of the strophe is the same, only the order of the second and third lines has been inverted; but it is hard to see the necessity of such a change, which affects neither the meter nor the Latinity.

This version, first presented as facultative (1629), was incorporated three years later into the official text of the Roman Breviary (in the Bull *Divinam psalmodiam*, January 25, 1632), and with the Bull *Cum alias* (April 27, 1643) it became obligatory in the city of Rome and its environs.[69] However, this was only for those who used the Roman Breviary; the religious and monastic orders who had their own rites, the Benedictines,[70] Cistercians, Carthusians, Premonstratensians, Dominicans, the Calced Carmelites, and the Franciscans of the provinces of France kept the traditional Hymnarium.[71] The canons of St. Peter's Basilica, who were so strongly attached to liturgical tradition that they had not accepted the introduction of the Vulgate Psalter but had maintained the use of the ancient Roman Psalter,[72] also kept the original texts of the hymns in the version of Paul V.[73]

Acceptance of the revision varied; there were of course many who applauded the work. Many felt, however, that they had in many cases lost the poetic meaning of the original which was linked both to the state of the Latin language in use and to the chant (the Roman cantors protested that the correctors were more familiar with the "muses" than with "music"), and there were those who said that with the new version, *accessit latinitas, recessit pietas.* Nevertheless the two claims of such a statement need some clarification. On the one hand (*pietas*), it is undeniable that, generally speaking, the fundamental

69. Cf. Bäumer, *Histoire du Bréviare*, vol. II, 291.

70. The Benedictine congregation of Saint Maur is the only that, after several variations, has finally adopted Urban VIII's revision. On the other hand, the text of the hymns of the Solesmes Benedictine Dom Joseph Pothier's *Monastic Breviary* (1885) does not reflect the traditional text either, because it includes a few number of variations that cannot be found in the older editions and coincide with Urban VIII's revision. Cf. Delaporte, *Les Hymnes du Bréviaire Romain*, 248, n. 3.

71. In France, the dioceses that rejected the introduction of the Neo-Gallican rites and preserved the authentic Roman rite in general used the old version. Few French editions of the breviary before 1789 can be found with the new versions; however, they are frequently found in an appendix. By contrast, the editions published after the second half of the nineteenth century have only the revised hymns. Cf. P. Guéranger, *Institutions liturgiques*, 2 vols. (Paris: Palmé, 2nd edn, 1878–1880), vol. I, 518.

72. *Romanum psalterium a Pio V Romae abolitum, adhuc perdurat in vaticana ecclesia;* J. Grancolas, *Commentarius historicus in Romanorum Breviarium* (Venetii: Coleti, 1734), 87.

73. Cf. Delaporte, *Les Hymnes du Bréviaire Romain*, 248.

religious meaning of the text was retained, and when the text itself was changed, it was substituted for something analogous. It would be an exaggeration however to speak of a disappearance of piety as a characteristic of this version.

On the other hand (*latinitas*), which was allegedly advantageous, was understood here in a restricted way; behind it was the predominantly Renaissance idea of classical purity, which considered the only "good Latin" and "good poetry" to be from the classical period. "Christian Latin," with its own particular vocabulary, methods of expression, grammar and poetical system, was totally and utterly ignored. Latin in the Middle Ages was a living language (and as such it was *sui generis*), one which accordingly found means of expression that were adaptable to a living language and not to a previous and often over-idealized version of it; even the classic writers of the golden age themselves took certain liberties in lyric poetry by sometimes departing from traditional meter.[74] This is how a system based on stressed rhythms, assonance and rhyme was developed, all characteristics that are easily understood by one who knew the spoken language but on which the music to which the poetry was sung depended. As Dag Norberg, one of the leading authorities on medieval poetry, said, "A rhythmical poem is one where the old system is replaced by a new, not one whose characteristics are barbarism and an absence of rules."[75] In this sense, it is certain that "Ambrose and Prudentius took something classical and made it Christian; the revisers and their imitators took something Christian and tried to make it classical."[76]

What Pope Urban VIII really did was to impose upon future generations of Catholics not a classical understanding, which as we have seen is debatable, but a seventeenth century view of classical Latin poetical construction. In fact, a poet of the classical era who limited himself to the norms of metrical feet and meter was justified because the sound of the text when declaimed was pleasant and

---

74. Bäumer, *Histoire du Bréviaire*, vol. II, 290.

75. D. Norberg, *Introduction à l'étude de la versification latine médiévale*, Studia Latina Stockholmiensia 5 (Stockholm: Almqvist & Wiksell, 1958), 94.

76. J. Connelly, *Hymns of the Roman Liturgy* (Westminster, MD: The Newman Press, 1957), cited by V. A. Lenti, "Urban VIII and the Revision of the Latin Hymnal" in *Sacred Music* 120 (1993), 30–33; also available on http://www.ewtn.com/library/liturgy/revishym.txt.

harmonious to hear; versifying without this effect can be a proof of ingenuity, but not poetry. Similar to this was another "prejudice" of the Renaissance, the fashion for white statues with eyes that had no pupils but just an empty stare. They considered these to be in the purest classical style, and they imitated it as such, but we now know that both Greek and Latin classical sculpture was colored, and that the ancients considered an unpainted statue imperfect.[77]

With that, let us recall the words of Batiffol: "Urban VIII thought that he was responding to the desire of his age by correcting the prosody, or so-called prosody, of the Church's hymns. It was thus that Barberini and so many others re-sculpted the disfigured limbs of the ancient statues rather than the secular mutilations of their own marble!"[78] A more exact comparison would perhaps be to say that it is as if they had adjusted the "Beau Dieu d'Amiens," modifying the dimensions in order to make it fit with the "canon" of Phidias.

Today, nobody would dare correct the plays of Shakespeare and adjust them to the classical theatrical principles of Aristotle's *Poetics*. The reality of this situation was becoming more and more obvious, and when in the nineteenth century there was a renewed interest in Church Fathers, there was at the same time a rediscovery of patristic and medieval Christian poetry. Many specialists in literature, liturgy and liturgical music displayed an awareness of the situation and even proposed initiatives for the return of the traditional texts.[79]

During the first part of the twentieth century these studies continually gained greater force and depth and the revaluation of the aesthetics proper to medieval poetry became continually more widespread. Finally during the Second Vatican Council, a return to the Christian Latin of the liturgical texts was proposed, something which was recognized in *Sacrosanctum Concilium*, 93, where it says, "*Hymni, quantum expedire videtur, ad pristinam formam*

---

77. Cf. A Gramoccia–H. Bankel, *I colori del bianco: policromia nella scultura antica*, Collana di studi e documentazione 1 (Roma: De Luca, 2004).

78. Batiffol, *Histoire du Breviaire Romain*, 336.

79. Dom Réginald Biron, who translated Bäumer's famous *History of the Breviary* into French, says: "We know for sure that the members of the Commission for Gregorian chant, instituted by Pius X and reunited for a congress in September 1904 at Appuldurcombe [Isle of Wight], have also announced their wish to return to the ancient text of the hymns, which would allow for the use of the Gregorian melodies"; translation of Bäumer, *Histoire du Bréviaire*, vol. II, 293, note.

restituantur." In the new *Liturgia Horarum* published in 1971 the
texts revised under Pope Urban were put aside completely.

Perhaps one of the most outstanding speeches on this subject
was that of Luigi Maria Carli, then Bishop of Segni: "I propose it
should be decreed that Christian Latinity is always to be observed in
Latin liturgical texts, both in re-editing and in composing anew . . . .
Thus 'Christian Latin,' as it is commonly labeled today even in
pontifical documents (cf. the 'Norms' for implementingthe Apostolic
Constitution 'Veterum sapientia'), embraces that species of Latin,
called a 'special language' by the philologists, which was developed
and brought into the use of the Church by the older Latin Christian
authors for this reason, to adapt the speech of the Romans to the
requirements of the new religion. This Christian Latin flourished in
the Middle Ages and the most perfect examples of it are found in the
old liturgical texts. Its use in editing liturgical books is encouraged for
these reasons. This Christian Latin is especially outstanding because,
whether on account of its technical vocabulary corresponding to
Christian doctrine, or its simplicity joined with nobility of style, or the
spirit of piety with which it is deeply imbued, it is suited to the needs
of Christian worship in a wonderful way. It would seem odd if, just
as this type of Latin is more and more esteemed by educated men, the
Catholic Church were to neglect it. This is equally, if not more, the
case because, after more recent studies and so many philological documents we have today a very extensive quantity of material to enable
the liturgical texts to be returned to their original beauty"; *Acta
synodalia sacrosancti Concilii Oecumenici Vaticani II. Vol. I: Periodus
prima. Pars 2: Congregationes generales X–XVIII* (Civitas Vaticana:
Typis Polyglottis Vaticanis, 1970), 463–65.

Nevertheless, the hymns that appear in it do not always reflect
the original texts; quite a few textual changes were made (more than
140 corrections in some 250 hymns), although this time they were not
inspired by the classicist prejudices of the Renaissance but rather by
other motives, some of them very debatable. Let us cite some criteria
for these changes: there was an aesthetic or literary motive behind
a great number of them, especially with regard to poetic and musical
rhythm (it is of course difficult to see such criteria as being separable
from the editor's subjective taste); other changes include the elimination of certain turns of phrase that could sound profane or that were

associated with "paganism"; elsewhere it is a desire for a certain "theological" correction, or a move toward a certain exegetical position, which is the motive behind a change. To give an example, when checking the "vast tradition of hymnography" (sic) in honor of Saint Mary Magdalene it was noted that she is identified as both Mary the sister of Martha and as the sinner of Luke 7:37, and so they felt obliged to create special hymns for her feast which were in accord with the "certain" details provided by the Gospels.[80] Finally, some phrases were modified if they were not considered "politically correct": certain "antiquated" expressions or concepts (65, 34, 93, 60, 65, 67, 214) or "scholastic" terms (34) were thus changed, and in particular concepts regarded as "antiquated," such as any reference to the link between "night" and "sin" (7, 10, 30), or the traditional discipline of fasting (92, 93, 94, 277), or phrases thought to be "inadequate" (7, 34, 37, 44, 49, 50, 65, 30, 74, 226, 248, 72, 165, 113, 140, 248) or shocking on account of their "harshness" (272). In the same way, those phrases that expressed a negative attitude toward the world (284) or could represent difficulties for ecumenical relations (109, 195, 226, 233) were modified or simply removed. In other cases, it is harder to find explanations for the changes (cf. hymns 96, 113, 153, 165, 183, 194, 217). Finally, we mention the case of hymn 241 which was almost entirely re-written.[81] But besides the judgement on the changes made with regard to the original text, this new Hymnarium has an important defect, one which is found also in the Urbanian revision but which is perhaps more grave from a liturgical perspective, and that is the fact that an original creation—the product of the study, work and reflection of some people—was imposed in such an abrupt manner. Let us examine the figures: the Tridentine Breviary contained some 90 hymns; Saint Pius X's version had 150; the current Breviary has 291 hymns. Of these, 217 were composed between the fourth and fifteenth centuries (about 150 are anonymous, and the other 70 are the works of 29 different authors). As for the remainder, 20 were composed between the sixteenth and nineteenth centuries (9 by known

---

80. Cf. A. Lentini, *Te decet hymnus. L'innario della "Liturgia horarum"* (Civitas Vaticana: Typis Polyglottis Vaticanis, 1984), notes on hymns 179 and 180, see also the note on hymn 70.

81. See Lentini, *Te decet hymnus*, XXVII, and the comments of L. Dobszay, *The Bugnini-Liturgy and the Reform of the Reform*, Musicae Sacrae Meletemata 5 (Front Royal, VA: Catholic Church Music Associates, 2003), 14–15.

authors and 5 anonymous), and 12 were written by 5 authors at the beginning of twentieth century. Anselmo Lentini, osb (1901–1989), who headed *Coetus* VII (that is, the group of specialists appointed by the *Consilium* to prepare the new Hymnarium), composed no less than 42 hymns: Lauds of Tuesday of the first and third weeks, Vespers of Wednesday of the second and fourth weeks, the Office of Readings of the Nativity, Lauds of the feast of the Holy Family, all the hymns for the solemnity of the Most Holy Trinity, the rest for the separate feast of the Proper of the Saints. This represents 15 percent of the total, and 30 percent of the hymns written by known authors, which makes him the main author of the current Hymnarium followed, far behind, by Aurelius Prudentius (ten hymns), Saint Peter Damian (nine), and Saint Ambrose (eight). The remainder of the 43 known authors is generally only represented by one, two or three hymns each. John Henry Newman, whose conversion was so importantly influenced by the Roman Breviary and especially its hymns, wrote the following in the prologue to his edition of the *Hymni Ecclesiae e Breviario Parisiensi* (Oxford: J.H. Parker, 1838), while he was still an Anglican:

> The Roman Hymns, whether good or bad, were the work of no one generation, much less the outpourings of one mind. They were not the contents of one collection, published all new in a day according to the will of man. They were the gradual accumulation of centuries, bearing in old and new upon one treasure-house. When there was a call to reject them, there was nothing to be done but begin again. We could not be young and old at once. It was a stern necessity alone which could compel us to change from what we were; but being changed, so far we were not what we were, and must be what the primitive Church was in these respects, poor and ill-furnished. We began the world, again. This is the proper answer to inconsiderate complaints and impatient interference. There have before now been divines who could write a Liturgy in thirty-six hours. Such is not our Church's way. She is not the empiric to make things to order, and to profess to anticipate the course of nature, which, under grace, as under Providence, is slow. She waits for that majestic course to perfect in its own good time, what she cannot extort from it; for the gradual drifting of precious things upon her shore, now one and now another, out of which

she may complete her rosary and enrich her beads, beads and rosary more pure and true than those which at the command of duty she flung away.[82]

CONCLUSION

This historical review of the development of Christian poetry and its relations with the liturgy manifests two tendencies which were opposed from the beginning, one or other predominating through the course of history: on the one hand a tendency toward slavish imitation of the classical model marked by a certain sentiment of inferiority which leads to scrupulously avoiding the Christian elements and which endures a greater or lesser lack of liberty for poetic inspiration. On the other hand, poetic inspiration and the enthusiastic experience of the faith[83] have produced a more authentic poetry, in an artistic and human sense, even when accompanied by frequent defects of form and idiomatic expression. In certain moments these two tendencies were able to harmonize, a model of this equilibrium between both elements being achieved without a doubt by Saint Ambrose.

Finally, the Urbanian correction of the hymnal must not be seen as an isolated fact which concerns only the metrical or the aesthetical poetry according to the first of the tendencies mentioned above, but rather as one that is placed in the context of a wider understanding of the culture proper to the Renaissance. The spirit of the sixteenth century was entirely different from that of the medieval "renaissances": in the Carolingian renaissance, "the learned followed the example of Prudentius as well as that of Virgil; Cicero was no more a model than Saint Augustine, Saint Jerome, or Saint Gregory. It was Christian Latin culture that Charlemagne wanted to spread and tried to raise up a level."[84] In this way, the literary potential of language was revived in a true renaissance, in something similar to the second medieval "renaissance" of the twelfth century. On the

---

82. Cf. Withey, *John Henry Newman: The Liturgy and the Breviary*, p. 151.

83. Christine Mohrmann suggests that primitive Christianity, the Christianity of the heroism of the martyrs and of the faith of the apologists did not use the poetic genre, not out of hostility to poetry or to art in general, but because it did not find it possible to have the expression of its living faith through an erudite poetry reduced to a mere technique: "La poésie était incapable d'être l'interprète des sentiment chrétiens: elle était disqualifiée par son manque de sérieux, par un certain dilettantisme pédantesque"; Mohrmann, *La langue et style de la poésie Chrétienne*, 153.

84. D. Norberg, *Manuel pratique de latin médiéval* (Paris: Picard, 1968), 50.

other hand, from the Renaissance humanists' point of view, Christian Latin was considered a sort of corruption of classical Latin that was merely kept out of reverence for the scriptures and the liturgy.[85] This archaeological restoration resulted in the death of the Latin tongue: "Before they had ceased talking of a rebirth it became evident that they had really built a tomb."[86] In fact, by rejecting every form of Latin that departed from the classical models, the language ceased to attract the true poets, who found more liberty in the romance tongues than in a language whose ruling principle was imitation, enforced by a rigorous, artificial and aesthetically ineffective regime of norms. At that moment, in the phrase of Norden, the *history* of the Latin language ends and its *study* begins.[87]

Permit me to end with a text from one of Oxford's outstanding figures, C. S. Lewis, who beautifully synthesizes what we have seen: "It is largely to the humanists that we owe the curious conception of the 'classical' period in a language, the correct or normative period before which all was immature or archaic and after which all was decadent. Thus Scaliger tells us that Latin was 'rude' in Plautus, 'ripe' from Terence to Virgil, decadent in Martial and Juvenal, senile in Ausonius. Vives says much the same. Vida, more wildly, makes all Greek poetry after Homer a decline. When once this superstition was established it led naturally to the belief that good writing in the fifteenth or sixteenth century meant writing which aped as closely as possible that of the chosen period in the past. All real development of Latin to meet the changing needs of new talent and new subject matter was thus precluded; with one blow of 'his Mace petrific' [Milton, *Paradise Lost*] the classical spirit ended the history of the Latin tongue. This was not what the humanists intended."[88]

---

85. See Norberg, *Manuel pratique*, 50, and C. Mohrmann, "Le dualisme de la latinité médiévale," in *Revue des Études latines* 29 (1952), 330–348, at 348.

86. C. S. Lewis, *English Literature in the Sixteenth Century, Excluding Drama* (Oxford: Clarendon Press, 1954), 21.

87. Cf. E. Norden, *Die antike Kunstprosa vom VI. Jahrhundert v. Chr. bis in die Zeit der Renaissance*, 2 vols. (Leipzig: Teubner, 2nd edn, 1909), vol. II, 767, see also 951.

88. Lewis, *English Literature*, 21.

Chapter 4

The *Proprium Missae* of the Roman Rite

László Dobszay

The Roman rite is more than the *Ordo Missae*. And although the Roman rite is historically linked to the Latin tongue, that rite itself is more than the language of the liturgy. Recall the fact that the eastern liturgies were translated repeatedly, whilst the rites themselves changed much less frequently over the centuries than did the Roman rite.

Also included in the Roman rite are the many texts of the *Proprium Missae*. In addition, the Roman rite is the order of the pericopes, the collection of prayers and orations and their distribution, the structure of the Divine Office, and the texts for celebrating the sacraments. Furthermore, the Roman rite is also the Mass Antiphoner (*Graduale)* and the Office Antiphoner (*Antiphonale*). I wish to stress this last aspect too, since discussions of the traditional liturgy tend to neglect the recent changes in the Office, which after all ought to be an integral, indeed an eminent part of the liturgy, without which there can be scarcely any liturgical education, any liturgical life, any liturgical renewal, and any pastoral-liturgical activity.

In this chapter, however, I shall confine my remarks to the chants of the *Proprium*, to their special features, and to some general conclusions. But we must begin with a brief historical survey of the Mass chants before we arrive at the conclusions, some of which will exceed the narrow limits of this presentation.

Mass Chants

Table 4.1 (pp. 104–111) lists a few selected days and their Proper Mass chants from sources of varying dates. The "equals" sign in the table (=) means that the given item is identical with the corresponding piece in the so-called Tridentine rite as indicated at the beginning of each line.[1] Pieces which differ are marked with only a reference letter (in capitals); the full text can be read in the footnote (printed in bold). A question mark (?) means the source offers no clear assignment. The first column following the incipit quotes the Antiphonary of the Old Lateran (Roman) use,[2] followed by the most ancient (and some later) Gregorian Mass antiphoners.[3] The last column points to the *Ordo Cantus Missae*[4] and the Missal of Paul VI.[5] The letter-codes identifying the various sources are explained above the table. The *Graduale Simplex*[6] was not taken into consideration because its chants are basically different from this system. What can we see in this table?

1.   The *continuity* of the Roman Mass chant tradition from the earliest sources up to the twentieth century emerges very clearly from these data. The Old Roman source testifies that the chants sung at Rome before the rite was transmitted to the Franks were identical to those found in the Tridentine Mass. It is certainly possible to trace this tradition back at least into the eighth century, which is only a *terminus post quem non.*[7] The identical nature of these sets of chants is convincing not only with respect to quantity but also in *quality*, since it covers all the cardinal points of the liturgy. And the *differences* confirm

---

1. I follow the *Graduale Sacrosanctae Romanae Ecclesiae* (Romae: Typis Vaticanis, 1908).

2. B. Stäblein, *Die Gesänge des altrömischen Graduale: Vat. lat. 5319*, Monumenta monodica medii aevi 2 (Kassel: Bärenreiter, 1970). Cf. M. Lütolf, *Das Graduale von Santa Cecilia in Trastevere: Cod. Bodmer 74* (Cologny: Bodmer, 1987).

3. For their list and sigla see Table 4.2.

4. *Missale Romanum: Ordo Cantus Missae,* Editio typica (Civitas Vaticana: Typis Polypglottis Vaticanis, 1972).

5. *Missale Romanum ex decreto Sacrosancti Oecumenici Concilii Vaticani II instauratum auctoritate Pauli PP. VI promulgatum*, Editio typica (Civitas Vaticana: Typis Polyglottis Vaticanis, 1970).

6. *Graduale Simplex in usum minorum Ecclesiarum* (Civitas Vaticana: Typis Polyglottis Vaticanis, 1967).

7. J. McKinnon, *The Advent Project: The Later-Seventh-Century Creation of the Roman Mass Proper* (Berkeley: University of California Press, 2000), with further literature.

this essential sameness, while only adding nuances to the picture.
To give a few examples:

    2.   In the Offertories we observe the presence or absence
of the *verses* (marked with "v" in the table), which in spite of their
rich significance unfortunately disappeared from the Roman liturgy
approximately during the twelfth and thirteenth centuries.[8] Some
of the ancient sources also included a so-called *versus ad repetendum*[9]
to the Introit, which wonderfully illuminate the selection of that
psalm on the given day (marked with "v" in the table), and a reference
to the Communion psalm (marked with "p"). In other cases the difference results from omission of a verse in some Alleluias. Double verses
occasionally appear in the ancient Roman liturgy;[10] this was simplified in the Curial rite and consequently in the Tridentine Missal
as well. Thus, for instance, the amputation of the verse *Epulemur* from
the Easter Sunday Alleluia seriously mutilated the full meaning of
the chant.

    3.   Some of the items in the table are in boldface, meaning
that one or more sources differ considerably from the Missal of Saint
Pius V. It will be instructive to examine them more closely. Though
in the recent reform the inter-Lectionary chants remained the only
obligatory Mass chants, we can see that the tradition is not uniform at
precisely these points. In the various individual usages the selection
of the Alleluia is anything but arbitrary, but the Roman rite as a whole
is not quite uniform in this respect. As some of the ancient liturgical
books put it: *Alleluia quale volueris*,[11] which of course does not mean
that these items were left to the creative will of individuals, but rather
permitted the worshipping community to select the chant from an
already established collection. Closer inspection of these cases reveals,
for example, that the Old Roman rite used only two Alleluias for
all of Advent, alternating from week to week.[12] The Gregorian sources
place these two Alleluias on the first and third Sundays (reversing the

---

    8. P. Wagner, *Einführung in die gregorianischen Melodien: Ein Handbuch der Choralwissenschaft*, 3 vols (Leipzig: Breitkopf & Härtel, 1911–1921), vol. I, 107–13 and vol III, 418–34. D. Hiley, *Western Plainchant: A Handbook* (Oxford: Clarendon Press, 1993), 121–130.

    9. R.-J. Hesbert, *Antiphonale Missarum Sextuplex* (Rome: Herder, 1935).

    10. Stäblein, *Die Gesänge*, 629–77, Nr. 3, 80a, 81b, 82b, 83b, 86b, 87n, 96, 102, 106, 126.

    11. *Antiphonale Missarum Sextuplex*, 82–85, 88–91, 107–10; lists without distribution: 199.

    12. Stäblein, *Die Gesänge*, 629–630.

order of the Old Roman rite) and added new pieces for the second and fourth Sundays. And it is precisely on these two Sundays that we can discern ambiguity between the sources.

Furthermore, the Old Roman rite had a limited set of Alleluias (*Dominus regnavit, Adorabo ad templum, Venite exsultemus,* etc.) which were used both on great solemnities and on ordinary Sundays.[13] The Gregorian sources assigned these few Old Roman Alleluias to the feasts,[14] and created a series of new Alleluias for the period *per annum,* arranged in an orderly linear sequence. Owing to some differences at the beginning and end of this series, and also because of a few insertions, the individual chants may shift position by a week or two depending upon the *consuetudo* of the particular local usage (see the two examples at the end of the table).[15] There are a few differences also in the case of the other inter-Lectionary chant, in the Graduals of the Sundays after Pentecost.

4.   There is another reason for the difference between the Old Roman and the Gregorian sources on the Fourth Sunday of Advent. In the Old Roman rite, because of the long vigil service on Ember Saturday, this day was specified *Dominica vacat.*[16] When the custom of the lengthy vigil on this day died out, it was necessary to compose a Proper for the Sunday which had become "free," and so one was assembled from the chants of other days. In some communities the Mass of the Ember Wednesday was repeated on the following Sunday, and this is how the *Rorate* became the Introit of the Fourth Sunday of Advent. In Transalpine regions, however, a new chant was provided for that day, and thus one of the most beautiful pieces was created: the Introit *Memento nostri* (whose melody is new, though

---

13. For example, *Alleluia Dominus regnavit decorem* is sung in the Second Mass of Christmas, on the Sunday after Christmas, on the Third Sunday after Epiphany, on the feasts of the Invention and of the Exaltation of the Holy Cross, on the eighth and the twenty-fourth Sunday after Pentecost.

14. For example, *Dominus regnavit* appears in the oldest manuscripts on different days (*Antiphonale Missarum Sextuplex*, 240), in the *Klosterneuburg Graduale* (Graz 807) similarly to the post-Tridentine choir books, only in the Second Mass of Christmas and the following Sunday.

15. Cf. D. Hiley, "Post-Pentecost Alleluias in Medieval British Liturgies," in S. Rankin and D. Hiley (ed.), *Music in the Medieval English Liturgy* (Oxford: Clarendon Press, 1993), 145–174.

16. McKinnon, *The Advent Project*, 129–131.

the text was chosen on the basis of a traditional interpretation which dates back to Saint Augustine).[17]

To summarize: the repertory and distribution of the Proper chants *per anni circulum*—what we may call chant pericopes—is an integral part of the Roman rite. The system as a whole was common throughout the *universal* Roman rite, accepted everywhere and at every epoch from the earliest documented beginnings—even if some few pieces were fixed in their place by the tradition of a *local* church institution such as a diocese or a religious order. In other words, the chant was not merely an accompaniment but an important component of the liturgy, indeed, of the *daily* liturgy. The chants had their function in delivering the contents of the liturgy. In other words, to the liturgy of a given day there *belong* the chant texts, no less than the prayers and readings, and therefore omission of the daily chanted texts truncates the message of the liturgy.

This statement, however, calls for refinement. Twentieth-century commentators on the liturgy often tended to analyze all the items of a given Mass as transmitting a homogeneous intellectual message. Thus they would explain how an Introit fits with the Gospel of the day, how the Gradual is linked to the Epistle, and so forth. However, this approach is flawed, because the cycle of the individual liturgical genres was composed separately in the course of the year, and the fixed series of texts often shifted away from one another.[18] Moreover, this approach encouraged the construction of rational "themes" for each day, with the danger of regarding the Mass (in Enlightenment fashion) merely as an illustration of catechetical or moral lessons. Since the Roman rite did *not* fulfill such expectations, the post-conciliar reform sought to make it more "consistent" in this respect. A striking example of such questionable harmonization is the

17. Augustine, *Enarrationes in Psalmos*, 105: CCL 40,1552–69; see also *Sermo de calendis ianuariis contra paganos* (Mainz 62/Dolbeau 25 [198 augm.]): ed. F. Dolbeau, *Augustin d'Hippone: Vingt-Six Sermons au Peuple d'Afrique retrouvés à Mayence*, Collection des Etudes Augustiniennes, Série Antiquité 147 (Institut d'Études Augustiniennes: Paris, 1996), 366–417.

18. J. A. Jungmann, *Missarum Sollemnia. Eine genetische Erklärung der Römischen Messe*, 2 vols (Wien: Herder, 5th edn, 1962), vol. I, 555–56; McKinnon, *The Advent Project*, 47–59, with further literature.

three-year system of responsorial psalms.[19] This system is guided
by the notion that reading and psalm together form some sort
of a dialogue: first God speaks to man and then man replies to God
according to the ideas or "trends" elicited by the reading. However,
this notion falls short of the fact that the liturgy is a "dialogue" in *each*
of its genres: *all* of its moments are God's gift, his word to the Church,
and they all include simultaneously the response of the Church.
God teaches also in the Gradual chant, and the Church hearkens also
to the reading in a spirit of continuous prayer and reflection.

PROPER CHANTS

How can one say that the Proper chants are "part" of the daily liturgy?
What does it mean to claim that those Proper chants are a decisive
element of the Roman rite which cannot be omitted? There are three
dimensions or principles which justify the thesis.

    1.   It is a peculiarity of the *Ritus Romanus* that most of its
chants have texts taken from Holy Scripture. Though to us this seems
self-evident, the liturgical usage of the Eastern Church makes it clear
that this is a special characteristic of the Church in the West and of
Rome in particular. This practice became possible because the Apostles
interpreted not only the words of the Lord in the Gospels, but also the
entire Scriptures, including the Psalter, and this *interpretatio Christiana*
was enriched by the theological reflection of the Church Fathers
during the succeeding centuries. Many of the faithful became familiar
with the biblical commentaries of Origen, Augustine, Ambrose or
John Chrysostom. But this type of interpretation really became the
common property of the Church *in and through the liturgy*. The
Church as a living community comprehended the Bible when it was
prayed in chant day by day. It was this understanding of the Sacred
Page which inspired the Church to sing a given passage, but at
the same time the *adoption* of that passage clarified the meaning of it.

---

19. *Psalmus responsorius unicuique lectioni respondeat*; *Missale Romanum ex decreto Sacrosancti
Oecumenici Concilii Vaticani II instauratum auctoritate Pauli PP. VI promulgatum Ioannis Pauli PP. II
cura recognitum*, Editio typica tertia (Civitas Vaticana: Typis Vaticanis, 2002), *Institutio Generalis*,
no. 61.

Thus, for instance, Psalm 2 and the solemnity of Christmas mutually interpret each other.

2.   The Christological reading of the Bible in general has become more accurate and refined by theological reflection when many verses of scripture were linked with specific mysteries and consequently with specific liturgical occasions. It was not at all as though someone searched out an appropriate text to be sung on a given Advent Sunday. Prior to being chosen, the particular Biblical *locus* was already associated with the mystery of the specific season. In this case, the "season" seems more important than the individual "day." Psalms 24, 79 and 84 recur again and again in the Masses and Offices of Advent; therefore, they should not be understood chiefly in the context of the *day* (and its other chants and readings), but rather in the larger framework of general Advent references. And then it becomes clear why *Excita* or *Ostende* (which recur at so many points of the Advent Office) are entirely appropriate texts to serve as an Alleluia verse, even though they are assigned differently to Sundays in the Old Roman and Gregorian systems.[20] Permit me to illustrate the relationship between the Patristic interpretation and the liturgical use by one cogent example, the Introit of Easter Sunday.

People of our time are perhaps unmoved by the enigmatic psalm verse of this Introit: *Resurrexi, et adhuc tecum sum*. Perhaps they would be more easily stirred by the triumphal sounds of a late medieval *cantio* or a Lutheran chorale that begins: "Christ ist erstanden . . . des solln wir alle froh sein." In order to understand the choice of this verse for the Easter Sunday Introit, let us consider Saint Augustine's explanation of Psalm 138.[21] It is difficult to summarize this text in a few sentences, but I can at least hint at its Paschal meaning.

Augustine's sermon begins with an admonition to search out in the words of the Prophet the same truth proclaimed in the Gospel, since the *sacrificium vespertinum* of Christ on the cross rent the curtain of the Temple, revealing its secrets. Christ addresses the Father as his "Lord" because here he speaks to the Father as someone less: "though he was in the form of God, did not count equality with God a thing to be grasped, but emptied himself, taking the form of a

---

20. As can be seen in Table I.
21. Augustine, *Enarrationes in Psalmos*, 138: CCL 40, 1990–2011.

servant" (Philippians 2:6–7). It is *this* Christ who says to the Father: "I arise, and am still with Thee" (Psalm 138:18). And further: "Thou hast searched me out, and known me" (v. 2)—not as though the Father had not known him before, but because the Father's knowledge is powerfully active: it *effects* what he *knows*. "Thou knowest my down-sitting, and mine up-rising" (v. 2). When a man takes a seat, he lowers himself, "humiliates" himself. The Savior "sat down" in his sacred Passion and "rose up" on Easter morning because the Father "has laid his hand" (v. 5) upon Christ. When Christ, the new Adam lay down and slept (Psalm 3:5), there emerged from his side (*ex corde scisso*) the new Eve, the Church (*nascitur Ecclesia*), and they become two in one flesh. Consequently the "sitting down and rising up" of the Head is also the Passion and Resurrection of the body. Thus the Head and the Body say together to the Father, "I arose, and am still with Thee: Thou hast laid Thine hand upon me: Thy knowledge is become wonderful" (Psalm 138:18, 5–6). And so we see that the Easter Introit not only *announces* Christ's Resurrection ("Christ ist erstanden"), but also joins together the voice of the Risen One with the voice of the Church. Together they speak to the Father in that unparalleled intimacy in which only the Son of Man might address the Father by means of his divinity.

When the Church achieved the deeper understanding of the full mystery of Holy Scripture, when the "secrets of the Temple" had been revealed (*sacrificium vespertinum crucis Domini conscidit velum, ut pateant iam templi secreta*), then also the mouth of the Church could open to chant praise to God with the appropriate words at the right time, proclaiming but also addressing him. Hence it belongs to the integrity of worship, to the fullness of the cult, to include at the apposite points of liturgical time the chanting of appropriate, well-understood texts.

3.   From the foregoing observations one might, of course, conclude that it would suffice to present a list or collection of biblical texts along with a scheme for distributing them over the appropriate seasons of the year. Close study of these chants has documented the fact that there was an historical period in which the Church contented herself with *seasonal collections*, which is to say, with the principle of "sets." This means that the festal periods had their own Proper chant repertories, while during "ordinary" time (*tempus per annum*) the

singers worked their way through a store of selected chants arranged in numerical order. Traces of this "set principle" can still be found in the pre-1970 missals, the Lenten Communions for example,[22] or the fact that the Introits, Alleluias, and Offertories of the first sixteen Sundays after Pentecost follow each other in successive numerical order of the psalms. Even clearer is the arrangement in the Ambrosian Mass Antiphoner where, even today, "ordinary" time is provided for by a 12-item set of *propria dominicalia*.[23]

One more dimension of the *Proprium* chants remains to be considered, however: it is the psychological one. As early as the sixth and seventh centuries the Church found it appropriate and desirable to distribute the sets of chants which had been collected, assigning them to individual days of the year. In fact, there is a scholar who argues that this arrangement and distribution of the Proper chants was the real beginning of the linear arrangement of the Church year itself.[24] In any case, a similar phenomenon can be observed when we study the other components of the Mass. For instance, an analysis of the sermons of Saint Gregory the Great reveals that in his time each Sunday had a fixed Gospel, in the majority of cases identical to those that are still found in the 1962 Missal. The transition from the principle of "sets" to the principle of *Proprium* chants in the strict sense brought great benefits. Among them were the cessation of an improvisatory style of liturgical chanting; introduction of a quiet and peaceful order into the liturgical celebration; formation of a barrier against arbitrariness; effective promotion of unity at the precise moment when the liturgy of Rome became the liturgy of half a continent; opportunity for singers and ministers to prepare themselves both technically and spiritually for the liturgy of the day because they could repeat at regular intervals the same chants on the same day every year. And so, as the annual sequence of orations and readings became fixed in the Sacramentary and the Lectionary, there arose also a bond of *association* amongst all the items prayed and chanted on a

---

22. J. McKinnon (ed.), *Antiquity and the Middle Ages* (London: Macmillan Press, 1990), 104–106.

23. *Antiphonale Missarum juxta ritum sanctae Ecclesiae Mediolanensis* (Romae: Desclée, 1935), 277–323.

24. McKinnon, *The Advent Project*, 24.

particular day. But that does not contradict what has just been explained, because this bond or link is not a premeditated, speculatively calculated coordination of the *Proprium* chants, but rather a bond whose nature is spiritual and emotional. One became accustomed to, and began to like, the fact that in the Mass whose Gospel recounts the miraculous raising of the widow's son of Naim, the Introit *Protector noster* is regularly chanted. Here, there is something more than mere routine: the fixed constellation produced a great many spiritual and psychological fruits.

In the mature form of the Roman rite, the order of *Proprium* chants is the result of three principles or factors completed by a fourth, a musical principle. The first factor is the tradition of the *interpretatio Christiana;* second is its manifestation in the *principle of sets*; the third factor is the transformation of the repertory into a cycle *per anni circulum*. And the fourth, musical component may be termed the principle of *genre*, the fixation of musical expression linked to individual liturgical moments and types of events. This principle of Gregorian musical forms explains why an Introit cannot be replaced by a Gradual and vice versa, even if their texts be identical.

Let us now examine how the liturgical reform that followed the Second Vatican Council affected the continuous tradition of the *Proprium* chants in the Roman rite. At first sight, very little: scarcely more than the non-essential changes wrought during earlier centuries. The new *Ordo Cantus Missae*, which determined the order of Mass chants as well as its implementation in the new *Graduale Romanum* of 1974, is similar to the *Ordo Antiquus* in many places, in spite of the relocation of a good many chants as a consequence of changes in the church calendar. The influence of the new three-year cycle of readings upon the arrangement of the chants led to the predominance of what we have seen to be a misleading concept (namely the idea of complete coordination within each daily liturgy) over the traditional order.

The changes in the new *Missale Romanum* are more numerous. Although the texts of the Gradual also appear in the Missal over a great part of the year, there are two conspicuous differences.

The *first* difference is the remarkable number of instances where the assignment in the Missal differs from that in the *Ordo*

Cantus Missae.[25] Before, the Antiphoner fixed the text and melody of
the chant, and the Missal quoted the texts from the choir book, after
the fashion of a libretto or "text-book." This is the first time in the
long history of the *Ritus Romanus* that choir book and altar missal do
not overlap or coincide. The separation of the two Mass books is not
(yet) as detrimental as it is in the case of the Divine Office, but it
tends in that direction.

The *second* novelty is the selection of new texts for the Introits
and Communions of some Masses. New texts also emerged, of course,
in past centuries, chiefly for new feasts instituted over the years.
But here, old and traditional Mass texts have been replaced, thereby
changing the contents of the liturgy at "cardinal" points.

Two other radical innovations need to be mentioned. The
Offertory chant has been eliminated from the new Missal, and the
inter-Lectionary chants transferred into the Lectionary where a new
three-year system, with totally new texts to be chanted, has been
constructed, thereby causing many problems which unfortunately
I cannot discuss at this time.

Another choir book published after the last Council under the
title of *Graduale Simplex* in order to follow the intentions of Vatican II
(SC, 117) attempted to adapt the principle of sets to modern times—
but in doing so, severed all ties to the centuries-old Mass Antiphoner.

The real shift began, however, not with these publications,
but in three seemingly innocuous words of the *General Introduction to
the Roman Missal* (GIRM), first issued in 1969. In addition to chanting the *Proprium* texts from the *Graduale Romanum* or the *Graduale
Simplex*, today, according to the GIRM paragraphs 48, 74 and 87, one
may substitute *alius cantus congruus* or *aptus*.[26] Since today 99 percent
of Masses throughout the world are celebrated without the participation of a schola capable of chanting the Roman Gradual, and since the
Simple Gradual has practically nowhere been effectively introduced,
alius cantus congruus has prevailed over the Proper chants of the
Roman Mass. There is no norm regulating or specifying what should
be regarded as *congruus* or *aptus*, and consequently the Roman
Proprium chants are hardly sung at all. This means that the Church

25. For example, most of the Communions in Lent, in Easter, and for *per annum* Sundays.
26. Cf. L. Dobszay, *The Bugnini-Liturgy and the Reform of the Reform*, Musicae Sacrae
Meletemata 5 (Front Royal, VA: Catholic Church Music Associates, 2003), 86–87.

today no longer speaks through the chants of the Mass: that the chants effectively have no part at all in forming the liturgy and delivering its message. In other words, the Proper chants ceased to be part of the liturgy. Today, the majestic phrases of the Constitution on the Sacred Liturgy sound almost ironic: "As sacred song united to the words, it forms a necessary or integral part of the solemn liturgy"; "sacred music is to be considered the more holy in proportion as it is more closely linked with liturgical action"; "the sacred Council, keeping to the norms and precepts of ecclesiastical tradition and discipline" (SC, 112). "The treasure of sacred music is to be preserved and fostered with great care" (SC, 114). "The Church acknowledges Gregorian chant as specially suited (*proprium*) to the Roman liturgy: therefore, other things being equal, it should be given pride of place in liturgical services" (SC, 116). If anything, even less valid today are the warnings of St Pius X's celebrated Motu Proprio *Tra le Sollecitudini* of 1903: "Nothing should have place, therefore, in the temple calculated to disturb or even merely to diminish the piety and devotion of the faithful . . . nothing, above all, which directly offends the decorum and sanctity of the sacred functions and is thus unworthy of the House of Prayer and of the Majesty of God. . . . As the texts that may be rendered in music, and the order in which they are to be rendered, are determined for every liturgical function, it is not lawful to confuse this order or to change the prescribed texts for others selected at will, or to omit them either entirely or even in part."[27]

Chant ceased to be an integral part of the liturgy. And the grievous damage is not repaired if *alius cantus congruus* is to become a juridically accepted part of the liturgy. Those three short words opened the pathway for the many kinds of *cantiunculae*, pious but liturgically inappropriate "popular" songs, as well as light music and pop tunes, poems foreign to the Church's textual tradition. One may criticize the 1974 *Graduale Romanum*, but the damage was done by the *General Introduction to the Roman Missal* and by the Instruction *Musicam Sacram* of 1967.[28]

---

27. Pius X, Motu Proprio sulla Musica Sacra *Tra le Sollecitudini* (November 22, 1903), introduction and no. 8.

28. Sacred Congregation of Rites, Instruction on Music in the Liturgy *Musicam Sacram* (March 5, 1967), especially no. 32.

Why were the words, *alius cantus congruus* inserted into the GIRM? One should of course presuppose that the changes were introduced with the best of intentions, as is the case with the liturgical reform as a whole. One may surmise that there were two basic aspirations, more or less correct, which led to the concession of *alius cantus congruus*. First, in the great majority of parish churches there is no qualified cantor or group of singers who could perform the chants of the Roman Gradual (or even the Simple Gradual) in its entirety, week after week, Mass by Mass. What then is to happen in the great number of Masses celebrated in spite of the lack of such cantors? One of the great temptations of our own day is that lovers of the liturgy and its *musica sacra* attend the Masses with the best music they can find, and ignore all the others. And so the liturgy has frequently been fractured and split into a "high" church music and "low" church music.[29] Secondly, there was the call to extend "active participation" to the chant, including the Proper chants.

In the present situation, it is not enough to invoke the great tradition of *musica sacra* without offering concrete proposals for those thousands of Masses that are celebrated every day throughout the world. In order to reconnect church music with the liturgical rite, an accurate diagnosis is required, and for this purpose, we need to provide a brief historical summary of Mass chant.

A BRIEF HISTORY OF MASS CHANT

In the earliest centuries, the Proper chants of the Mass consisted of but two pieces: the inter-Lectionary chant(s) and the Communion, both performed by the *psaltes*, the trained solo singer. The role of the congregation was to join in the responses, the Ordinary as a special kind of response, and the repeated refrains of the responsorial psalmody. On the basis of the ancient reports and descriptions, confirmed by the surviving practice of the Eastern Church, we can conclude that in the earliest times the true field of *participatio actuosa externa* for laypeople was the Divine Office.

This situation changed in a fundamental way when the *scholae* were founded. In the very beginning, these were little more than a

---

29. Cf. Chapter 7: "High Church–Low Church: The Split of Catholic Church Music," in Dobszay, *The Bugnini-Liturgy*.

gathering, a "workshop" of psalm singers, which made possible their occasional singing as a group. We do not know when and where such gatherings of singers emerged, but it was surely no earlier than the late fourth or early fifth century, and then only in some of the larger churches. Today it is generally believed that as a regular institution, the Roman schola was founded in the sixth or seventh century.[30] One should not imagine that there was a schola in every parish church: at first, only two or three papal basilicas possessed the infrastructure and the financial resources required for the support of such an active ordinary institution. In the parish churches at Rome, the so-called *tituli*, musical practice remained in the hands of the precentors. The papal schola, as a body of selected young people who lived a *vita communis* and learned the liturgy and its chant as a vocation, flourished amidst exceptionally favorable conditions which made it possible to develop a new and more demanding style of Mass Proper chants. Although melismatic chanting, too, had flourished earlier (one thinks of the improvised Tract or Communion of the solo singers), it was the *individuality* of the tunes which demanded such great skill and diligence.[31] The new pieces were not mere adaptations of standard musical models; in the new situation each text had its own tune, and mastery of these involved an enormous task for the memory, particularly in an age when notation had not yet developed. These singers did not chant only once a month, and they could not decide for themselves which items of the Mass would be performed on a given day. They were required to sing by heart each of the four or five *Proprium* chants of the particular Mass, and even a new piece week after week—or even every day, as for instance in Lent. It is not surprising that those who from early childhood grow up in such a school later chose the service of the liturgy as their lifelong vocation. And in this sense it may be said that the chanting at Mass in the Roman basilicas was of a "clerical" nature from the sixth or seventh century onward. The only way to transmit these chants to a wider

---

30. J. Dyer, "The Schola Cantorum and Its Roman Milieu in the Early Middle Ages," in P. Cahn and A.-K. Heimer (ed.), *De Musica et Cantu: Studien zur Geschichte der Kirchenmmusik und der Oper. Helmut Hucke zum 60. Geburtstag*, Musikwissenschaftliche Publikationen/Hochschule für Musik und Darstellende Kunst Frankfurt/Main 2 (Hildesheim: Olms, 1993), 19–40.

31. L. Dobszay, "Two Paradigms of Orality: The Office and the Mass," in T. Bailey and A. Coolk Santosuosso (ed.), *Music in Medieval Europe: Studies in Honour of Bryan Gillingham* (Aldershot: Ashgate, 2007), 1–10.

environment was through visits of the papal schola in the various parish churches, where they would chant the entire liturgy on the stational days. Otherwise, the precentor or *psaltes* remained the chief executant of the chant in the many local churches.

It was the evangelizing efforts of the missionaries from the seventh century onward which spread the liturgy of Rome throughout the European continent. In the monasteries and cathedrals, abbots and bishops imitated Rome by establishing their own *scholae* which trained professional singing masters and a cadre of good singers. The prelates did not fail to urge the entire liturgical community to join in chanting at least some pieces. The best institution to implement this ideal, of course, was the cathedral or monastic school, where boys could be systematically prepared to chant the liturgy. The typical liturgical choir consisted of priests, young men and boys, up to a hundred or more in the cathedrals, 20 or 30 in the cities, or only two or three, in the smaller town or village churches. All the singers together, or in smaller groups, performed the obligatory chants of each day, and this took three or four hours of the day, in addition to an hour or two of preparation. Maintaining such a system on a level that assured its functioning required *stable* institutions, with material and intellectual backing. This is to say that large estates, endowments and strict regulations assured the regularity of liturgical singing in each ecclesiastical centre, over decades and centuries. In their turn, these institutions promoted further development of *musica sacra* over many years during which Gregorian chants were embellished or completed with polyphony, and later supplanted by polyphonic masterworks. Since the liturgy regulated the texts, such pieces remained lawful even if the texts were not delivered on their Gregorian tunes. During this period of history, congregational participation was at a minimum, if it existed at all.

In the middle of the sixteenth century, this vibrant liturgical life came to an abrupt end. The collapse of institutions in the Protestant revolution, lack of material resources (or their redirection to new purposes), the radical change in the educational system, widespread secularization—all these factors converged in a perfect storm to destroy the basis of regular liturgical chanting. Actual liturgical praxis was sharply divided: in some wealthier churches groups of professional musicians graced the High Mass with exquisite art music (often of a character increasingly alien to worship), and Gregorian chant became the domain of experts. On the other side of the great divide, in a great majority of Masses the text of the liturgical chant became a prayer read by the celebrant: silence in the sanctuary became the norm. The few monasteries and religious houses that preserved in practice a remnant of the regular Proper chants were small and insignificant islets in the great stream of the Church's life.

The *cantilena Romana* had developed and grown into an enormous liturgical and spiritual treasury. But that treasure was not shared in equal degrees by the entire Church. As a sung reality it resonated in the praxis of some monasteries and cathedrals and their *scholae*, though the medieval institutions like the system of schools (with their strong staff and reliable financial support) had made a good beginning on the process of making chant the possession of all the faithful. But after the sixteenth century, liturgical chant became a *hortus conclusus* for congregations as well as choirs in most churches, for it remained present in the Mass only as a prayer, surrounded by other texts and covered over by non-liturgical music.

During the course of the last century, as a growing number of laypeople achieved a higher educational and cultural level, there emerged a new opportunity for improving the status quo. Fostering literacy, comprehension and music-making would have greatly aided endeavors to transform a great number of the communities into some type of liturgical bodies.

Which is to say that the medieval "liturgical choir" could have been broadened and enlarged so as to include educated laypeople and eventually, by processing gradually, the whole congregation.[32] To achieve this, the common elements of church life such as catechesis, preaching, singing classes in the church-run schools, activity of the choirs and indeed most institutional aspects of church life should have been adapted to the great purpose. It would have required a definite focus for pastoral activity, the training and employment of suitable leaders, promulgation of diocesan statutes and the establishment of apposite foundations and endowments in order to elevate the regular chanting of the Divine Liturgy from the level of short-lived individual initiatives to its rightful place as an integral part of a flourishing

---

32. One may note in passing that it was precisely this noble goal which motivated Justine Bayard Ward to devise her ingenious method of musical formation, in the spirit of Saint Pius X.

religious life—which, I may add, also includes involving popular participation in the Divine Office.

For a great many Roman Catholics, highly profitable "participation aids" such as "missalettes" have become an intermediary transmitting the message of at least the text of many Proper chants. Because of the isolation into which Latin has been forced, however, the texts of the Proper chants lack their directness and immediacy of contact. No missalette can compensate for the loss of the *chanted Proprium*. Although the text as the voice of the praying Church was precious for many people, the Church as it really exists was only listening indirectly to this voice. The Proper chants of the Mass can communicate the full value of their message only as *chanted* texts; the *read* or recited Propers have a diminished function in the liturgy. That is to say, in practice the Proper chants had *de facto* dropped out of the liturgy well before the Second Vatican Council.

It was precisely in this situation that far-reaching changes were introduced. The validity of any criticism of these changes and their attendant results will depend on a view or approach that adheres to the tradition but at the same time is not blind in one eye to the legitimate goals that the post-conciliar liturgical reform ardently desired but that have not yet consistently achieved. After this historical sketch, let us examine what how the present situation can be remedied. After the publication of the Motu Proprio *Summorum Pontificum* in 2007, there is reason to hope that Pope Benedict XVI's wish that "the two Forms of the usage of the Roman Rite can be mutually enriching"[33] will lead to a recovery of the *Proprium* chants in the Ordinary Form of the Roman rite, given their stable presence in the Extraordinary Form.

CONTINUED DEVELOPMENT

One possibility would be simply to allow the present state of affairs to continue, which is to say: organize magnificent Gregorian days, courses, and conventions, solemn Masses with majestic chant performed by professional singers—and then to extend pious wishes with a blessing for all the other churches and all of their Masses.

---

33. Benedict XVI, *Letter to the Bishops that accompanies the Motu Proprio Summorum Pontificum* (July 7, 2007).

But is it even possible to resolve the contradiction between preserving the inherited Roman repertory, and obstacles of its regular use? Finding a resolution requires that we think over the situation carefully and formulate purposeful provisions leading to a liturgical reform that extends also to the field of chant and includes both the musical material and the institutional background. I would like to discuss only the first aspect in five proposals:

Proposal 1. The formula *alius cantus congruus* as a substitution for the Roman Gradual or the Simple Gradual must be removed from the normative text of the *General Introduction to the Roman Missal.*

Proposal 2. The highest degree of vocal participation in the Mass Proper is of course chanting the full *Proprium* with its Gregorian tunes. One could accept certain minor corrections and alternative options to the Missal of Trent, for instance the restitution of the Offertory and Communion verses; the use of double Introit *Rorate* and *Memento* for the Fourth Sunday of Advent, etc.

The Missal must contain the same text printed in the choir books. Official authoritative instructions should be issued to regulate matters such as these: where and when is the chanting of the full Proper obligatory? What kind of simpler forms are permitted? When and where? How can and *should* individual churches provide a *psaltes/* cantor or a schola for the parish Masses? How can it be guaranteed that the faithful actually receive the message of the Proper chants through authentic translations? What tools or aids can be offered to the clergy in order to insure an obligatory systematic introduction to the understanding of these texts in the framework of local catechesis, preaching, and spiritual reading?

Proposal 3. Although the most splendid sonic vesture of the Proper texts is contained in the *Graduale Romanum* which "should be given pride of place in liturgical services" (SC, 116), it is in confor- mity with church tradition that those texts may also resound in other worthy settings such as the polyphonic elaboration of the texts, or *alternatim* compositions combining polyphony with Gregorian chant.

On the other hand, collections of less difficult musical settings can also be approved which enable choirs with less training (or even the entire congregation) to chant the canonical texts, that is, the texts contained in the Gradual and not some other substitute. The best of these will be settings that adapt melodic models to different texts (like the ancient antiphons of the Roman Office) so as to render the liturgical chant more widely accessible. And on occasion the chanting of antiphons might even be simplified somewhat by introducing some less accentuated motives in the text into the verses.[34] The question of liturgical and musical norms must be relegated to another forum.

Proposal 4. For churches that are less well provided with good cantors for Mass, or are just beginning the process of introducing liturgical chant, permission might be given to return to the old "set principle," which is to say using a collection of set pieces for an entire season, analogous to the Simple Gradual but based upon the traditional Gradual. In such cases the celebrant, the ministers, and/or the congregation should, after chanting that "set" piece, pray the Introit (or Offertory, etc.) proper to the day. In an "emergency situation" like that, the Introit *Ad te levavi,* for instance, could be sung throughout Advent, followed by recitation of Introit proper of the day. I would call this form a "regulated use of sets" because it allows the necessary freedom to the local community without sacrificing the liturgical canon.

Proposal 5. The "regulated use of sets" is a step above the lowest level, which could be adopted chiefly in weekday Masses or at Masses with a small congregation. It involves congregational recitation of the antiphons, with the verse read out by a lector or server (facing the altar and not the congregation). If these texts were recited *recto tono* on one pitch (or even with a soft organ accompaniment), worshippers might be reminded that the text is properly a chant. Indeed, before or after the text of (for example) the Introit, a well known hymn which is appropriate to the liturgical day could also be sung. But the catalogue of hymns allowed for the use of a specific type of community should be accurately fixed and officially approved.

I have eschewed a comprehensive discussion of the "language problem." The vernacular can be useful for the Proper chants (cf. SC, 36). However, this option should, I believe, be combined with the

---

34. For instance, in some medieval churches the Introit *Gaudete* was sung with verse taken from the same biblical paragraph instead of the psalm. If the Introit itself happens to be abbreviated (for example, *Gaudete . . . Dominus enim prope est;* cf. the *Missale Romanum* of Paul VI, *Dominica Tertia Adventus*) the omitted parts could be transposed to this recitative section. Similarly in an easy version of the Introit *Ad te levavi* the middle section (*in te confido . . . inimici mei*) could be transferred to the psalm-section.

rules governing a regular (and suggested) use of the Latin tongue. For such complementary use of the mother tongue I propose four tools. 1) Specified types of churches are obliged to celebrate the Mass, according to a fixed schedule, with Latin Propers. 2) Latin and vernacular in combination, for example, the soloist/cantor chants the Latin Gregorian melody of the Introit at the beginning of the Mass, after which the congregation repeats it in their mother tongue on a simple tune, as a "sung translation," so to speak. 3) A third possibility is to follow a custom as development of the use in the "Tridentine rite": the congregation or a small schola sings the Proper chant in the vernacular while the priest as the "mouthpiece" of the Church prays the required Latin text. 4) The fourth tool is the use of *bilingual* choir books or notated Missals, thus permitting the faithful to see the original Latin (read by the celebrant) whilst the same text is chanted in the vernacular.

Restraints of space do not permit me to discuss at this point the musical style of vernacular Proper chants. What is of primary importance, either in reciting or chanting, is to use a worthy translation which renders the meaning quite precisely while preserving the traditional biblical-liturgical style of the particular native tongue. The best way of doing this would be a slight and tactful modernization of the old translations. (I never cease to wonder why it has not occurred to post-conciliar English-speaking Catholics to use Palmer's admirable choir books with the English versions of the Sarum chant.[35])

A differentiated praxis such as I have just outlined, would ensure preservation of the full Roman chant repertory while also permitting those chants to resound even in the poorest and simplest circumstances. Each level uses the same texts; the same thoughts are pronounced, but differently, depending upon the local circumstances. These forms resemble an ascending staircase: those who stand on the lowest step and are still unable to climb higher, celebrate the same liturgy as those standing higher—and they can see before their eyes (and ears!) the steps to which their community can rise. To adapt the well-known saying of Saint Pius X: they are not singing something during the Mass, but singing the Mass itself. It would be mistaken to

---

35. G. H. Palmer, *The Diurnal After the Use of the Illustrious Church of Salisbury: Lauds and the Hours* (Wantage: S. Mary's Convent, 1926).

regard this gradation as a degradation of the full Latin Gregorian *Proprium* chanted by the schola! Let the classic chant remain in its majestic state, but let us consider also the ordinary Masses in parish churches today—and appreciate the opportunity for improvement offered by these "tools."

By way of illustration, I have prepared a list of possible Proper chants for the four Advent Sundays (Table 4.2, pp. 116–117), showing some possible musical renditions (music examples). And all of this is no mere wishful thinking, for in Hungary, despite very adverse conditions, a widespread practice of chanting the *Proprium* has in fact been achieved. And not only in the urban parishes does the ancient biblical-liturgical message resound, but in small rural villages as well—often on the lips of little children.[36]

Permit me to offer a concluding observation. I fear that my suggestions may have set off a two-front war. For the champions of the post-conciliar liturgical reforms, my adherence to the tradition might be cause for reproach; and for the friends of the older form of the Roman rite the practical measures I have suggested, may seem too opportunistic. I think, though, that the "Tridentine" liturgy will remain a source of joy *only for a few*, and hence have little impact upon the general usage of the Church because of this isolated position, unless we recognise that while maintaining its identity, the traditional Roman rite could—and did!—live, change, and develop over the centuries. The question is: what does this "change" mean? If it is not to demolish the Roman rite but to make it more vigorous and alive, then the change is justified not only by the Liturgy Constitution of the Second Vatican Council, but by the *tradition itself.* Remain the same, by the force of change—this should have been the true motive of the post-conciliar reform. What I am calling for is not a compromise or an admixture of New and Old, but rather a way to surmount their conflict, and it seems to me that this is what Pope Benedict wants to achieve with *Summorum Pontificum.* We must return to the rite of 1962, not in order to call a halt at that point, but in order to locate the true reform of which we have been deprived.

---

36. Helped by the alternative Folk Hymnal *Éneklő Egyház (The Chant of Church)* (Budapest: Szent István Társulat, 1985). A full edition of proper chants for all Sundays and solemnities: *Graduale Hungaricum* (Gödöllő: A Premonterei rend Gödöllői Kanóniája, 2007).

In this respect, I think that what has been said about the chant might offer a model for restoration of other elements of the Roman liturgy such as the readings, the sacraments, the Office, the Calendar, etc. I consider this to be the best and most accurate meaning of the formula: reform of the reform.

Table 4.1

Sources: OR = Old Roman,[37] **R** = Rheinau (eighth–ninth century), **MB** = Mont Blandin (eighth–ninth century), **Co** = Compiègne (ninth century), **Cor** = Corbie (ninth–tenth century), **S** = Senlis (ninth century), **L** = Laon 239 (ninth–tenth century), **Ch** = Chartres 520 (thirteenth–fourteenth century), **Be** = Benevento 34 (eleventh–twelfth century), **Bo** = Bologna (eleventh century), **Kl** = Klosterneuburg, Graz 807 (twelfth century), **Le** = Leipzig (fourteenth century), **Str** = Strigonium/Esztergom (fourteenth century), **OCM** = *Ordo Cantus Missae* (1972), **MP** = *Missale Paulinum* (1970).[38]

Abbreviations: v = with verse; **p** = psalm in the Communion

Dies		Missale Romanum Pii V	OR	R	MB	Co	Cor	S
ADV. Dom 1								
Intr.	1	Ad te levavi	=	=	=	?	=	=
Grad.	2	Universi qui te	=	=	=	?	=	=
Allel.	3	Ostende nobis	E[39]	=	=	?	=	=
Offert.	4	Ad te (Domine) levavi	= v[40]	=	= v	?	=	= v
Comm.	5	Dominus dabit	=[41]	=	=	?	= p	= p

	L	Ch	Be	Bo	Kl	Le	Str	OCM	MP
1	=	=	=	=v[42]	=	=	=	=	=
2	=	=	=	=	=	=	=	=	—
3	=	=	=	=	=	=	=	=	—
4	= v	=	= v	= v	= v	=	=	=	—
5	= p	=	=	= p	=	= p	=	= p	=

Dies		Missale Romanum Pii V	OR	R	MB	Co	Cor	S
Dom 2								
Intr.	6	Populus Sion	= v[43]	=	=	?	=	=
Grad.	7	Ex Sion species	=	=	=	?	=	=
All.	8	Laetatus sum	O[44]	=	=	?	=	= + S[45]
Offert.	9	Deus tu conversus[46]	= v[47]	=	= v	?	=	= v
Comm.	10	Jerusalem surge	=[48]	=	= p	?	= p[49]	= p
Dom 3								
Intr.	11	Gaudete in Domino	= v[50]	=	=	= v	=	=
Grad.	12	Qui sedes Domine	=	=	=	=	=	=
All.	13	Excita Domine	=	=	=	=	=	=
Offert.	14	Benedixisti Domine	= v[51]	=	= v	= v	=	= v
Comm.	15	Dicite pusillanimes	=	=	= p	= v[52]	=	=[53]
QuT. f4								
Intr.	16	Rorate. Ps. Caeli	= v[54]	=	=	= v	=	=
Grad. 1	17	Tollite portas	=	=	=	=	=	=
Grad. 2	18	Prope est Dominus	?	?	=	=	=	=
Offert.	19	Confortamini et jam	= v[55]	=	= v	= v	=	=
vel Off.	20	—	—	—	Ave[56]	—	Ave	Ave v
Comm.	21	Ecce Virgo concipiet	=	=	=	= v[57]	= v[58]	=

	L	Ch	Be	Bo	Kl	Le	Str	OCM	MP
6	=	=	=	=	=	=	=	=	=
7	=	=	=	=	=	=	=	=	—
8	=	= +S	= +S	= +S / Vi[59]	= +S	= +S	R[60]	=	—
9	= v	=	= v	= v	= v	=	=	=	—
10	= p	=	=	= p	=	= p	=	= p	=
11	=	E[61]	=	=[62]	=	=	= E[63]	=	=[64]
12	=	=	=	=	=	=	=	=	—
13	=	=	=	=	=	=	=	=	—
14	= v	=	= v	=	= v	=	=	=	—
15	=	=	=	= p	=	= p	=	= p	=
16	=	=	=	= v[65]	=	=	=	M[66]	Ve[67]

	L	Ch	Be	Bo	Kl	Le	Str	OCM	MP
17	= .	=	=	=	=	=	=	I[68]	—
18	=	=	=	=	=	=	=	—	—
19	= v	—	= v	= v	= v	=	=	Au[69]	—
20	Ave	—	—	—	—	—	—	—	—
21	= p	=	=	= v	=	= p	=	Ve[70]	E[71]

Dies		MR	OR	R	MB	Co	Cor	S
Qu.T. f6								
Intr.	22	Prope es tu	= v[72]	?	=	=[73]	=	=
Grad.	23	Ostende nobis	=	?	=	=	=	=
Offert.	24	Deus tu conversus	Ad[74]	?	=	= v[75]	=	=
Comm.	25	Ecce Dominus veniet	=	?	=	= v[76]	= v[77]	=
Qu T. S.								
Intr.	26	Veni et ostende	= v[78]	=	=	= v[79]	=	= v
Grad. 1	27	A summo caelo	=	=	=	=	=	=
Grad. 2	28	In sole posuit	=	=	=	=	=	=
Grad. 3	29	Dñe Deus virtutum	=	?	=	=	=	=
Grad. 4	30	Excita Domine	=	=	=	=	=	=
Hymn.	31	Benedictus es	=	?	?	?	?	?
Tractus	32	Qui regis Israel	=	=	?	=	=	=
Offert.	33	Exsulta satis	= v[80]	=	= v	= v	=	= v
Comm.	34	Exsultavit ut gigas	= v[81]	=	= v	=	= v[82]	= v
Dom 4								
Intr.	35	Rorate Ps. Caeli	—[83]	V[84]	—	M[85]	—	=
Grad.	36	Prope est	—	A[86]	—	=	—	=
All.	37	Veni Domine et noli	—	?	—	=	—	=
Offert.	38	Ave Maria gratia	—	E[87]	—	= v[88]	—	= v
Comm.	39	Ecce Virgo	—	=	—	=	—	=

	L	Ch	Be	Bo	Kl	Le	Str	OCM	MP
22	=	=	=	= v[89]	=	=	=	Ve[90]	E[91]
23	=	=	=	=	=	=	=	A[92]	—
24	=	=	=	Au[93]	= v	=	=	Ex[94]	—
25	= p	=	=	= p	=	= p	=	Ex[95]	S[96]
26	=	=	=	= v[97]	=	=	=	M[98]	=
27	=	=	=	=	=	=	=	Ex[99]	—
28	=	=	=	=	=	=	=	—	—
29	=	=	=	=	=	=	=	—	—
30	=	=	=	=	=	=	=	—	—
31	?	Om[100]	=	=	=	=	=	—	—
32	=	=	=	=	=	=	=	—	—
33	= v	=	=	= v	= v	=	=	Ex[101]	—
34	= p	=	=	= p	=	= p	=	Ex[102]	Ec[103]
35	—	M	M	= / M	M	M	M	=	=
36	—	T[104]	=	=	=	=	=	=	—
37	—	=	= A[105]	F/L[106]	= /P[107]	=	= / P	=	—
38	—	C[108]	= v	= v	= v	=	=	=	—
39	—	=	=	=	=	= p	=	= p	=

Dies		MR	OR	R	MB	Co	Cor	S
NAT.D.								
Missa 1								
Intr.	40	Dominus dixit ad me	= v[109]	=	=	=	=	= v[110]
Grad.	41	Tecum principium	=	=	=	=	=	=
All.	42	Dominus dixit ad me	=	=	=	=	=	=
Offert.	43	Laetentur caeli	= v[111]	=	= v	= v	=	= v
Comm.	44	In splendoribus	= p[112]	=	= v[113]	=	= p	= v
Missa 2								
Intr.	45	Lux fulgebit	= v[114]	=	=	= v	=	=
Grad.	46	Benedictus qui	=	=	=	=	=	=

Dies		MR	OR	R	MB	Co	Cor	S
All.	47	Dominus regnavit	=	=	=	=	=	=
Offert.	48	Deus firmavit	= v^{115}	=	= v	= v	=	= v
Comm.	49	Exsulta filia Sion	=	=	=	=	=	= v^{116}
Missa 3								
Intr.	50	Puer natus est	= v^{117}	=	=	= v	=	= v
Grad.	51	Viderunt omnes	=	=	=	=	=	=
All.	52	Dies sanctificatus	=	=	=	=	=	=
Offert.	53	Tui sunt caeli	= v^{118}	=	= v	= v	=	= v
Comm.	54	Viderunt omnes	=	=	=	=	= p^{119}	= v^{120}
D2 p. Ep.								
Intr.	55	Omnis terra	In^{121}	=	=	=	=	= v^{122}
Grad.	56	Misit Dominus	=	=	=	=	=	=
All.	57	Laudate Dnm omnes ang.	Ad^{123}	=	=	=	=	=

	L	Ch	Be	Bo	Kl	Le	Str	OCM	MP
40	=	=	=	=^{86}	=	=	=	=	= /G^{125}
41	=	=	=	=	=	=	=	=	—
42	=	=	=	=	=	= /N^{126}	=	=	—
43	= v	=	= v	= v	= v	= v!	=	=	—
44	= p	=	=	= p	=	= p	=	= p	V^{127}
45	=	=	=	= v^{128}	=	=	=	=	=
46	=	=	=	=	=	=	=	=	—
47	=	=	=	=	=	=	=^{129}	=	—
48	= v	=	= v	= v	= v	= v!	=	=	—
49	= p	=	=	= p	=	= p	=	= p	—
50	=	=	=^{130}	= v^{131}	=	=	=	=	=
51	=	=	=	=	=	=	=	=	—
52	=	=	=	=Ve^{132}	=	=	=	=	—
53	= v	=	= v	V	= v	= v!	=	=	=
54	= p	=	=	= p	=	= p	=	= p	=
55	?	=	=	= v^{133}	=	=	=	=	=
56	?	=	=	=	=	=	=	=	—
57	?	Do^{134}	O^{135}	=	Do	Do	=	=	—

Dies		MR	OR	R	MB	Co	Cor	S
Offert.	58	Jubilate Deo universa	Ju2[136]	=	= v[137]	= v	=	=
Comm.	59	Dicit Dominus implete	Mi[138]	=	=	=	= p[139]	= v[140]
D.Palm.								
Intr.	60	Domine ne longe	= v[141]	=	=[142]	=	=	=
Grad.	61	Tenuisti manum	=	=	=	=	=	=
Tract.	62	Deus Deus meus	=	=	=	=	=	=
Offert.	63	Improperium	= v[143]	=	= v	= v	=	= v
Comm.	64	Pater si non potest	=	=	=	= p[144]	= p[145]	=
Cena								
Intr.	65	Nos autem gloriari	= v[146]	= p[147]	= p	= p	=	= p
Grad.	66	Christus factus est	=	=	=	=	=	=
Offert.	67	Dextera Domini	= v[148]	=	= v	= v	=	= v
Comm.	68	Dñs Jesus postquam	=	=	=	= v[149]	= p	= p

	L	Ch	Be	Bo	Kl	Le	Str	OCM	MP
58	?	=	= v	= v	=	=	=	=	—
59	?	=	=	= v[150]	=	= p	=	L[151]	P / N[152]
60	=	=	=	= v[153]	=	=	=	—	—
61	=	=	=	=	=	=	=	D[154]	—
62	=	=	=	=	=	=	=	Ch[155]	—
63	= vc	=	= v	=	= v	=	=	=	—
64	= v[156]	=	= v[157]	= v[158]	=	= p	=	= p	=
65	=	=	=	=	=	=	=	=	=
66	=	=	=	=	=	=	7=	O[159]	—
67	= v	=	=	=	= v	=	=	U[160]	—
68	= p	=	=	= p	=	= p	=	H[161]	H

Dies		MR	OR	R	MB	Co	Cor	S
Intr.	69	Resurrexi et adhuc	$= v^{162}$	$=$	$= v$	$= v$	$=$	$= v$
Grad.	70	Haec dies	$=$	$=$	$=$	$=$	$=$	$=$
All.	71	Pascha nostrum	$= +E^{163}$	$= +E$	$= +E$	$= +E$	$= +E$	$= +E$
Offert.	72	Terra tremuit	$= v^{164}$	$=$	$= v$	$= v$	$=$	$= v$
Comm.	73	Pascha nostrum	$=$	$=$	$=$	$=^{165}$	$=$	$= v^{166}$
D 17 Pe								
Intr.	74	Justus es Domine	$= v^{167}$	$=$	$=$	?	$=$	$=$
Grad.	75	Beata gens	T^{168}	B^{169}	T/B	#	U^{170}	U
All.	76	Domine exaudi	L^{171}	L	?	#	?	D^{172}
Offert.	77	Oravi Deum meum	$=$	$=$	$=^{173}$	#	$=$	$= v^{174}$
Comm.	78	Vovete et reddite	$=$	$=$	$=$	#	$=$	$=$
D 20 Pe								
Intr.	79	Omnia quae fecisti	$= v^{175}$	$=$	$=$	#	$=$	$=$
Grad.	80	Oculi omnium	$=$	E^{176}	$= /E$	#	$=$	$=$
All.	81	Paratum cor	Q^{177}	A^{178}	?	#	?	?
Offert.	82	Super flumina	$= v^{179}$	$=$	$= v^{180}$	#	$=$	$= v^{181}$
Comm.	83	Memento verbi tui	$=$	$=$	$=$	#	$=$	$=$

	L	Ch	Be	Bo	Kl	Le	Str	OCM	MP
69	=	=	=	?	=	=	=	=	=/S[182]
70	=	=	=	?	=	=	=	=	—
71	= +E	= +E	= +E	?	= +E	= +E	= +E	=	—
72	= v	=	= v	?	= v	= v!	=	=	—
73	=	=	=	?	=	= p	=	= p	=
74	=	=	=	=	=	=	=	=	=
75	=	=	U	=	=	=	=	=	—
76	Q[183]	P[184]	=	P	Di[185]	Di	P	=	—
77	= v	=	= v	= v	= v	=	=	=	—
78	=	=	=	=	=	=	=	=	Qu/E[186]
79	=	=	=	=	=	=	=	=	=
80	=	=	=	=	=	=	=	=	—
81	De[187]	Qui[188]	N[189]	Do/M[190]	Qui	Qui	De	=	—
82	= v[191]	=	= v	= v	= v	=	=	=	—
83	=	=	=	=	=	=	=	=	= /I[192]

37. *Graduale Lateranense* (12th century); see fn. 2 in the main text.

38. OR R, MB, Co, Cor, S: R.-J. Hesbert, *Antiphonale Missarum Sextuplex* (Rome: Herder, 1935). **L:** *Le Codex 239 de la Bibliothèque de Laon*, Paléographie musicale 10 (Abbaye Saint-Pierre-de-Solesmes: Les Éditions de Solesmes, 3rd edn, 2001). **Ch:** *Missale Carnotense (Chartres Codex 520)*, ed. D. Hiley, Monumenta monodica medii aevi 4, 2 vols (Kassel: Bärenreiter, 1992). **Be:** *Le Codex VI 34 de la Bibliothèque Capitulaire de Bénévent*, Paléographie Musicale 15 (Abbaye Saint-Pierre-de-Solesmes: Les Éditions de Solesmes, 1992). **Bo:** *Le Codex 123 de la Bibliothèque Angelica de Rome (XIᵉ siècle): Graduel et tropaire de Bologne*, ed. J. Gajard, Paléographie musicale 18 (Berne: Lang, 1969). **Kl:** *Graduel de Klosterneuburg*, ed. J. Froger, Paléographie musicale 19 (Berne: Lang, 1974). **Le:** *Graduale der Sankt Tomaskirche zu Leipzig (14. Jahrhundert) als Zeuge deutscher Choralüberlieferung*, ed. P. Wagner, Publikationen älterer Musik 6-7, 2 vols (Leipzig: Breitkopf & Härtel, 1930-1932). – **Str:** *Missale Notatum Strigoniense ante 1341 in Posonio*, ed. J. Szendrei – R. Rybarič, Musicalia Danubiana 1 (Budapest: Institute for Musicology, 1982). – **OCM:** *Missale Romanum: Ordo Cantus Missae*, Editio typica (Civitas Vaticana: Typis Polypglottis Vaticanis, 1972). **MP:** *Missale Romanum ex decreto Sacrosancti Oecumenici Concilii Vaticani II instauratum auctoritate Pauli PP. VI promulgatum*, Editio typica (Civitas Vaticana: Typis Polyglottis Vaticanis, 1970).

39. Excita

40. V1: Dirige me in veritate. V2: Respice in me.

41. Ps. 84. V. Veritas.

42. V. Qui non vis mortem. V. Scimus quia non reliquis.

43. V. Excita.

44. All. **Ostende.**

45. V2. Stantes erant.

46. Vel: Domine tu convertens.

47. V1. Benedixisti. V2. Misericordia et veritas. (MB: V3 Veritas de terra) OR: Benedixisti. 2. Redemisti. 3. Misericordia.

48. "psalmus ut supra."

49. Ps. 147.

50. V. Ostende nobis.

51. V1. Operuisti omnia. V2. Ostende nobis Domine.

52. Ps. 84. V. Ostende nobis.

53. V. Deus manifeste veniet.

54. V. In sole posuit.

55. V1. Tunc aperientur oculi. V2. Audite itaque.

56. Offert. **Ave Maria.** V1. Quomodo in me. V2. Ideoque quod nascitur.

57. Ps. 18. V. In sole posuit (= Bo).

58. V. Exsultavit ut gigas.

59. All. **Virtutes caeli.**

60. All. **Rex noster adveniet Christus.**

61. Gaudete. V. **Et pax Dei.**

62. V. Et pax Dei. V. Laetemur angelica turba.

63. V. **Et pax Dei.**

64. Textus abbreviatus.

65. V. Caeli laetentur.

66. Intr. Memento nostri.

67. Intr. Veniet Dominus et non tardabit.

68. Grad. In sole posuit.

69. Audi Israel.

70. Comm. **Veni Domine.**

71. Comm. **Ecce Dominus noster.**

72. Ps. 118. V. Beati qui scrutantur.

73. Ps. 118. V. Tu mandasti.

74. Ad te Domine levavi.

75. Sicut in Dominica II.

76. Ps. 118. V. Tu mandasti.

3977. V. A solis ortu.

78. Ps. 79. V. Excita.

79. Ps. 79. V. Excita.

80. V1. Loquetur pacem. V2. Quia convenio/venio.

81. Ps. 18. V. In sole posuit.

82. Ps. 18. V. Nec est qui se abscondat.

83. Dominica vacat.

84. Intr. Veni et ostende (= Qu. Temp. Sabb.).

85. Intr. **Memento nostri Domine.** Ps. Peccavimus cum patribus.

86. Gr. **A summo caelo.**

87. Off. Exsulta satis (= Qu. Temp. Sabb.).

88. V1. Quomodo fiet. V2. Ideoque et quod nascetur.

89. V. Bene est prophetatum.

90. Intr. **Veni Domine.**

91. Intr. **Ecce Dominus veniet.**

92. Grad. **A summo caelo.**

93. Off. **Audi Israel.** V. Israel si me.

94. Offert. **Exsulta satis.**

95. Comm. **Exsultavit ut gigas.**

96. Comm. **Salvatorem exspectamus.**

97. V. Quousque exspectavimus.

98. Intr. **Memento nostri.**

99. Grad. **Excita.**

100. Hy. **Omnia opera Domini.**

101. Off. **Exsulta satis.**

102. Comm. **Exsultavit ut gigas.**

103. Comm. **Ecce venio cito.**

104. Grad. **Tollite portas.**

105. Alleluia alia: **Ave Maria.**

106. Alleluia **Festina ne tardaveris,** vel: **Levate capita.**

107. vel All. **Prophetae sancti praedicaverunt.**

108. Offert. **Confortamini.**

109. Ps. 2. V. Postula.

110. Ps. 2. V. Astiterunt.

111. V1. Cantate Domino canticum (BS). V2. Confessio et pulchritudo (B). V3. Cantate Domino benedicite (S).

112. Ps. 109.

113. Ps. 109. V. Tecum principium.

114. Ps. 92. V. Parata sedes tua.

115. V1. Dominus regnavit. V2. Mirabilis in altis/excelsis.

116. Ps. 147. V. Quoniam confortavit.

117. Ps. 95. V. Notum fecit.

118. V1. Magnus et metuendus. V2. Misericordia et veritas. V3. Tu humiliasti.

119. Ps. 97.

120. Ps. 97. V. Recordatus est.

121. Intr. **In excelso throno** (Omnis terra: D1 p.Ep.).

122. Ps. 65. V. Dicite Deo.

123. All. **Adorabo ad templum.**

124. V. Cum dilexisset me.

125. Vel Intr. **Gaudeamus omnes.**

126. Vel All. **Natus est nobis hodie.**

127. Comm. **Verbum caro factum est.**

128. Ante saecula natus.

129. Melodia propria.

130. Tropi!

131. V. Multiplicabitur ejus imperium.

132. Alleluia **Verbum caro.** Vel: **Natus est nobis.**

133. V. Tibi laus Deus noster.

134. Alleluia **Dominus regnavit exsultet.**

135. Alleluia **Omnis terra!**

136. Offert. **Jubilate Deo omnis** (Jubilate Deo universa: D1 p. Ep.).

137. V1. Reddam tibi. V2. Locutum est os meum.

138. Comm. **Mirabantur omnes.**

139. Ps. 65.

140. Ps. 65. V. Qui convertit mare.

141. V. Libera me.

142. V. Diviserunt.

143. V1. Salvum me fac Deus. V2. Adversum me exercebantur. V3. Ego vero orationem.

144. Ps. 21.

145. Ps. 115.

146. Ps. 67! V. Sicut deficit.

147. Ps. 95 (R, B, Co, S).

148. V1. In tribulatione. V2. Impulsus.

149. Ps. 118. V. Tu mandasti.

150. V. Manifestavit gloriam suam.

151. Comm. **Laetabimur** Ps. 96.

152. Comm. **Parasti in conspectu.** Vel: **Nos cognovimus.**

153. V. Sciens autem Jesus omnia.

154. Tract! **Deus Deus meus.**

155. Grad! **Christus factus est.**

156. V. Et hymno dicto.

157. V. Verumtamen non sicut.

158. Cumque consummassent omnia.

159. Grad. **Oculi omnium.**

160. Hymn. **Ubi caritas.**

161. Comm. **Hoc corpus.** ps. 22.

162. V. Ecce tu Domine (B: Tu cognovisti. Co, S: Intellexisti).

163. V2. **Epulemur.**

164. V2. Notus in Judaea. V2. Et factus est in pace. V3. Ibi confregit.

165. Ps. 138. V. Et omnes vias.

166. Ps. 117. V. Dextera Domini.

167. Ps. 117. V. Justifica.

168. Grad. **Timebunt gentes.**

169. Grad. **Bonum est confidere.**

170. Grad. **Unam petii.**

171. All. **Laudate nomen Domini.**

172. All. **Deus judex justus.**

173. B: V1. Audivi vocem dicentem. V2. Ecce me loquente.

174. S, L, Be, Bo, Klo: V1. Adhuc me loquentem. V2. Audivi vocem dicentem.

175. V. Sicut audivimus.

176. Grad. **Eripe me Domine.**

177. All. **Quoniam confirmata.**

178. All. **Adorabo ad templum.**

179. V1. In salicibus. V2. Hymnum cantate. V3. Si oblitus fuero. V4. Memento Domine.

180. V1. Si oblitus fuero. V2. Memento Domine.

181. S, Be, Bo, Klo: V1. In salicibus. V2. Si oblitus fuero. V3. Memento Domine.

182. Vel Intr. **Surrexit Dominus vere.**

183. Alleluia **Qui timent Dominum.**

184. Alleluia **Paratum cor meum.**

185. Alleluia **Dilexi quoniam.**

186. Comm. **Quemadmodum desiderat.** Vel: **Ego sum lux.**

187. Alleluia **Dextera Dei fexit.**

188. Alleluia **Qui confidunt** (cum tropo).

189. Alleluia **Non nobis Domine.**

190. Alleluia **Domine Deus salutis.** Vel: **Magnus Dominus.**

191. V1. In salicibus. V2. Si oblitus fuero.

192. Vel Comm. **In hoc cognovimus.**

Table 4.2

Graduale Romanum	*Graduale Parvum*

Dominica I.

Introitus: Ad te levavi. Ps. 24. V. Vias tuas, Domine. V. Dirige me in veritate.	*Introitus:* Ad te levavi, Domine animam meam; etenim universi, qui te exspectant, non confundentur. Ps. 24. (2–3), 4b–5.
Graduale: Universi qui te exspectant. V. Vias tuas Domine.	*Graduale*: Universi qui te exspectant. V. Vias tuas Domine.
Alleluia: Ostende nobis Domine.	*Alleluia*: Ostende nobis.
Offertorium: Ad te Domine levavi. V1. Dirige me in veritate. V2. Respice in me.	*Offertorium*: –
Communio: Dominus dabit benignitatem. Ps. 84. 2–3, 4 + 8, 9–10, 11–12.	*Communio*: Dominus dabit. Ps. 84. 2–3, 4+8, 9–10, 11–12.

Dominica II.

Introitus: Populus Sion. Ps. 79. V. Qui regis Israel. V. Excita potentiam.	*Introitus:* Populus Sion. Ps. 79. V. Qui regis Israel. V. Excite potentiam vel *Introitus:* Ad te levavi (= Dom. I)
Graduale: Ex Sion species. V. Congregate illi.	*Graduale*: Ex Sion species. V. Congregate illi.
Alleluia: Laetatus sum. V2. Stantes erant pedes vel *Alleluia:* Rex noster adveniet.	*Alleluia*: Laetatus sum. V2. Stantes erant pedes vel *Alleluia:* Rex noster adveniet.
Offertorium: Deus tu convertens. V1. Benedixisti Domine. V2. Misericordia et veritas.	*Offertorium*: —
Communio: Jerusalem surge. Ps. 147. 12–13, 14–15, 17–18, 19–20.	*Communio*: Dominus dabit. Ps. 84. 2–3, 4 + 8, 9–10, 11–12.

Dominica III.

Introitus: Gaudete in Domino. Ps. 84. V.
Benedixisti. V. Et pax Dei.

Introitus: Gaudete in Domino sem
per, iterum dico, gaudete; Dominus
prope est.
V1. Nihil solliciti sitis.
V2. Et pax Dei.
vel *Introitus*: Rorate caeli,
vel *Introitus*: Ad te levavi.

Graduale: Qui sedes Domine.
V. Qui regis Israel.

Graduale: Qui sedes Domine.
V. Qui regis Israel.

Alleluia: Excita, Domine, potentiam.

Alleluia: Excita, Domine, potentiam.

Offertorium: Benedixiti Domine.
V1. Operuisti omnia.
V2. Ostende nobis, Domine.

Offertorium: −

Communio: Dicite: Pusillanimes. Cant.
Isaiah 35, 1−2cd, 5−6ab, 6cd−7ab.

Communio: Dominus dabit (= D I)
vel *Communio*: Ecce virgo concipiet
(= D IV)

Dominica IV.

Introitus: Rorate caeli. Ps. 18. V. Caeli
enarrant. V. In sole posuit.
vel *Introitus*: Memento nostri Domine.
Ps. 105. V. Confitemini Domino. V.
Salvos nos fac.

Introitus: Rorate caeli. Ps. 18. V.
Caeli enarrant. V. In sole posuit.
vel *Introitus*: Memento nostri, Domi
ne, in beneplacito populi tui, visita
nos in salutari tuo. Ps. 105. Ad
videndum in bonitate. Salvos nos
fac.

Graduale: Prope est.
V. Laudem Domini.

Graduale: Prope est.
V. Laudem Domini.

Alleluia: Veni Domine et noli tardare.
vel *Alleluia*: Prophetae sancti praedicaverunt.
vel *Alleluia*: Levate capita vestra.

Alleluia: Veni Domine et noli tardare.
vel *Alleluia*: Prophetae sancti
praedicaverunt.
vel *Alleluia*: Levate capita vestra.

Offertorium: Ave Maria.
V1. Quomo fiet istud.
V2. Ideoque et quod nascetur.

Offertorium: −

Communio: Ecce virgo concipiet.

Ps. 18. 2−3, 4−5, 6−7.

Communio: Ecce virgo concipiet.

Ps. 18. 2−3, 4−5, 6−7.

Music Examples

1

Ad te Do- mi-ne le-va-vi a- ni - mam me-am:

ve-ni et e- ri- pe me, Do-mi- ne ad te con-fu-gi. (*Antiphonale Monasticum*)

2

To thee, O Lord, do I lift up my soul:

come & de-li- ver me,   for I flee un- to thee to hide me.

(Palmer, *The Diurnal Noted*)

3

Hoz-zád e- me- lem   az én lel- ke - met, U-ram,

mert kik té-ged vár- nak,   meg nem szé- gye- nül- nek.

Éneklő Egyház (The Chant of the Church) Hungarian Catholic Hymnal

4

Ad te, Do- mi- ne,   le- va- vi   a- ni- mam me-am,

qui- a qui te ex- pe-ctant, non con- fun- den- tur. (*Graduale Parvum*, proposal)

Chapter 5

Theological Foundations
of the Liturgy

Nicola Bux[*]

INTRODUCTION

The universal nature and characteristic sobriety of the Roman liturgy,
which for centuries had rendered it so eminently plantable in missionary lands, were being blurred by a misunderstood application of the
instauratio desired by the Second Vatican Council. The West became
infatuated with the idea that the eastern liturgies are much closer to
the people and thus more expressive of the local church, the continuity of apostolic tradition and the communion of saints, thereby
fostering a greater sense of community. The eastern liturgies were
considered true "icons" of the mystery and therefore of the heavenly
liturgy, in all its rich symbolism. It needs to be said that sometimes
the interest in these liturgies seemed to be motivated by a form of
exoticism, which originated from the idea that they contained features
which the Roman liturgy had either never possessed or had subsequently lost. More often than not, this judgment was owing to an
ignorance of the genius and the spiritual reach of the Roman liturgy.
However, when we reread today Romano Guardini's *The Spirit of
the Liturgy* (1919), or turn to its "aggiornamento" by Cardinal Joseph
Ratzinger,[1] we discover the profound unity of the Catholic liturgy
even in its historical variations. If we take a perspective that sees
eastern traditions not as alternative, but as complementary to the

---

[*] Translated by Andrew Wadsworth.
1. J. Ratzinger, *The Spirit of the Liturgy*, trans. J. Saward (San Francisco: Ignatius Press, 2000).

western traditions, we will be able to achieve a certain re-balancing of several aspects of the liturgical reforms of Vatican II.

For the project that has become known as a "reform of the reform," we have to take as our starting point the theology of the liturgy,[2] both east and west, outlined in the Constitution on the Sacred Liturgy *Sacrosanctum Concilium* and taken up again in the *Catechism of the Catholic Church*.[3] In this chapter, we will deal with some theological fundamentals of the liturgy.

The Lord's Presence in the Liturgy

What does the Church mean by *liturgy?* The book of Revelation describes the Church, in her divine-human reality, as permanently focused on the mystery of Jesus Christ present in her midst, understanding the physical liturgy here on earth to be an imitation of the heavenly liturgy. The distance from this prototype constantly obliges the Church to renew herself. This spirit is the basis for the Constitution on the Sacred Liturgy, which above all else exalts the nature and importance of the Catholic liturgy, the aim of which is the glorification and adoration of the Lord. It is the "place" where we meet the three divine Persons, the place where Christ meets us, the prayer which he, in unity with the body of the Church, offers up to the Father with the voice of the Bride;[4] above all, "it is the work of redemption,"[5] the act of earthly pilgrimage.[6]

The *Compendium of the Catechism of the Catholic Church* offers this definition: "The liturgy is the celebration of the mystery of Christ and in particular his Paschal Mystery. Through the exercise of the priestly office of Jesus Christ the liturgy manifests in signs and brings about the sanctification of humankind. The public worship which is due to God is offered by the mystical Body of Christ, that is by

---

2. I refer to the Second Vatican Council's Dogmatic Constitution on the Church *Lumen Gentium*, 23; Constitution on the Sacred Liturgy *Sacrosanctum Concilium*, 4, 21, 37–40; Decree on Ecumenism *Unitatis Redintegratio*, 4; also to Paul VI, Apostolic Exhortation *Evangelii Nuntiandi* (1975), 63–64; John Paul II, Apostolic Exhortation *Catechesi Tradendae* (1979), 53; and John Paul II, Apostolic Letter *Vicesimus Quintus Annus* (1989), 16.

3. *Catechism of the Catholic Church* (1992) (CCC), 1077–1112.

4. SC, 84.

5. SC, 1, 2, 104.

6. SC, 8.

its head and by its members."[7] All this says only one thing: in the liturgy we celebrate the Lord's love for us and our response to his love. Celebrating means that in the liturgy, the blood of the Mediator continues to be poured out in exchange for the freedom of man; in it, the covenant with God which is most appropriate to mankind is constantly renewed; in it we relive the tears of the disciples when they saw the crucified Christ and their joy at meeting him in his Resurrection, a joy which is the fruit of the presence of the Holy Spirit sent by the Father. All this constitutes the reason, the *pathos* and the attraction of the liturgy which is a fusion of faith, hope and charity.

The mystery of the three divine Persons at work in liturgical worship is defined as *Opus Dei*; its essential aim being to bless and adore the Father as "the source and end of the liturgy."[8] *Benediction* is, in Hebrew, the action of God as word and gift (in Latin *bene-dictio*, in Greek *eu-logia*) to which corresponds the action of man as adoration and offering of himself (*logike latria*) or thanksgiving.[9] It is uniquely the work of the glorified *Logos* and the Holy Spirit which flows from the right hand of the Father to make the offering *rational*, as I shall go on to explain shortly.

Jesus Christ, who is "the Lord," is present in and with the Church first and foremost in the liturgy whose intensely graded nature, according to the Constitution on the Sacred Liturgy, begins and ends in the sacrifice of the Eucharist, by means of its ministry, the sacraments, scripture, and prayer.[10] How can we understand and concentrate on acknowledging this presence in the liturgy?

The presence of Jesus on earth, which had begun with the Incarnation, was totally altered from the moment of the Ascension when it became a *noli me tangere* presence (John 20:17); his presence is a new reality. Pope Leo the Great explains that Christ did not disappear but opened the heavens: "It was then that . . . the Son of Man was known in the most sublime and holy way as the Son of God: having in fact withdrawn in glory to the majesty of his Father, he began in the most ineffable manner to be even more present (*praesentior*) in

---

7. *Compendium of the Catechism of the Catholic Church* (2005), 218.

8. Cf. CCC, 1077–1083.

9. CCC, 1078.

10. Cf. SC, 7; CCC, 1088–1089.

terms of his divinity, albeit more distant in terms of his humanity . . . .
When I have risen to be with my Father, then you will be able to
touch me in a more perfect and sublime manner."[11] Jesus said: "You
will not see me again, until you say, 'Blessed is he who comes in
the name of the Lord'" (Matthew 23:39); thus, the Lord showed us
how he will return: whenever we say: "Blessed is he who comes in
the name of the Lord." This happens in the liturgy: the act of blessing
which brings about the presence is the central constitutive act of
the liturgy.

The presence of God became hidden with the Passion of
Jesus: because neither he nor the Father received "praise or blessing"
from the people. This does not mean that man's "praise" constitutes
the condition for the Lord to be present; the presence "depends" on
the praise or blessing in the sense that it opens the door to the Lord
who knocks (cf. Revelation 3:20), praise is also the recognition that
he is present. His presence is not invasive. Christ is always present and
it is possible to recognize him wherever there are people who acclaim
him as "blessed." After Easter, the disciples "were continually in the
temple blessing God" (Luke 24:53); they had received a mission: that
of blessing and recognizing the gift of his presence. Christ himself
had made the Eucharist from the Jewish blessing (cf. Luke 24:30),
which, in other words, becomes a eucharistic blessing.

The chalice of blessing was taken up by the apostles when the
risen Christ returned to their midst. From that moment until the end
of time, the Church, whenever it gathers, will always acclaim him
"blessed." Gradually the liturgy absorbed this into the anaphora and
added, after the hymn of the triple *Sanctus,* taken from the liturgy of
the synagogue, the acclamation *Benedictus qui venit in nomine Domini.*
This is a truly Christian addition, which was first sung in Gaul from
the seventh century. Once the liturgy of the Church offers its praise
and blessing to Jesus Christ, from that moment it can be said that the
Lord has come into the Church and through the Church, into the

---

11. Leo the Great, *Sermo 2 de Ascensione*, 61(74), 4: SCh 74 bis, 280–282. With regard to the
presence of the Lord in the world, cf. J. Ratzinger, "Himmelfahrt Christi: II. Systematisch," in
Lexikon für Theologie und Kirche, 2nd edition, vol. V (Freiburg: Herder, 1960), 360–362, at 360;
K. Rahner, "Fest der Zukunft der Welt," in *id., Schriften zur Theologie* VII (Einsiedeln: Benziger,
1966), 178–82, at 181.

world. In the extraordinary form of the Roman rite, the priest makes the sign of the cross at the *Benedictus qui venit.*

The "blessing" of the disciples resulted in the presence of Christ. The sacrament of the Eucharist is the sacrament of the Presence, because when bread and wine are blessed[12] or consecrated, the Lord appears; he who has blessed the Father rejoicing in the Holy Spirit (cf. Luke 10:21–22) thus reveals the divine life in which he permanently abides, which is why his presence fills the Church. So we can then say that the new mode of Christ's being present is the eucharistic mode: a discreet, humble and yet more imposing and imminent presence. How are we to interpret what Jesus said: "I go away, and I will come to you" (John 14:28)? The withdrawal of the visible presence of Christ coincides with the imminence of his coming. He comes to us in the same instant in which he goes to his Father. He is the *Logos* glorified by the Father in the Holy Spirit. The Holy Spirit is the glory of Christ, since if Christ is not there, neither is the Holy Spirit.

We cannot hide the fact that an attempt was made to *empty* the Catholic liturgy of content as a consequence of un-Catholic thinking which tends to negate the humanity of Christ, borrowing Calvinist inspired expressions such as "dynamic presence" compared with the "static presence" attributed to the formulations of Trent— not to mention its symbolic reductions. The presence of Christ is a new reality which continues to dwell among us because it is given through grace and is identified with the gift of the Eucharist. It can thus be seen only if he is received and he can be received only if he is recognized or "blessed."

---

12. With reference to the terms *to bless* and *blessing*, and their use in relation to the Ascension and the Eucharist it is necessary to consider the relationship between *eulogein* (Luke 9:16 = Mark 6:41 = Matthew 14:19: the multiplication of the loaves and Luke 24:30, the Supper at Emmaus) and *eucharistein*, to praise giving thanks (Matthew 15:36 = Mark 8:6 = John 6:11 and 23) and also the institution of the Eucharist (Luke 22:17 and 19 that follows the common New Testament usage in Matthew 26:27 = Mark 14:23 = 1 Corinthians 11:24). In his Ascension, Christ gives his blessing leaving his Eucharist and returning to the Father with the aim of bringing it to completion.

THE *EFFICACY* OF CHRISTIAN WORSHIP

Jesus Christ is at one and the same time the Word and the outpouring
of the Holy Spirit. He is distinguished, however, from the latter in the
Eucharist. In the Eucharist, he gives of himself by himself, whereas
the Holy Spirit imparts a profound understanding of God. They are
two distinct, albeit very closely united and connected gifts. It is therefore necessary to clarify the relationship between Christ and the
Holy Spirit in the liturgy, which the *Catechism* presents as very closely
linked to the Church. To worship the Father through the action
of Christ and the power of the Holy Spirit is the "spiritual and perfect
sacrifice" (translation of *oblatio rationabilis* in the Roman Canon),
literally the "offering conforming to reason," since it is fulfilled through
words and acts accessible to our humanity. Sensible signs or sacraments
as they are traditionally called, whose greatest value is that of being
efficacious.[13] In fact, if Christ is glorified by the Holy Spirit, then man
too receives a deposit here and now through the liturgy, by way of
anticipation of future glory. In it, *Christus heri, hodie et semper* totally
involves man by means of *anamnesis*. In the *hour* of Christ, the unique
Paschal event does not come to an end because Christ through the
totality of his love has conquered death in such a way that he will
remain and have no end.[14]

To speak of the *efficacy* of worship and the sacraments means
making oneself comprehensible in everyday language (a good comparison would be efficacy of medicines): the sacramental efficacy of
the liturgy is due to *grace*, that is divine life poured out for humanity
by means of the Lord's Passion and the power of his Resurrection.
Thus, in the sacraments grace touches our humanity reaching down
into the soul causing it to be reborn. It thereby fortifies it, nourishes it,
pardons it, heals it, assists it, and loves it, and ultimately it saves it now
and for evermore, even preparing it for the resurrection of the body.

The definition of the sacraments as "memorial signs of saving
events" needs explanation to avoid reducing them to symbols evocative
of the past. If their saving efficacy does not depend on their human
symbolism, it means that their material element is essential because it
is the *form* into which the divine Word descends. As Saint Augustine

---

13. Cf. CCC, 1084.
14. CCC, 1085.

puts it so sublimely: *Accedit verbum ad elementum et fit sacramentum*.[15] If the sacraments make the *mirabilia Dei* present through gestures and words, it means that they are the continuation of the Word incarnate, glorified in the Holy Spirit, the *mimêsis*, the perceptible representation of the mysteries of Jesus Christ. The apostles administered the sacraments in the form of the eucharistic sacrifice around which the entire life of the liturgy revolves, in order to implement the *work* of salvation:[16] a work that concerns man presupposes created matter, namely, flesh. The sacraments are thus memorial signs in the sense that they are inhabited by the saving power of God, as the humanity of the visible Christ passed into them after the Ascension,[17] It is something extraordinary, an efficacious and stupendous sign, a *miracle*. For instance, what could be more sublime than baptism, observes Saint Ambrose, when in one single moment, the guilt of a whole people is wiped out![18] In what else would freedom consist? The miracle of making everything new is the Lord's. Are we afraid to say so?

The liturgy cannot be understood without the sacraments, in fact they are the fulfillment of its expression, by which God acts upon matter (water, oil, bread, wine) making it an instrument of salvation. If a sacrament has become difficult to understand, this is above all due to the fact that it is understood as an evocative symbol, perhaps because nowadays it is considered impossible for God to intervene in the material world. Parallels can easily be drawn between the Incarnation and the work of the Holy Spirit through the sacraments, but what cannot be deduced are the consequences for the humanity and the soul of man.[19]

The Paschal Mystery continues to operate in the sacraments of Christ due to its words and actions which are explained as "forces that emerge" from him who is ever-living and life-giving and as the working of the Holy Spirit within the Body of the Church.

---

15. Augustine, *Tractatus in Johannis Evangelium*, 80,3: CCL 36, 529.

16. Cf. SC, 6.

17. Cf. Leo the Great, *Sermo 2 de Ascensione*, 61(74), 2: SCh 74 bis, 278.

18. Cf. *Opera omnia di Sant'Ambrogio: Inni, Iscrizioni, Frammenti*, ed. S. Banterle, G. Biffi, I. Biffi, L. Migliavacca (Milano: Biblioteca Ambrosiana, 1994), 96–99.

19. In order to deepen an understanding of the role of matter in liturgical form and its relationship to the Incarnation: cf. Ratzinger, *The Spirit of the Liturgy*, 220–224; N. Bux, *Il Signore dei Misteri: Eucaristia e relativismo* (Siena: Cantagalli, 2005), 41–54.

For this reason, they are also sacraments of the Church.[20] It is indeed through this *efficacy* that the glory of Christ has been revealed from the very earliest days of the apostolic church: it receives glory because the Apostles *actualize,* by means of the eucharistic sacrifice and the sacraments, the very work of saving mankind and creation, announcing that as a consequence of such a Paschal Mystery, they would be taken into the kingdom of heaven.[21] Due to the power of sanctification conferred by the Holy Spirit, the Apostles are themselves a "sacrament" to be passed on to succeeding generations; it is here that we find the origin of the ecclesial *traditio* which is affirmed in the *Catechism* as: "this 'apostolic succession' which gives structure to the entire liturgical life of the Church which is itself sacramental, as it is transmitted through the sacrament of orders."[22]

The sacraments are the Church's confession of faith which precedes that of the believer: they are lived both as a *norma* of apostolic faith and as prayer (the famous dictum of Prosper of Aquitaine *lex orandi, lex credendi*); they do not permit, nor does the liturgy as a whole allow any room for manipulation, except when the authority of the Church has to update them in obedience to the faith and out of respect for the mystery.[23] The liturgy belongs to the tradition handed down to us and is to be transmitted both whole and enriched; in this respect, it is an *opus operantis* of the Church and derives its efficacy from the salvation wrought by Christ (*ex opere operato*), even if the fruits of this salvation *also* depend on the disposition of the faithful.

Thus, from the presence of the glorified Lord, there derives another fundamental element of the liturgy, its sacramental efficacy: if God did not disdain to take human flesh in order to redeem man through cosmic matter, creating it and giving it form by his word, it is understood that "matter and form" are both necessary for salvation: it is therefore of these two elements that the sacraments are made.[24] Human flesh is the *hinge* on which the salvation which begins

---

20. Cf. CCC, 1115–1121.
21. Cf. CCC, 1086.
22. CCC, 1087.
23. Cf. CCC, 1124–1125.
24. CCC, 1127–1129.

on earth and is intended to culminate in the resurrection and eternal life ultimately hangs: the sacraments are a pledge of this.

In the liturgy, through grace flowing from the efficacy of the Passion and power of the Resurrection, the mystery of the Lord glorified in the Holy Spirit renews all things.

PARTICIPATION IN THE LITURGY

The Holy Spirit and the Church work *together* in the liturgy, but in what sense? First of all, the Holy Spirit, who wants us to live the life of the risen Christ, *prepares* us to meet the Lord. He does so by revealing Christ who is hidden in the types (*typoi*) of the Old Testament, and by introducing us to the revelation of the New Testament.[25] This corresponds to the catechesis based on typology;[26] this "method of the Apostles" perpetuated by the Fathers of the Church, was intended to justify the faith to Jews and pagans. It was neither abandoned by the medieval doctors of the Church nor by the Roman liturgy itself. An example of this would be the hymns of Saint Thomas Aquinas and the sequence *Lauda Sion*, sung in praise of the Eucharistic Bread which is prefigured in the Old Testament by means of symbols (*in figuris praesignatur*). Thus, through Christ and the Holy Spirit we have the first stages of worship in spirit and truth which is achieved by means of an ascending hierarchy of experiences:

- Conversion to the Lord
- Entry into the Celestial Liturgy
- Offering of Oneself
- Piety and Devotion
- Communion within the Mystical Body

Conversion to the Lord

The aim of mystagogical catechesis in terms of types is unique in the way it uses every figure, allegory or symbol of the liturgy, through *preces et ritus*, to come closer to the mysteries of Christ and through them, the mystery of God. At the same time, the Holy Spirit expects to find within us the response of faith which the Holy Spirit himself

---

25. CCC, 1091–1092.
26. CCC, 1093–1094/1098.

inspires. His intention is not to leave things as they are but to get us to turn our eyes towards God, *conversi ad Dominum,* and thus to change our hearts. In other words, *participation* in worship must not remain merely external. The Constitution on the Sacred Liturgy affirms that faith and conversion are both necessary in order to be able to approach the liturgy.[27] The opposition which is sometimes set up between patristic and scholastic catechesis, based on the theory that the Fathers applied the catechism in church whereas the Scholastics applied it in places of learning, not only ignores differences of time and context, it overlooks the fact that coming face to face with the mystery necessarily requires a path of conversion to truth by means of faith and reason. For a renewal of mystagogical catechesis today, we should resume the approaches of *both* the Fathers *and* the Scholastics. Given that Western civilization today is marked by religious and intellectual relativism, the explanation of the mystery to which man has to be led has a sole objective: that of passing from the visible to the invisible, something which is brought about by faith, and a hope in things which cannot be seen.

The Holy Spirit, as a "living memory," reminds the Church of Christ, a function he fulfils by means of the *anamnesis* of the liturgy; the Holy Spirit guides the faithful to be mindful of Jesus Christ in order to give glory to the Father—hence, the doxology.[28] Through the *blessing and adoration* of Christians, the Holy Spirit himself is manifest as glorifying the Son.

Moreover the Holy Spirit manifests, makes present and *actualizes* the mystery of Christ: this means that the Lord's power comes into action to save mankind: and, as we have seen, its efficacy, like a medicine—*phármakon*—contains a potential yet to be activated within me.

A word should be added here: what can *actualize* mean? It means to re-present the mysteries of Christ, the facts, in the words of Saint Augustine: *in manibus scripta, in oculis facta*—in which we are implicated here and now—the *hodie* and the *hic* of scripture and of the liturgy—a work of the whole Trinity and not just the Holy Spirit. This *making present* is distinct from actualizing, but at the same

---

27. Cf. SC, 9.
28. Cf. CCC, 1099–1103.

time it is united to it: it implies that the mystery which has taken place once and for all time is not repeated chronologically, but it is always present and becomes in *actu* for us when we call it to mind. In a certain sense, actualizing means that *we make ourselves present to him* by calling him to mind.[29] All this happens through the supplication to the Father to send the Holy Spirit (*epiclesis*) so that the holy gifts and faithful are transformed by means of his power, as in the Incarnation, through the cooperation of the Word.[30] The work of the Holy Spirit happens "before" that of the Word, as in the Roman Canon after the *epiclesis* there follows the *anamnesis*, so that these "two hands" might return to the Father the man created and now saved by him.

Finally, as the Spirit of communion, the Paraclete unites the Church to Christ.[31] This is the aim of his mission, as previously stated: to unite the Church to Christ, the fruit of such a union being a communion of the Trinity with ourselves (the *epiclesis* is also this), our transformation as an offering, by means of a *logical* sacrifice bringing the truth and charity of Christ into the world. The center is the Trinity and at the center of the center stands Jesus Christ who became incarnate; the Holy Spirit does nothing without the Son but only reminds the faithful of what he has taught and witnessed even unto the shedding of his blood. Thus, the action of the Holy Spirit is fulfilled "after" that of the Son: the Holy Spirit also "proceeds" from him. It is understandable how, in terms of the scriptural as well as the liturgical economy, that the Holy Spirit is invoked before the consecration and again after it (the two *epicleses*). But this is not the moment for a deeper consideration of this question.

Thus, the Holy Spirit renews the face of the earth through the sacraments administered by the Church, the sacrament of Christ which is, in turn, that of the Father.

Entry into the Celestial Liturgy

A further fundamental element of our participation in the liturgy is our taking part in the celestial liturgy made possible by the presence

---

29. Cf. Bux, *Il Signore dei Misteri*, 73–81.
30. Cf. CCC, 1104–1107.
31. CCC, 1108–1109.

of Christ.[32] The *forma* of Christian worship descends (*katabasis*) from heaven with the Heavenly Jerusalem in order to enable us to ascend to heaven (*anabasis*).

Alluding to the vision of Jacob's Ladder (Genesis 28:12), Jesus proclaims that by his Incarnation—his "descent" to earth, and his Ascension, heaven has been opened (John 1:51), the Father enters into communion with mankind (the *admirabile commercium* of the divine/human exchange). The angels who ascend and descend represent the glory of the Father made manifest through the Son, before his resurrection by means of prodigious signs and after the Ascension through sacramental mysteries. According to commentators on the Eastern rites, deacons take the place of angels serving the heavenly banquet. The Apocalypse describes the Heavenly Jerusalem descending from heaven to earth and has at its center the altar of the Lamb. This vision is, in a certain sense, the *norm* which regulates Christian liturgy, as witnessed in the Roman Canon which proposes through the liturgy the uninterrupted presence of him who descended by means of the Incarnation and has ascended for our salvation, he who is the Risen and Living One, who renews and subsumes all of creation in himself. The liturgy nourishes faith in Jesus Christ by means of the incessant opening of mankind to God's entry into the world of men. In this way, Christian worship is revealed to us as the adoration of God with the aim of entering into communion with him.[33] It is precisely in the Eucharist that this wondrous exchange which saves mankind continues. It is this mystery which, according to Saint John Chrysostom, "transforms the earth for us into heaven. It shows us that what is above is more venerable than that which is here below. It shows us the very Lord of Angels and Archangels."[34] In the words of Pope John Paul II, the celebration of the Eucharist gives us "a powerful experience of its universal and, so to speak, cosmic character. Yes, cosmic! Because even when it is celebrated on the humble altar of a country church, the Eucharist is always in some way celebrated *on the altar of the world*. It unites heaven and earth. It embraces and permeates all creation."[35]

---

32. CCC, 1090.

33. SC, 8; John Paul II, Encyclical *Ecclesia de Eucharistia* (2003), 19.

34. John Chrysostom, *In Epistulam I ad Corinthias Hom.*, 24,5: PG 61,205.

35. *Ecclesia de Eucharistia*, 8.

Offering of Oneself

"Offer your bodies as a spiritual sacrifice" (Romans 12:1). This passage is decisive for the notion of Christian worship; the word "offer" (Greek *parastêsai*, Latin *exhibeatis*), indicates the act of the act of placing before God the sacrifice of oneself. This act of devotion is the offering, the culminating act of Christian worship and the fulfilled expression of the spirit of the liturgy. By contrast, the notion of devotionism indicates a reduction of that act to its merely formal and external elements. Is this not the most widespread malady among the Christians of today—doubt, absence or scarcity of faith, skepticism, ignorance of the presence of Christ and of his action through the Church and in the world by means of the Paschal Mystery, all of which can be traced back to the reasonable question which arises from the human heart?

Personal interior experience of the mystery of Christ is an absolute necessity. It seems that the emphasis placed on the community eclipses that of the individual. The passage from Romans is important for from it we derive the notions of: spiritual sacrifice, the living victim who makes spiritual worship possible by means of the conversion of the heart which includes charity towards the brethren. Saint Gregory the Great explains it thus: "I say boldly that we will not have any need of the saving sacrifice after death, if before death we have made ourselves a sacrifice for God."[36] In what way does the Church on earth celebrate the liturgy? The *Compendium of the Catechism* emphasizes this essential character of the members of the Church: the baptized offer themselves as a spiritual sacrifice.[37] Saint Augustine is right when he says that it is not sufficient to just reply *Amen* or to sing *Alleluia*![38]

This personal experience seems to occur precisely in the process of passing from the objective to the subjective. Cardinal Jean Daniélou applies this to the journey of faith stating that

> The Christian faith has but one object, the mystery of Christ who has died and is risen. The mystery subsists in different ways, it is prefigured in the

---

36. Gregory the Great, *Dialogi*, IV,62,3: SCh 265,206: *fidenter dico quia salutari hostia post mortem non indigebimus si ante mortem Deo hostia ipsi fuerimus.*

37. Cf. *Compendium*, 235.

38. Augustine, *In Epistulam Iohannis ad Parthos*, V,7: PL 35,2016.

Old Testament, it is historically fulfilled in the earthly life of Christ, it is contained in the mystery of the sacraments, it is mystically lived in the life of individual souls, it is fulfilled socially in the Church, and it is consummated eschatologically in the kingdom of heaven. Thus the Christian has within his grasp many possibilities, a multi-dimensional symbolism which expresses a single reality. All Christian culture consists in holding together in the closest union the connections between Scripture and liturgy, gospel and eschatology, mysticism and liturgy. The application of this method to the study of Scripture is called exegesis, as applied to the liturgy, it is called mystagogy. It consists of reading the mystery of Christ in the liturgical rites and contemplating the invisible reality that lies beyond the symbols.[39]

I ask myself whether it is possible to posit a notion of liturgical participation without an interior experience of Christ! *Sacrosanctum Concilium* observes: "The Church is greatly concerned that the faithful . . . learn to offer themselves."[40]

Piety and Devotion

If the liturgy is not everything,[41] between the *fons* and the *culmen* there is a river which must take its course! The Constitution on the Sacred Liturgy affirms that the liturgy does not exhaust the pastoral and spiritual life of the faithful;[42] there are therefore other sources: scripture and the exercises and devotions of popular piety. In his encyclical *Mediator Dei*, Pope Pius XII recalls that the objective must become subjective. The relationship between the individual conscience and the mind of the Church is always rather precarious—the Church is the "we believe" of a Christian, in such a way that a knowledge of belonging to the one Body must prevail, so that being a part of the Body enables one to participate in the liturgy (with all the necessary time and space required for examining oneself, discerning of the Lord's Body being an essential condition for communion). Personally, I see no separation between the liturgy of the Church and personal piety as each implies and necessitates the other.

---

39. J. Daniélou, "Le symbolisme des rites baptismaux," in *Dieu Vivant* 1(1945), 17–43, at 17.
40. SC, 48.
41. Cf. SC, 12.
42. SC, 9.

Liturgists want popular piety to renew its language in such a way that the liturgy expresses itself in the language of the people. Nowadays it is necessary to discover cultural expressions that give life to different modes of expression and correspond to that which Pope John Paul II called "the challenge of the new evangelization." In all times and places, whether geographical, social or cultural, Christians always find the same difficulty in proclaiming the Gospel of Jesus Christ. That this should be so is due to the synthesis which Christianity uniquely achieves between faith and reason. The faith in its essentials cannot be diminished but from time to time, with the aid of reason, it is assisted in finding the forms which enable it to be expressed and communicated.

The many *Guidelines* (*Orientamenti*) promulgated in recent years concerning the catechumenate, Christian Initiation and the various means of reawakening faith have created something of a short circuit, risking the theorization of a reality that does not exist, considering the unimaginable de-Christianization of Europe. Fortunately, the Christian people in their mission, which is increasingly expressed in a variety of new ecclesial movements, are able to go beyond these theories. Before witness to gospel values, there is the need for Christ "to be formed" in us, from this true devotion is born.

Thus, we are able to better understand the famous phrase of the Constitution on the Sacred Liturgy which states that the liturgy is "the source and summit of the Church's life."[43] We have to overcome the juxtaposition of liturgy and popular piety as well as action understood in terms of the individual and that individual as part of the Mystical Body. Here we find the motive for the crisis in our understanding of liturgical participation. In order that there is complimentality, the liturgy must be "of the people," integrated into the people, without any notion of being purely conceptual or elitist, but enabling us to live united to Christ in the Church.[44] This is the unifying principle in God's saving plan as evidenced in the variety of personal journeys. *Leiturgia* means the action of the holy people of God, characterized by *pietas*, since it is by nature popular. This *pietas*

---

43. SC, 10.

44. Congregation for Divine Worship and the Discipline of the Sacraments, *Directory on Popular Piety and Liturgy* (2002), 143.

towards God which is our recognition and adoration of him is the
spirit of the liturgy.

Communion within the Mystical Body

The oldest resurrection account of the Lord's appearance to more than
five hundred people (1 Corinthians 15:36) shows the Church to be
a *convocation* of the Lord. The term *assembly* should not be misunderstood in the democratic sense of the term—the assembly is convoked
from every part of Christ, *ek-klesis* (called forth) being the etymologi-
cal origin of the word "church." The Church is the work of redemption,
it necessitates, however, a knowledge of *being a part in order to take
part in the liturgy*; from this there emerges the necessity of formation
of the faithful and particularly the clergy.[45] From the catechism class
to the seminary, this is also the aim of the adaptation of liturgical
forms. If formation concentrates on this knowledge which emerges
from belonging to the ecclesial body, participation becomes active
and fruitful,[46] to the point that our offering of ourselves becomes an
eternal offering.[47] Since participation cannot be separated from the
sacramental journey[48] which is "source and summit" of the Christian
life, it must tend toward that perfection which is communion,[49]
establishing the necessary conditions for it and above all, faith.
Educating people towards participation means educating them in faith,
that is, responding to divine grace, either personally or ecclesially
(cf. 1 John 1:1–4). The faith of the individual reposes in the ecclesial
body. Christian liturgy is made up principally of persons and then
signs. With Christ we constitute the liturgy and by means of the
sacraments we are transformed by it: through baptism which makes
us purifying waters and healing and strengthening oil for others;
through the Eucharist which changes us in such a way that we
become Christ for one another and a witness to the world that does
not yet know him. In this way, he becomes visible through us

---

45. SC, 14.
46. SC, 11, 14.
47. SC, 12, 48, 105.
48. SC, 61.
49. SC, 55.

(Galatians 2:20). From this faith lived sacramentally there flows Christian morality.

Communion with the Mystical Body through the liturgy makes us philosophers as *faith and reason* flow together in our visible worship since the Roman liturgy and Christian liturgy in general, in contrast to that of other religions, is worship that conforms to reason. In this way participation becomes fruitful.

If the liturgy has its own language that is expressed in objects, in gestures and in silence, understanding it is important and not just on an intellectual level. The use of spoken language is not necessarily synonymous with comprehension and neither does understanding turn us into experts, but it does allow us the possibility of being involved. We will never totally understand the liturgy, not just because it is the mystery of Christ, but because the liturgy includes us in such a way that it is impossible for us to be objective about it. It is the heart which must understand and this implies so much more than merely grasping notions, rites and symbols in their biblical, anthropological or various other aspects. Beyond this understanding, the heart, the imagination and the memory are also all essential if we are to fully enter the mystery, as are the five senses. It has already been stated that we must hear as if there were nothing to be seen. More than explanations, the liturgy needs to be lived with faith.

In order to know the liturgy we need to enter into a relationship with the mystery of Christ and be touched by it—this is participation. It is not necessary to understand everything, but to allow oneself to enter it body and soul. Here is the meaning of the sacramental "symbol," uniting the visible with the invisible that is unutterable and making it perceptible. This is quite different from a sign that points to another, as the symbol contains the spiritual reality and guides us towards a contemplation of the invisible. In order to enter this, even psychologically, it takes time for the whole being to become involved and necessitates faith. Liturgical time is also necessary, which, like the returning seasons, allows salvific time to run in a linear way toward its fulfillment, involving the whole cosmos and history sacramentally. Without all this, the liturgy becomes so intellectual that the people of God prefer to perform rituals in a church in which they can make a tour of the statues and touch them, light a candle and leave flowers. Neither should we be surprised if people turn to esoteric cults in an attempt to encounter the mystery.[50]

The "Immutable Novelty" of Catholic Liturgy

From the elements considered thus far, it is evident that the liturgy cannot replicate the ways of the world, because it is an absolute novelty. Christian worship is Christ in his divine humanity,[51] who has introduced into the world a hymn of praise to the Father.[52] Since he is present in this,[53] the Holy Spirit makes this sacrifice of Christ possible, insofar as the risen Christ has entered time, once and for all, and is no longer limited by it. We need to think of this when we speak of eschatology in the liturgy and of the adoration of the Real Presence in the Eucharistic gifts. In Christ himself we find the complete unity of word, worship and Eucharist.[54] This memorial of Christ is made every Sunday and every day throughout the year. This is why the liturgy "is not some cold and lifeless representation of past events or a simple and empty reminder of the past. It is Christ himself always alive in his Church."[55] This is the exercise of his priesthood[56] which by means of the Holy Spirit emits the divine energy which is grace,[57] in such a way that the presence of Christ changes man in his essence, touching and sanctifying every moment in life,[58] uniting mankind and proposing the Church as the sign of salvation that gathers those who are scattered.[59]

The liturgy is the action of the whole Christ because it is catholic. In the Apocalypse, Saint John sees Christ at the center, seated on the throne, or standing upright as the immolated Lamb. From this center, there flows, as a river, the Holy Spirit. United to the Head

---

50. Cardinal Godfried Danneels returns to this point several times: see his "Comment entrons-nous dans la liturgie?" in *Pastoralia* 12/1995, 220–223.

51. SC, 5–6.

52. SC, 83.

53. SC, 7.

54. SC, 56.

55. Pius XII, Encyclical Letter *Mediator Dei* (1947); DS 3855.

56. SC, 7.

57. SC, 10.

58. SC, 61.

59. SC, 2.

and beneath him are the 24 witnesses of the Old and New Testaments, with the Mother of God, the martyrs and saints together with people of every nation.[60]

"It is in this eternal liturgy," as the *Catechism* affirms, "that the Spirit and the Church enable us to participate when we celebrate the mystery of salvation in the sacraments."[61] As a permanent visual indication of this, a person entering a church first sees an altar with a crucifix in the center (for the Eastern Churches this is the tomb from which Christ rises),[62] on it the tabernacle and book of the gospels. We *receive* the heavenly liturgy, which always precedes us as the celebration of the universal Church mentioned in the diptychs of the saints and of the faithful departed, which are read during the anaphora. However, we also *receive* the earthly liturgy in the diptych prayers for the living, in particular in those for the bishops. The Pope reaches each particular church from within, expressing the mutuality between the Universal Church and each particular church.[63] The bishop is the visible principle of unity in a particular Church, in communion with which each priestly celebration of the Eucharist finds its legitimacy. Due to the fact that we *receive* the liturgy, we can only serve as its ministers.

In brief, we have described the liturgy in its prototypical form, from which all other liturgies find their source in such a way that they cannot but be Catholic. This prototypical liturgy constitutes "the immutable part of the divine institution,"[64] which is untouched by restoration or reform across the centuries, as regards its ritual forms, must be the subject of careful investigation.[65]

We can state, together with Jungmann, Gamber, Bouyer and Ratzinger that such an investigation is still awaited. As an example, we can cite the Constitution on the Sacred Liturgy, which recommends: "The rites should be distinguished by a noble simplicity; they should be short, clear, and unencumbered by useless repetitions; they

---

60. CCC, 1136–1138.

61. CCC, 1139.

62. CCC, 1182.

63. Cf. Congregation for the Doctrine of the Faith, Letter to Bishops of the Catholic Church on some aspects of the Church understood as Communion *Communionis notio* (1992), 9.

64. SC, 21.

65. SC, 23.

should be within the people's powers of comprehension, and normally should not require much explanation."[66] Instead one assists at liturgies where the eloquence of the signs is submerged in a sea of words and explanations that prevent the signs from speaking directly to the hearts of the faithful.

A further example would be the invitation to restore that which has fallen into disuse. Here I am thinking about the use of Latin, an expression of the immutable part of the liturgy, or in the interests of variety, Gregorian chant.[67] Sacred music is a ministerial task.[68] It is "sacred" precisely because it has an objectivity that surpasses the subjective consideration of taste, even if it makes use of it. In order that the Church might assess the value of elements that could be admitted to the liturgy, she reserves to herself the right to be arbiter in relation to artistic forms.[69]

In the liturgy, we "enter" into adoration, we do not create it; liturgical creativity is possible only if it harmonizes with this characteristic of faith, otherwise the liturgy has no meaning. It comes from above; it is celebrated by the Church but inspired by scripture and tradition. The liturgy serves but is not subjugated to it. The sole agent of the liturgy is Jesus Christ. We are but guests; otherwise, it would be a theatrical spectacle. It is his epiphany, the prolonging of his mysteries from his birth to his resurrection; it is a mystical reality which also involves my birth, my life and my death. The liturgy educates man by means of Christ our Teacher and the Church our Mother, introducing to us the meaning of reality in its irreducible form, providing a dramatic backdrop to our struggle with evil.

The unceasing novelty of worship is in its continual conversion of man to God.

THE DIVERSITIES OF THE LITURGY IN RELATION TO ITS MISSION

In the liturgy there is the unchangeable part established by divine institution that the Church must protect and those parts which are

---

66. SC, 34; see also 35.3 and 59.
67. SC, 50, 36.1, 37, 116, 117.
68. SC, 112.
69. SC, 122.

susceptible to change which the Church "has the power, and sometimes also the duty, to adapt to the culture of peoples who have been
more recently evangelized."[70] The Paschal Mystery is unique but the
form and rituals of the Church are manifold, dating back, to various
degrees, to the faith of the apostles, even if none of these rituals in
themselves exhaust its expression. Their story demonstrates compli-
mentarity insofar as various Churches were enriched as long as they
remained in communion, otherwise they were impoverished.[71] In each
case, the cause of ritual diversity was not cultural exoticism but rather
the missionary development of the churches. Even today the revelation to all peoples of the mystery of Christ must guide the work
of adaptation of the liturgy in accordance with the mind and culture
of different peoples.[72] In the churches of Europe and those continents
evangelized by them, the Latin rite, including the Roman rite, the
Ambrosian rite and the rites of local churches and religious orders
should be conserved and developed.[73]

Furthermore, the diversity of rites is a demonstration of the
Catholicity of the liturgy. The rite, particularly in its liturgical symbolism, expresses the manner of one part of the Church in a given
geographical and cultural area in celebrating the mystery of Christ.
The Church is Catholic precisely due to the fact that she is able
to integrate and thereby purify cultural riches—on the one hand the
liturgy is expressed through culture without becoming subject to it,
on the other hand the liturgy generates and molds culture.[74]

As long as this diversity is a source of enrichment and not
tension, misunderstanding and schism, it fosters unity. It must therefore express itself in a manner which is faithful to the faith commonly
held, to the sacramental signs which the Church has received from
Christ and to hierarchical communion of the Church.[75] The criterion
which assures unity in plurality of liturgical traditions is fidelity to the
apostolic tradition, in other words, communion in the faith and the
sacraments received from the apostles which is signified and guaranteed

---

70. CCC, 1205.
71. Cf. CCC, 1200–1201.
72. Cf. SC 37–40; CCC, 1204.
73. CCC, 1202–1203.
74. CCC, 1207.
75. CCC, 1206.

by the apostolic succession—*lex credendi*. To the extent that this criterion is not observed a rite loses its appearance.[76] The rites must follow the organic progress of the development of dogma; on the old trunk, the new branch sprouts forth, but not to supplant it. For this reason, it makes no sense to hold that the *Novus Ordo* of Pope Paul VI abolished the Missal of Saint Pius V.

CONCLUSION

How do we consider the 40 years since Vatican II in the light of the two thousand year history of the Church? The idea that the Council was a complete innovation, a break with the past, has resulted in provoking the polarization of two legitimate and complimentary positions: sensitivity to tradition and sensitivity to the incarnation of our own day. One of the fields of conflict has been the Roman liturgy, often dismantled in an arbitrary way incompatible with its essence, appearance and form, which is more ancient than that of the Eastern rites. The sobriety which is characteristic of this rite, distinguishing it from all others, is based on the idea of "worship conforming to reason" that is the human response to the divine word. It is precisely this original characteristic that suggests the notion of a *reform of the liturgical reform*, to use the now famous expression of the then Cardinal Ratzinger, to clarify above all the necessity of an educational process that will re-establish the notion that the liturgy is a gift and not purely a demonstration of human ability, not human property, but rather the eruption of the divine presence on the earth. Secondly, there should be a reflection on the present liturgical forms to evaluate whether they have in some sense become deformed in relation to the original intention and if so to restore them. Liturgy, as theology, does not live by that which is thought, but that which is received and as such is not susceptible to manipulation. Reflection on the spirit of the Christian liturgy leads us logically to ask whether it is not essentially the adoration of God. Such is the principal intention of this conference.

In his book *The Spirit of the Liturgy*, Cardinal Ratzinger, now Pope Benedict XVI, defines it as the offering of everything to God,

---

76. According to Klaus Gamber, that is what has happened to the Roman Rite: cf. *La réforme liturgique en question* (Le Barroux: Sainte-Madeleine, 1992), 81–87.

history, the cosmos, and ultimately ourselves. Such a formulation leads us to deduce certain points of priority for *the reform of the reform*:

1.   The adoption once again of the orientation of the prayer of the faithful *ad Dominum* in contrast to the present situation, taking up the apostolic tradition of east-ward orientation of Christian buildings and the consequent liturgical practice where possible.

2.   Restoring the relationship of the tabernacle to the altar. Adoration is not opposed to communion and should not be sidelined. This should lead to a further consideration of the so-called "conflict of signs" that has resulted in the decentralization of the tabernacle, relegating it to a secondary position or even placing it in the position of the priest's chair.

3.   To re-establish the relationship between Christian art and the Incarnation, which happened in order to draw mankind into a process of ascent. New churches are often functional but rarely capable of transmitting beauty.

4.   To withdraw liturgical music from any risk of shrouding the Christian event in a sort of generic mysticism, leading the way to Gnosticism and the New Age.

5.   To understand correctly participation in the liturgy as wished by the Council. In the Roman liturgy there exists the expression *facti participes*, that is, being rendered participants by an action which is not human, even if it is carried out in a human context. Without this knowledge of being made participants, there is no liturgical participation. To such participation eminently belong actions such as kneeling or bowing profoundly—the principal bodily disposition indicating adoration, linking Catholics to orthodox and Jews to Muslims. It is also a return to the Scriptures where these things have a central importance. In the New Testament alone there are 59 references of which 24 are found in the book of the Apocalypse, the book of the heavenly liturgy which is presented to the Church as a model and criterion for the earthly liturgy. Finally, applause which assimilates the liturgy to a sort of religious entertainment should be avoided.

All this signifies having the necessary courage to go against the trend, and yet to stay within the furrow of the bi-millennial tradition of the Church, in the footsteps of those theologians of the

Liturgical Movement who wanted to renew the spirit of Christian liturgy as adoration of the Father through the Holy Spirit in the truth of Jesus Christ. The demands of the application of such a reform of the reform, however, are not satisfied by instructions, but it is necessary to have exemplary places where the liturgy is lived with faith and consequently celebrated faithfully. Churches which, by their Rite of Dedication, are removed from profane use and consecrated to God cannot function as concert halls or museums in which the treasures of the past are displayed in a vainglorious manner. To do so would end in depriving the people of today of the possibility of encountering the divine and thereby of the conversion which is the concrete finality of the liturgy. We therefore favor the debate, without prejudice or omission, as a way of increasing our understanding that in every generation a right understanding of the liturgy necessarily implies a worthy celebration of the Christian liturgy.

Chapter 6

Liturgies of the Military Religious Orders

Cristina Dondi

The military religious orders were a novelty for medieval society, which was used to keeping military and religious activities well separate. The first orders originated at the turn of the twelfth century as a consequence of the First Crusade, which had been set up to free Jerusalem and the Holy Land (1099): Templars and Hospitallers came into being to protect the pilgrims on their way to and in the holy places, and to care for the sick. Other military religious orders developed later, in the Holy Land and in Europe, with different purposes. Time, place, goal, founding members and spiritual guidance were factors that shaped the liturgy each of these orders would practice: sometimes creating a use with original features, sometimes adopting or adapting an already existing one from a diocese or a religious order.

The unequivocal way to establish which liturgical use was practiced by the military orders, institutions whose religious history is often not as clear as it is the case for other religious orders, is to analyze their liturgical books. While I have conducted a survey on Hospitallers' and Templars' sources,[1] liturgical manuscripts or printed books belonging to other military orders have not yet been systematically located and studied: therefore, their liturgical practice has to be inferred by direct or indirect references generally found in rules, statutes, and confirmation bulls.

---

1. C. Dondi, *The Liturgy of the Canons Regular of the Holy Sepulchre of Jerusalem: A Study and a Catalogue of the Manuscript Sources*, Bibliotheca Victorina 16 (Turnhout: Brepols, 2004), and "Hospitaller Liturgical Manuscripts and Early Printed Books," in *Revue Mabillon* N.S. 14=75 (2003), 225–256.

A number of the less known military orders, moreover, had a varied existence, their condition shifting from independent to dependent. It can only be assumed that part of the process of change included a liturgical change. I have tried to offer a systematic survey of the liturgy of all military religious order in an entry which I prepared for the *Dictionnaire des ordres militaires au Moyen Âge,* published in 2009.[2] There I deal with the orders established in the Holy Land, such as those of Saint Thomas, of Saint Lazarus, and confraternities such as the *Societas Vermiliorum* and the confraternity of Saint Edward the Confessor, as well as the religious military institutions not founded in the Holy Land, namely the Spanish orders of Calatrava and Alcántara, the order of Santiago, of Montjoy, and of Montesa.

In this chapter, I will be concentrating on the better documented military orders which were founded in the Holy Land in the twelfth century, Templars and Hospitallers. The Templar order was founded in Jerusalem in 1120 and subsequently confirmed by Innocent II in 1139, while the Hospitallers, as a religious order, had already received papal confirmation in 1113. These orders practiced the liturgy of the Church of the Holy Sepulcher of Jerusalem, the practice established by the Latins after 1099 in the cathedral church of Jerusalem, which from 1114 was officiated by canons regular. The diocese of Jerusalem observed the principle of diocesan uniformity formulated in 517 at the Council of Gerona, a custom which, promoting a centralizing attitude, was later particularly suited to the ideals of the reformed papacy. According to the principle of diocesan uniformity a new foundation generally conformed its office to that of the cathedral within whose diocese the foundation was established.[3] The application of this principle within the diocese of Jerusalem is evident by the canonical organization of the Templars and Hospitallers, as attested by their rule and statutes, and by the adoption of the liturgy of the cathedral church of the Holy Sepulcher, as attested by their extant manuscripts.

---

2. C. Dondi, "Liturgie," in *Dictionnaire des ordres militaires au Moyen Âge,* ed. N. Bériou–P. Josserand (Paris: Fayard, 2009), s.v.

3. *Ut institutio missarum sicut in metropolitana ecclesia agitur ita in Dei nomine in omnibus provinciis tam ipsius misse ordo quam psallendi vel ministrandi consuetudo servetur; Collectio tripartita,* A. 2.32.c.1.

The liturgy of the Holy Sepulcher survives in eighteen manuscripts, which were written from the twelfth to the fourteenth century in Jerusalem, Acre, Caesarea, Tyre, Antioch, and Cyprus. Its composite nature, with offices derived from the western uses of Évreux, Bayeux, Chartres, Paris, with the addition of some English elements not yet clearly defined, reflects the influence of different characters active in the cathedral chapter in the early years: the patriarch Arnulf of Cocques (1112–1118), Ansellus de Turre (1112–1138), *cantor* of the church of the Holy Sepulcher, and Fulcher of Chartres, also a canon of the Holy Sepulcher from 1114. Therefore, the liturgy of the Holy Sepulcher is completely western, and more precisely Gallo-Roman; the only pre-conquest liturgical feature retained in their calendars and sanctorals is the veneration of some Palestinian and specifically Jerusalem feasts such as Timothy (January 24), Bishop of Ephesus; Ignatius (February 1), Bishop of Antioch; the Forty Martyrs (March 11); Athanasius (May 2), Bishop of Alexandria; Matthias (January 30), eighth Bishop of Jerusalem; Alexander (March 18), fourth Bishop of Jerusalem; Quiriacus (May 4), Bishop of Jerusalem in the fourth century; Zacchaeus (August 23), Bishop of Jerusalem in the second century; Cleophas (September 25), disciple of Christ and martyr in Emmaus; Abraham, Isaac, and Jacob (October 6); Mark (October 22), first Bishop of Jerusalem; Narcissus (October 29), third Bishop of Jerusalem; Peter (November 25), Bishop of Alexandria; and Saba (December 5), abbot in Jerusalem.

A new office was composed in the Holy Land to celebrate the day of the liberation of Jerusalem (July 15), a date that from 1149 coincided with the dedication of the newly built church of the Holy Sepulcher.[4]

Although no manuscripts have yet been identified as coming from the Hospitaller motherhouse in Jerusalem or Acre, nor from Limassol, we still have some 80 extant manuscripts, written from the thirteenth to the seventeenth century, in Rhodes, Malta, and various Hospitaller houses in Europe. Moreover the breviary of the order was printed in 1480, 1495, 1517, 1547, and 1551, while their missal was printed in 1505, 1528, 1551, and 1553. From a liturgical point of view, these Hospitaller sources show that there is absolute consistency with

---

4. A. Linder, "The Liturgy of the Liberation of Jerusalem," in *Medieval Studies* 52 (1990), 110–131.

the use of the Holy Sepulcher as far as the chant repertory of the liturgical office is concerned. In the calendar, sanctoral and litanies of certain manuscripts, however, the presence of local saints venerated in the area where the Hospitaller communities were established is evidence of a minimal degree of adaptation to the local environment. The only known exception, the Hospitaller sisters of Sigena, had by the sixteenth century (date of their extant breviary) changed some of their core offices, for All Saints' Day and the Office of the Dead in · particular, according to Spanish traditions.

Finally, special Hospitaller offices and masses were composed to celebrate saints and events related to the history of the order. The feast of Saint Pantaleon (July 27) began to receive a special commemoration within the order because on that day in 1480 Pierre d'Aubusson, Grand Master of the Hospitallers (1479–1503), and his troops defeated the Turks who were attacking Rhodes. The special commemoration of St. Pantaleon is first recorded in the first edition of the Hospitaller Missal printed in Strasbourg in 1505.

Another feast specifically relating to the order is the commemoration of the presentation of the relics of Saint John the Baptist on November 21. Relics were known to belong to the order in the fourteenth century in various places. The entry appears in a number of manuscripts from the German area, where according to Paolo Maria Paciaudi relics of Saint John the Baptist were venerated in Passau, Munich, and Trier. A relic of the arm of Saint John the Baptist was translated from Constantinople to Rhodes in 1484, when it was presented to Pierre d'Aubusson by the Sultan Bayezid II (1481–1512).

TEMPLARS

That the Templars of Jerusalem and Acre were practicing the liturgy of the Holy Sepulcher is witnessed by extant manuscripts: the Ordinal of the Holy Sepulcher (Rome, Biblioteca Apostolica Vaticana, ms. Barb. lat. 659, 1153–1157), was used by the Templars of Jerusalem as is shown by the obituary notes added to the calendar, while the Breviary of the Holy Sepulcher (Paris, Bibliothèque nationale de France, ms. lat. 10478, 1256–1261), was used by the Templars of Acre as is evident from extracts of the *retrais* (part of Templar legislation) added to a leaf in the manuscript. It was only in their houses throughout Europe that such liturgical connection would have ceased. This can be inferred with almost certainty on the basis of the liturgical features of two manuscripts which had been used by two different Templar communities established in Modena, Italy, and somewhere in Cambridgeshire. The two manuscripts, a Sacramentary (Modena, Biblioteca Capitolare, ms. O.II.13, the end of the twelfth or the beginning of the thirteenth century) and a Calendar (London, British Library, ms. Cotton Cleopatra, B. III. [3], twelfth century) do not contain any of the typical characteristics of the liturgy of the Holy Sepulcher; instead they present liturgical elements pertaining to the local dioceses where the Templar commanderies were established. This points toward a less centralized approach in liturgical matters, in line with the administrative organization of the order itself. Unlike the Hospitallers, liturgical conformity to the Church of Jerusalem was not perceived by the Templars as an important unifying factor and integral part of the order's heritage.

The Teutonic order was founded at Acre in the aftermath of Henry VI's crusade in 1198 and was confirmed by Innocent III with a bull dated February 19, 1199. By adopting the rule of the Templars the order was to practice the rite of the church of the Holy Sepulcher of Jerusalem. However, from 1244 the Teutonic order adopted the Dominican Breviary (probably a sign of the increasing presence and influence of the Dominicans in thirteenth-century Acre), to which they brought some modifications, confirmed in 1257 by Pope Alexander IV as *Notula Dominorum Teutonicorum*. Teutonic liturgical manuscripts retain only some of the Jerusalem feasts in their calendar. The Teutonic Breviary was printed six times between 1484 and 1500, then in 1504 and 1609. The Teutonic Missal was printed in 1499, 1504, 1519 and 1520.

I would like now to move to the period defined by the invention of printing and the Council of Trent: a period which includes roughly one hundred years, from the printing of the first liturgical books, namely, the Roman Breviary printed in Venice in 1474[5] and the first assigned Roman Missal printed in Milan in 1474,[6] to the

---

5. *Breviarium Romanum* (Franciscan use) (Venice: Jacobus Rubeus, 1474). 8°. *ISTC* no.: ib01117000.

6. *Missale Romanum* (Milan: Antonius Zarotus, December 6, 1474). Folio. *ISTC* no.: im00688450. This edition was preceded by three unassigned editions, a *Missale Fratrum*

edition of the first Tridentine Roman Breviary printed in Rome in 1568[7] and Roman Missal printed in Rome in 1570.[8]

The advent of printing was of fundamental importance for the unification and standardization of liturgical books, and so it was perceived from very early on.

According to the data collected by the Incunabula Short-Title Catalogue (ISTC), a very thorough but still not complete database of fifteenth-century editions, from 1474 to 1500 444 different editions of breviaries and 370 different editions of missals were produced. Among the breviaries, we can count 373 editions of diocesan use, of which 84 are Roman, and 71 editions that belonged to breviaries of religious orders.

Among the missals, we find 345 editions of diocesan use, of which 94 are Roman, and only 25 missals of religious orders. The sixteenth century sees a general escalation of numbers.

It is often possible to evaluate the process which brought into print the text of a given religious order or diocese, and to discover the historical and religious context surrounding it. The mandate for publication, generally printed as the opening of a liturgical text, contains information about the person who commissioned an edition, generally the abbot of the motherhouse of a religious order or an archbishop or bishop of a diocese. It also contains the reasons and sometimes includes even more detailed information on the editorial process, such as the person in charge of the revision of the text, or the manuscript exemplar used to prepare the edition. Among the most enthusiastic supporters and users of the new printing invention surely has to be remembered the abbot of Citeaux, Jean de Cirey (d. 1503), who commissioned the abbot of Baumgarten, Nicolas de Saliceto, to edit the Cistercian Breviary printed in Basel in 1484,[9]

Minorum (Central Italy?: n.pr., c. 1472?). Folio. *ISTC* no.: im00643000; a *Missale Speciale* (Basel: Printer of the *Missale Speciale* [Johann Meister?], c. 1473?). Folio. *ISTC* no.: im00732500; and a *Missale Speciale Abbreviatum* (Basel: Printer of the *Missale Speciale* [Johann Meister?], c. 1473?). Folio. *ISTC* no.: im00735500.

7. *Breviarium Romanum ex decreto ss. Concilii Tridentini* (Rome: Manutius, 1568).

8. *Missale Romanum ex decreto ss. Concilii Tridentini restitutum, Pii V Pont. Max. jussu editum* (Rome: apud heredes Bartholomei Faletti, Joannem Variscum, 1570).

9. *Breviarium Cisterciense* (Basel: Peter Kollicker and Johann Meister, November 4, 1484). 8º. *ISTC* no.: ib01135000.

and in Strasbourg c. 1487,[10] the Cistercian Missal printed in
Strasbourg in 1487,[11] and who also personally edited a collection
of privileges of the order, which appeared in Dijon in 1491.[12]

Much more should be said on the early involvement of
religious institutions with the early presses. As mentioned, from the
very beginning it was clear to most of them the great potential for
unifying communities separated by great physical distance by produc-
ing books which would finally really offer a unified liturgy. Rudolf
Hirsch noticed that there were at least seven monastic presses in
German areas by 1470s.[13] Lotte Hellinga has shown that the establishment of the press in Subiaco, central Italy, may have been more
connected with plans for monastic reform than is evident from
what it produced, or from what survives of its production. In 1471,
Benedict Zwink of Ettal, a Benedictine monk who resided in the
abbey of the Sacro Speco, adjoining Santa Scolastica, wrote to the
abbot of Göttweig, near Melk, in connection with plans to extend the
Benedictine congregations of Bursfeld and Melk to include those who
observed the rules of Subiaco and Montecassino.

> Since it might be difficult for all monasteries to compare and edit brevia-
> ries, it will be easy to produce 100 or 200 copies on the presses, just as we
> have also produced 200 copies of St Augustine's *De Civitate Dei* in the
> form of type as enclosed. In the monastery of the Sacro Speco we can
> make use of this technique to the full, for we have the equipment and the
> people [who know how to use it]. If we could form part of this religious
> union [the extended congregation], all books, whatever the number
> required, could be printed and distributed to all monasteries which in their
> turn would have joined the congregation, with the equipment which is

---

10. *Breviarium Cisterciense* (Strasbourg: Johann [Reinhard] Grüninger, [not before 1487]). 8⁰.
ISTC no.: ib0113600.

11. *Missale Cisterciense* (Strasbourg: Johann [Reinhard] Grüninger, September 4, 1487). Folio.
ISTC no.: im00635000.

12. *Privilegia Ordinis Cisterciensis* (Dijon: Petrus Metlinger, July 4, 1491). 4⁰. *ISTC* no.:
ip00976000. A book of hours for the Cistercian use was also printed in Paris by Philippe
Pigouchet for Simon Vostre in c. 1500 (8⁰; *ISTC* no.: ih00343500), a very rare example of hours
for the use of a religious order.

13. R. Hirsch, *Printing, Selling and Reading 1450–1550* (Wiesbaden: Harrassowitz, 2nd edn,
1974), 54.

available on the spot, and with the help of five brethren who could be instructed in this technique.[14]

Sometimes the appearance of a printed missal of given use is simply the result of the work of itinerant printers, who were wandering from place to place offering their services. More often, however, the printing of liturgical books was accompanied by a process of evaluation and emendation of the textual tradition of the liturgy pertaining to that order or diocese: the printing of the Hospitaller texts falls into this interesting category.

Before examining how the Hospitallers responded to the chance offered by the printing press I also would like to underline one fact about the use of printing in the fifteenth century. As for editions of other texts, classical, literary, etc., fifteenth-century liturgical editions do not always or necessarily represent the beginning of a homogeneous tradition, but simply the tail-end of an individual one. And this fact is very clearly exemplified by the differences between the fifteenth- and sixteenth-century editions of the Hospitaller Breviaries and Missals.

HOSPITALLERS

The Hospitaller Breviary was first printed in Mainz in 1480,[15] then in Speyer in 1495.[16] In the sixteenth century, the third edition was printed in Lyon in 1517,[17] a fourth edition appeared in Zaragoza in

---

14. Abbey of Melk, MS 91; see L. Hellinga, "The Codex in the Fifteenth Century: Manuscript and Print," in N. Barker (ed.) *A Potencie of Life: Books in Society, The Clark Lectures 1986–1987* (London: British Library, 1993), 63–88, at 73–74 (English paraphrase). The original Latin text is published by B. Frank, "Tipografia monastica sublacense: per una confederazione benedettina," in *Il sacro speco* 74 (1971), 69–72.

15. *Breviarium Hierosolymitanum* (Mainz: Printer of the "Darmstadt" Prognostication, c. 1480). 8°. *ISTC* no.: ib01143300; Dondi, *Hospitaller Liturgical Manuscripts*, 248 no. B.81.

16. *Breviarium secundum consuetudinem domus hospitalis Hierosolymitani s. Johannis* (Speyer: Peter Drach, 1495). 8°. *ISTC* no.: ib01143310; Dondi, *Hospitaller Liturgical Manuscripts*, 248–250 no. B.82, with a transcription of the mandate for publication.

17. *Breviarium secundum consuetudinem domus hospitalis Hierosolymitani s. Johannis* (Lyon: Cyriacus Hochperg, 1517). 8°; Dondi, *Hospitaller Liturgical Manuscripts*, 250–51 no. B.83, with a transcription of the mandate for publication.

1547,[18] and finally a fifth one in Lyon in 1551.[19] As far as the missals are concerned, no editions were printed in the fifteenth century, but four in the following century: the first in Strasbourg in 1505,[20] the second in Zaragoza in 1528,[21] the third in Lyon in 1551,[22] the last in Lyon in 1553.[23]

The two Spanish editions were printed specifically for the house of Hospitaller sisters of Sigena, in the province of Huesca, and they are representative of a tradition apart.

As far as I am aware, the case of the sisters of Sigena is the only one, within the Hospitaller tradition, where the typical liturgical use of the Holy Sepulcher of Jerusalem, which was adopted by the Hospitallers,[24] has been varied to adjust to a local tradition. Variation is noted in the calendar, which contains only a few saints of the Holy Sepulcher, but mainly local Spanish ones, in the short office of the Virgin, Dedication of the Church, and above all in the office for All Saints, for which similarities are found with Valencia and Tudela, and in the office for All Souls, for which the Sigena Breviary presents a Spanish series, found in Oloron, Huesca, Zaragoza, and Valencia. This series, a derivation from Toulouse, was probably introduced to Spain from Oloron. Whatever the origin, it clearly shows how the Hospitaller sisters of Sigena, by the sixteenth century, had adapted the original Hospitaller use to a Spanish local one.[25]

18. *Breviarium secundum ritum Sixene monasterij: Ordinis sancti Joannis Hierosolymitani sub regula beati Augustini* (Zaragoza: George Coci, [*industria vero* Petri Bernuz], November 4, 1547). 8°; Dondi, *Hospitaller Liturgical Manuscripts*, 251–252, no. B.84.

19. *Breviarium secundum usum ordinis s. Joannis Hierosolymitani* (Lyon: Cornelius a Septemgrangiis *expensis* Haeredum Jacobi Junctae, 1551). 8°; Dondi, *Hospitaller Liturgical Manuscripts*, 252–253, no. B.85.

20. *Missale secundum institutionem ordinis hospitalis s. Johannis Ierosolymitani* (Strasbourg: Johannes Prüss zum Thiergarten, 1505). Folio; Dondi, *Hospitaller Liturgical Manuscripts*, 253–254, no. B.86, with a transcription of the mandate for publication.

21. *Missale secundum ritum Sixene monasterij: Ordinis sancti Joannis Hierosolymitani sub regula beati Augustini* (Zaragoza: George Coci, 1528). Folio; Dondi, *Hospitaller Liturgical Manuscripts*, 254 no. B.87.

22. *Missale sacri ordinis s. Joannis Hierosolymitani* (Lyon: Cornelius a Septemgrangiis, 1551). Folio; Dondi, *Hospitaller Liturgical Manuscripts*, 254, no. B.88.

23. *Missale sacri ordinis s. Joannis Hierosolymitani* (Lyon: *Sumptibus haeredum* Jacobi Juntae *speciosis characteribus apud* Cornelium a Septemgrangiis *excusum*, 1553). Folio; Dondi, *Hospitaller Liturgical Manuscripts*, 254–255, no. B.89.

24. Dondi, *The Liturgy*, 40–44.

25. See above, notes 18 and 21; K. Ottosen, *The Responsories and Versicles of the Latin Office of the Dead* (Aarhus: Aarhus University Press, 1993), 169 and 320. In the prologue at the opening

The only surviving copy of the first edition of the Hospitaller Breviary, printed in Mainz c. 1480, is not complete. This copy, now in the British Library, contains the summer part only.[26] We do not know who commissioned the work, information which, if present, was presumably contained in the opening of the winter part, something that can be seen in the 1495 edition. Its content, however, shows that this breviary was certainly printed from a manuscript exemplar coming from a German Hospitaller house. In the calendar, sanctoral, and litanies, in addition to the traditional feasts of the Holy Sepulcher, are listed a number of saints venerated in German areas: we find Lubentius (October 13) and Maximin (May 29) of Trier; Boniface (June 5) and Alban (June 21) of Mainz; Gereon and companions (October 10) and the 11,000 virgins (October 21) of Cologne; Gingulfus (May 13), venerated in Bonn; Lambert (September 17) of Liège; Servatius (May 13) of Maastricht; Arbogast (July 21) and Florence (November 7) of Strasbourg; Ulrich (July 4) and Afra (August 7), patron saints of Augsburg; and Kilian (July 8) of Würzburg.

The second edition of the Hospitaller Breviary is a result of the Provincial Chapter of the order held in Strasbourg in 1495 by Pierre d'Aubusson; it was commissioned by Rudolf Graf von Werdenberg (d. 1505), Prior of Germany (1481–1505) and *Commendator* of Heitersheim.[27] The mandate for publication at the beginning of the winter part states that it was edited by the Strasbourg *Commendatores* of the order of Saint John. This suggests that at the Council the *Commendatores* of Strasbourg were working on the basis of the previous, 1480 edition, and their emendations consist in the insertion of antiphons between the Psalter and the Gradual Psalms, some further prayers for the suffrages, and a proper office for Saint Arbogast, Bishop of Strasbourg, clearly a reflection of the importance of the Strasbourg house.

Of the seven extant copies of this breviary, we have evidence of early use within the Hospitaller environment for three. A copy was kept in the Strasbourg house, in whose library it still appeared in 1749, when Johann Nicholas Weislinger prepared the catalogue of the

---

of the Breviary the prioress of the community, Elisabeth de Alagon, states the purpose of the publication and fixes the price at 32 "*solidi*."

26. London, British Library, IA.322; see above, note 15.

27. See above, note 16.

library, and it is now preserved in the National and University Library of Strasbourg.[28] A second copy was used by the Hospitallers of Heitersheim and is now preserved in the University Library of Freiburg, which acquired the Hospitaller library in 1802.[29] A third copy was probably used within the Hospitaller house of Cologne, *SS. Johannes et Cordula*.[30]

To this period of German influence on the early printed editions can be ascribed also the publication of the first missal, printed in Strasbourg in 1505 by Johannes Prüss zum Thiergarten.[31] The mandate for publication states that a member of the Hospitaller house of Strasbourg, whose name is not mentioned, moved by the exiguous number of missals conforming to the Hospitaller use, and by the necessity for a religious order to profess the same liturgical practice, prepared a text which conformed to the ordinal of the order and handed it to the printer. This editor was aware of the inclusion of some typically German feasts, which he justified by the devotio *terre* and *provincie observantia*. The edition appeared under the patronage of Emery d'Amboise, Grand Master of the order in the years 1503–1512, Rudolf Graf von Werdenberg, Prior of Germany, Johann Heggenzer, Grand Bailiff of Rhodes and later Prior of Germany (1505–1512), and Erhardus Kienig from Ettlingen, *Commendator* of Strasbourg. The mandate closes with an appeal to the *preceptores* and *locatenentes* of the order not to save a paltry sum but to buy this missal, and to use it as an exemplar to correct and emend the books they have previously been using.

A copy of this missal was kept in the Strasbourg house and is now preserved in the Library of the Seminary of Strasbourg.[32]

---

28. *Armamentarium Catholicum perantiquae rarissimae ac pretiosissimae Bibliothecae quae asservatur Argentorati in celeberrima commenda eminentissimi ordinis Melitensis Sancti Johannis Hierosolymitani*, ed. J. N. Weislinger (Strasbourg, 1749), 640–641 (*pars hiemalis et aestivalis*). Weislinger (1691–1755) was also the owner of a manuscript Hospitaller Breviary, datable to 1450–1500, now in Munich, Bayerische Staatsbibliothek, Clm. 10111; see Dondi, *Hospitaller Liturgical Manuscripts*, 232–233, no. A.12.

29. Freiburg i. Br., Universitätsbibliothek, Ink. O 9535, d.

30. San Juan, Puerto Rico, La Casa del Libro, no pressmark.

31. See above, note 20.

32. Strasbourg, Bibliothèque du Grand Séminaire, A 599; Weislinger, *Armamentarium Catholicum*, 251.

Another copy was used by the Hospitallers of Haarlem, and is now kept in Haarlem City Library, where it was transferred in 1625.[33]

In the calendar and sanctoral, still of German basis, the most substantial innovation is the addition of the feast of Saint Pantaleon (July 27), celebrated to commemorate the victory over the Turks in Rhodes in 1480. In the sanctoral, from the rubric we read that July 27 is celebrated with a double feast for the great victory obtained by Cardinal Pierre d'Aubusson, Grand Master, of the people of Rhodes (1479–1503) against the Turks. Five years later Innocent VIII, with the bull *Redemptor noster*, dated May 31, 1485, made Saint Pantaleon's day a solemn feast day in perpetuity[34] and gave an indulgence of 50 years attached to the office of the saint. The full text of the mass, however, is not in this 1505 edition, but can be found in the 1551 edition of the Hospitaller Missal.[35]

With the turn of the century, but mostly under the mastership of Emery d'Amboise, a substantial shift in liturgical policies takes place. At the General Council of the order held in Rhodes on February 1, 1510, the need was pointed out to reinstate the uniformity of liturgical observance within the houses of the order which were now celebrating their office according to different uses, literally, *sub vario stilo*. With the death of Rudolf Graf von Werdenberg, Prior of Germany, in 1505, the man who had clearly realized the importance of printing for the unity of the order, but had concentrated only on the Continental, and mostly German component of it, the concern for a truly international uniformity hits the headquarters of the order.

For sake of clarity, it has to be pointed out that the proper liturgical use of the Hospitallers, as given by the chant repertory of the major feasts, derived from that of the Holy Sepulcher of Jerusalem, this was never changed. The evidence which I have collected from 80 liturgical manuscripts used by the Hospitallers from the thirteenth to the sixteenth century in various parts of Europe, together with the early printed editions, shows that they all share the same chant

---

33. Haarlem, Stadsbibliotheek, 165 A 9; A. de Vries, *Catalogus Bibliothecae publicae Harlemensis* (Haarlem: Enschedé, 1848), 179, no. 28.

34. K. Setton, *The Papacy and the Levant 1204–1571*, 4 vols. (Philadelphia, Pennsylvania: American Philosophical Society, 1976–1984), vol. II, 357, n. 37.

35. Dondi, *Hospitaller Liturgical Manuscripts*, 228, n. 12 for the text of the indulgence, n. 13 for the text of the office.

repertory. There occurred, however, some local variation, identifiable in the calendars, sanctorals, and litanies, that is to say within those parts of the text where it is easier to adjust to some local influence. And that materializes, in practice, in the celebration of the office for different saints in certain days of the liturgical year. It is this kind of variation that the General Council refers to and wants to eliminate, to conform to the early practice of the order which adopted the liturgy of the church of the Holy Sepulcher of Jerusalem.

In the mandate for publication of the 1517 edition of the Hospitaller Breviary[36] we read that the Grand Master of the Order Emery d'Amboise, together with the other members of the General Chapter held in Rhodes on February 1, 1510, notify that they had been informed that in the various churches of the order the office of the canonical hours was celebrated under different styles, so generating confusion when members from these houses attended the service in the conventual church of the order in Rhodes. For this reason the Chapter had ordered the institution of a commission to investigate the matter. The commission was composed by Leonardo Balestrieri, OFM OBS, Latin Archbishop of Rhodes (1506–1539), the Spanish Ramon Riolx, Prior of the conventual church of the Collachium of Rhodes (1507—at least 1519), and Guillaume Quignon, *helemosinarius* of Emery d'Amboise,[37] Preceptor of Arnhem, in the Netherlands (1510–1527),[38] and *Stamparum generalis Hospitalis Militiae per Galliam Procurator*.[39]

The commission reported to the Chapter that the breviary of the order was in many points confusing and defective. In the text the breviary is referred to as *antiquum breviarium ecclesie sancti Iohannis* and I believe it has to be taken as the fifteenth-century printed edition of the breviary. On the advice of the commission and at the request of the Chapter, Antonius Beriat was assigned the task of transcribing a

---

36. See above, note 17.

37. J. M. van Winter, *Sources concerning the Hospitallers of St John in the Netherlands, 14th–18th centuries*, Studies in the History of Christian Thought, 80 (Leiden: Brill, 1998), 77.

38. Van Winter, *Sources*, 77–80.

39. According to the preface addressed to him by J. Quintin, which opens the work of A. Geuffroy, *Estat de la court du Grand Turc, l'ordre de sa gendarmerie, et de ses finances* (Antwerp: Steels, 1542); see A. Luttrell, "The Hospitallers' Historical Activities: 1530–1630," in *Annales de l'Ordre Souverain Militaire de Malte*, 26 (1968), 57–69; reproduced in A. Luttrell, *Latin Greece, the Hospitallers and the Crusades 1291–1440* (London: Variorum, 1982), no. III, 58.

good exemplar of a breviary extracted from the ordinal of the conventual church of Rhodes so that this could be given to the printer, Cyriacus Hocpreg of Lyon. Finally the Chapter decrees and orders that this breviary must be adopted by all houses of the order to reinstate everywhere the proper use. The final outcome is a breviary which, while it has been cleared of almost all German feasts, now includes some Carmelites feasts, such as Cyril of Constantinople (March 6); the prophet Elisha (June 14); Phocas (July 14), Bishop of Sinope, whose relics were venerated in Constantinople and in Antioch; and Elijah (December 1). This occurrence clearly suggests that the exemplar used to prepare this edition must have been a breviary of the Holy Sepulcher previously used by Carmelites. Nothing surprising in that, considering that the Carmelites, like the Hospitallers, had adopted the liturgy of the Holy Sepulcher of Jerusalem, and that more than one liturgical manuscript of the Holy Sepulcher, written in Jerusalem, Acre, or Cyprus in the twelfth or thirteenth century ended up being used by Carmelite communities after the loss of the Holy Land. The only liturgical variant introduced at this stage, probably through the Carmelite exemplar, occurs in the short office of the Virgin, where the *Capitulum* at None now presents a form common to the Roman use. This variant, not present in the previous editions of the Hospitaller Breviary based on German exemplars, can also be found in a few Hospitaller manuscripts, previously of unknown origin, which can now be ascribed to Rhodes or descending from a Rhodes exemplar.[40] A copy of this breviary was owned by the Hospitaller Mathias Molitor in 1586.[41]

In 1551, Cornelius a Septemgrangiis prepared a new edition of the Hospitaller Breviary, very similar in text to the 1517 Breviary,

---

40. *Liber horarum*, beginning of the fourteenth century (after 1309), London, BL, MS Additional 41061. Probably written in Rhodes for an English Hospitaller; see Dondi, *Hospitaller Liturgical Manuscripts*, 237–238, no. A.57.

Psalterium-Liber horarum, 1455–1488, Oxford, St. John's College, MS 131. Probably written for John Weston (d. 1489), Castellan of Rhodes 1470–1471, Turcopolier 1471–1476, Prior of England 1477–1489; see Dondi, *Hospitaller Liturgical Manuscripts*, 247–248, no. A.80.

Liber horarum, c.1460, Paris, BnF, MS lat 1400. With an early unidentified coat of arms of f. 29r: azure, in chief a cross couped gules between letters BC and CB, argent; in base a double-headed eagle, or; crest, a helmet in profile with mantling surmounted by three plumes, gules, or, and argent; see Dondi, *Hospitaller Liturgical Manuscripts*, 239, no. A.62.

41. London, Library of the Venerable Order of Saint John, A. 3. 7.

and a new edition of the Hospitaller Missal.[42] These two 1551
editions present the same calendar, which is identical to that found in
the 1517 Breviary revised by the General Council of Rhodes in 1510.
Therefore, in comparison with the first edition of the missal, of 1505,
this missal no longer contains the German entries.

In 1553, a final edition of the Hospitaller Missal appeared, a
reprint of the 1551 text.[43] While we do not have information on early
use for the only surviving copy of the 1551 Missal, we know that
a copy of the 1553 Missal was used by the Hospitallers of Siracusa,
Sicily, and that, after having been used also by the Capuchines
of the same town, it entered the Municipal Library in 1886, at the
time of the suppression of the monasteries.[44] Another copy was used
by the Hospitallers of Arles, and it is now preserved in the city's
Municipal Library.[45]

To sum up, while the first fifteenth-century editions of
Hospitaller liturgical texts represent the tail-end of the manuscript
tradition of the large and influential German houses of the order, it is
with the beginning of the sixteenth century, and in particular with
the clear liturgical policies defined by the General Council of Rhodes
in 1510, that the Hospitallers produce a truly standard breviary and
missal to be used by all their houses, and more closely representative
of their ties with the Holy Land.

At the Council of Trent, the Grand Master of the Order,
engaged in the military defense of Malta, was represented by Martin
Rojas Portalrubei. Summoned by a brief of Pope Pius IV of November
7, 1561, he was officially received on September 7, 1563, when he
made his address, published in Brescia by Ludovicus Sabiensis. None
of the privileges and immunities of the order was revoked by the
Council, though the decrees of the Council brought some modification to their religious activities, with regard to the administration of
sacraments and pastoral care.[46]

---

42. See above, note 19 and 22.

43. See above, note 23.

44. Siracusa, Biblioteca Comunale, α 2 7; G. Agnello, "I cavalieri di Malta a Siracusa:
Convento e chiesa di S. Francesco. La chiesa di S. Leonardo. Il Messale dell'Ordine," in *Per l'Arte
Sacra* (maggio-agosto 1936), 27–33.

45. Arles, Bibliothèque Municipale, RB 40.

46. A. C. Breycha-Vauthier de Baillamont, "L'Ordre au Concile de Trente," in *Annales de
l'Ordre Souverain Militaire de Malte*, 20 (1962), 82–84.

As far as liturgy is concerned, the Hospitallers' proper of saints was still published in 1659,[47] 1739,[48] and 1759.[49] What the advent of printing in the late fifteenth century undeniably brought is a general quest for order. The Roman liturgy was at the forefront in this respect and the appearance of the printed Roman breviaries and missals stimulated one of two reactions: their availability widened the circle of their users to those places that did not engage in the printing of their own liturgical texts; secondly, the Roman editions must have been taken as example of what could be done to preserve the liturgical identity for present and future benefit, and in this process efforts were made to put some order in a sometimes messy liturgical tradition. Both processes, the adoption of the Roman use and the philological revision of the non-Roman rites, came to constitute the chief principles emanated by the Council of Trent on the subject of liturgical observance, 100 years later.

---

47. *Officia propria sanctorum ordinis S. Joannis Hierosolymitani Melitensis in usum domus Coloniensis S.S. Joannis et Cordulae seorsim edita* (Coloniae Agrippinae: Antonius Metternich, 1659); a copy in Strasbourg, Bibliothèque du Grand Séminaire, GS. 1 Ddi 55.

48. *Officia propria sanctorum recitanda a religiosis utriusque sexus Ordinis S. Johannis Hierosolymitani* (Strasbourg: Melchior Pauschinger, 1739); see F. de Hellwald, *Bibliographie méthodique de l'Ordre Souverain de St. Jean de Jérusalem* (Rome: Imprimerie de la Propagande, 1885; reprinted Farnborough: Gregg, 1968), 266.

49. *Officia propria sanctorum recitanda a religiosis utriusque sexus Ordinis Militaris Sancti Joannis Jerosolymitani* (Malta: Nicola Capaci, 1759); reprinted by Johannes Mallia in 1785; see Hellwald, *Bibliographie méthodique*, 266.

Chapter 7

The Calendar and *Corpus Christi:* An Historical and Theological Consideration of the Church's Sacred Year

Lauren Pristas

INTRODUCTION

The Church's sacred year took shape slowly. Here we shall trace the history of its development in order to enhance our theological understanding.

From the very beginning all churches celebrated the weekly Sunday and some the annual Pasch. From the fourth century, feasts commemorating mysteries of the Lord's life were added, as well as feasts of our Lady, the martyrs and the saints. Later, feasts that some say celebrate truths rather than events, the so-called doctrinal feasts, made their appearance. The feast of the Most Blessed Trinity is perhaps the earliest and finest example. Many classify the feast of *Corpus Christi* as a doctrinal feast, and we shall discuss the historical reasons why the feast of *Corpus Christi* was placed on the universal calendar.

The history of the liturgical calendar illumines the relationship between the weekly celebration of the Lord's Day and the annual celebration of the Church's cycle of feasts and seasons. The historical origins of the feast of *Corpus Christi* shed light on its place in the Church's sacred year.

Part I: The First Christian Centuries: Weekly Lord's Day and Yearly Cycle of Feasts

History

We begin with four questions:

1. When did Christians begin celebrating the Lord's Supper on the Lord's Day?
2. When and where did Christians begin observing an annual Pasch?
3. Have Christians always and everywhere observed an annual Pasch, and was it always observed on Sunday?
4. What did the liturgical calendar at Rome look like in the first decades of the fourth century?

On the night before Christ died, a Thursday, he instituted the sacrament of the Eucharist when he gave his Body and Blood to the apostles under the form of bread and wine and instructed them to repeat what he had done in his memory. Shortly thereafter, on the first day of the week, Christ was raised from death. The first day became the Christian day of worship, which brings us to our first question: when did Christians begin hallowing the first day of the week by celebrating the Lord's Supper?

Our answer follows two guides: Camille Callewaert, a Catholic priest professor who published an essay on the origin of Sunday in 1938,[1] and Willy Rordorf, a Reformed Patristic scholar whose history of Sunday in the earliest Christian centuries appeared in 1962.[2] Callewaert and Rordorf examine basically the same corpus of biblical and non-biblical texts, that is: a) New Testament passages in which the words "the Lord's Supper," "breaking of bread," or "Lord's Day" appear, or which speak of the post-resurrection appearances of Christ; b) Christian and non-Christian writings of

---

1. C. Callewaert, "La synaxe eucharistique à Jérusalem, berceau du dimanche," in *Ephemerides Theologicae Lovanienses* 15 (1938), 34–73.

2. W. Rordorf, *Sunday: The History of the Day of Rest and Worship in the Earliest Centuries of the Christian Church*, trans. A.A.K. Graham (Philadelphia: Westminster Press, 1968). Rordorf's work is the published version of the doctoral dissertation that he wrote under O. Cullman and in which he investigates hypotheses previously published by Cullman. See *Urchristentum und Gottesdienst* (Zürich: Zwingli-Verlag, 2nd edition, 1950) or *Early Christian Worship*, trans. A. Stewart Todd and J. B. Torrance, Studies in Biblical Theology 10 (London: SCM, 1953). The relevant pages in the English edition are 15–18.

the late first and early second century that speak of Christian Sunday observance.

At first glance the biblical evidence does not seem to witness unequivocally to the universal celebration of the Lord's Supper on the Lord's Day, but interpreting the witnesses is more difficult than one might initially suppose because three systems of reckoning days were in use during apostolic times: Jews reckoned from sundown to sundown; Romans from midnight to midnight; and Greeks from sunrise to sunrise.[3] After carefully examining texts that we cannot discuss here,[4] both Callewaert and Rordorf agree that the first and following generations of Christians converts, both the Jewish Christians of Jerusalem and the Gentiles of the Pauline churches, celebrated the Lord's Supper weekly on the Lord's Day. Callewaert dates the practice from Pentecost on the basis of passages in Acts 2,[5] and Rordorf traces it back to the evening meals that the Lord took with his disciples on the first day on which he rose as well as at least one other first day of the week.[6]

The practice of celebrating the Lord's Supper on the Lord's Day dates from New Testament times, certainly from Pentecost, and maybe even from the Sunday upon which Christ rose from death. To put the same point another way: there is no record of a development which resulted, finally, in Christians hallowing the first day of the week with the celebration of the Lord's Supper—as far as we know, it has been so from the beginning.

After the weekly Sunday, the first feast to develop was the annual celebration of the Christian Pasch and our next questions are about its origins: when did Christians begin observing an annual Pasch? Have they always and everywhere observed it? And was it always observed on Sunday? We have far less information about this than we do about the weekly celebration of the Lord's Day.

The earliest reference we have to the annual Pasch at Rome is found in the records of a controversy about when the Paschal fast was

---

3. See, for example, Callewaert, *La Synaxe*, 36, and Rordorf, *Sunday*, 200–202.

4. 1 Corinthians 16:1–2; Acts 20:7; and Revelation 1:10, among others.

5. Callewaert, *La Synaxe*, 63.

6. Rordorf, *Sunday*, 233–237 and 303. See also John 20:19–29. In Rordorf's view, this is also *why* the early Christians celebrated the Lord's Supper on Sunday rather than on Thursday or Friday, the days of the Lord's last supper and death, respectively.

to be kept.[7] The custom in the Christian East was to fast on the fourteenth and fifteenth days of Nisan, that is, on the anniversary of Christ's death regardless of the day of the week upon which it fell. The Roman custom was to break the Paschal fast only on the Sunday following the fourteenth of Nisan, and always to celebrate the annual feast of the Lord's resurrection on a Sunday.

The controversy erupted at Rome in the last decade of the second century. Christians who had migrated to Rome from the East had continued to observe the Paschal fast on the fourteenth and fifteenth of Nisan, and Pope Victor I, Bishop of Rome at the time, wanted them to adopt the Roman way.[8] The fact of the controversy suggests that each practice was, at least relatively speaking, well-established. Scholars are not agreed, however, about when an annual observance of the Pasch began to be celebrated at Rome.

Some hold that Rome celebrated the annual Pasch on Sunday from apostolic times. Others believe that Paschal observance at Rome began during the reign of Pope Soter and, correspondingly, that Rome knew only the weekly observance the Lord's Day until at least AD 167.[9]

This very brief and select historical survey is presented to show that while the Lord's Supper has been celebrated on the Lord's Day always and everywhere from the beginning, the annual observance of the Christian Pasch has not. For, while there are places in which the Christian Pasch was observed from the beginning, this is not the case everywhere. First there was Sunday, always and everywhere; then there was the Pasch, observed in some places from the beginning but adopted in other places later. And then other observances came to be added, which brings us to our last question.

We skip ahead to the fourth century. What did the liturgical calendar at Rome look like in the first decades of the fourth century? The answer, as far as we know, is that it featured only the weekly celebration of the Lord's Day and the annual celebration of the Christian Pasch. The earliest documentary evidence we have for the

---

7. Cf. T. Tally, *The Origins of the Liturgical Year* (New York: Pueblo, 1986), 5–13.

8. R. Cantalamessa, *Easter in the Early Church: An Anthology of Jewish and Early Christian Texts*, ed. and trans. J. M. Quigley–J.T. Lienhard (Collegeville, Minnesota: The Liturgical Press, 1993), 9–10.

9. Cantalamessa, *Easter in the Early Church*, 10–11.

December 25 celebration of Christmas at Rome comes from the year AD 354[10] and the rest of the Roman liturgical calendar developed subsequently.

If Rome knew only the weekly Sunday and the annual Pasch until sometime after 325, and only the weekly Lord's Day was always and everywhere celebrated in Christendom, why do the liturgical calendars before and after the Second Vatican Council have so many feasts? The answer lies in the relationship between the Sunday celebration of the Lord's Supper and all the others feasts and seasons on liturgical calendars.

Theology

Our discussion of the relationship between the Sunday celebration of the Lord's Supper and the various feasts and seasons relies on the theological insights that Odo Casel presents in *The Mystery of Christian Worship*.[11]

It is a truth of Catholic faith that the whole mystery of our redemption is celebrated at Mass—at the Lord's Supper. The Mass contains the very source of our redemption, the death and resurrection of the Lord, for at Mass Christ's sacrificial death and resurrection are mystically carried out in the presence of the faithful.

Three aspects pertain: first, the nature of the Paschal Mystery; second; the way the mystery unfolds in time; third, the way the mystery unfolds in the Church's sacred year.

First, the mystery itself. The *Sacramentum Paschale*, or Paschal Mystery, is an indivisible whole, a single mystery, hidden in God from eternity, revealed in time, and now re-presented in the Church.[12] It is a divine mystery, not a human thing at all. The mystery is none other than the whole reality of our salvation given by God to his Church to celebrate and possess.[13]

---

10. Tally, *The Origins of the Liturgical Year*, 85.

11. O. Casel, "The Church's Sacred Year," in *Id.*, *The Mystery of Christian Worship and Other Writings*, editor, B. Neunheuser (Westminster, Maryland: Newman Press, 1962; reprinted with an introduction by A. Kavanagh, New York: Herder and Herder, 1999), 63–70.

12. Casel, *The Church's Sacred Year*, 67–68.

13. Casel, *The Church's Sacred Year*, 66.

Second, the mystery unfolding in time. Here there are two aspects—one pertains to the life of Christ and the other to our human nature.

The Word became flesh that we might be saved—more specifically, the very Son of God became man to die on the cross for us. While the immediate source of our salvation is the Passion, death, and Resurrection of Christ, every moment of the human life of the Son of God, from the Incarnation to his Resurrection and Ascension, belongs to the mystery of our salvation and cannot be separated from it.[14] And this must be affirmed without prejudice to what we just said about the mystery being an indivisible whole.

The paradox of this twofold assertion, that the mystery is an indivisible whole and that all the different moments of Christ's human life belong to it, derives from the differences between eternity and time and between God's nature and our own. Eternity is not endless duration but an ever present *now*. As baffling as it is to us, there is no before or after in God, but only *now*. All of history is present to him as *present*; in him there is no process or unfolding. Whatever was, is, or will be is ever and always wholly present to him.

But this is not the case for us. And when the Son of God is conceived and born a man, his life, like ours, unfolds in time. Further, even as Christ's redemption of all men was accomplished in principle once and for all on Good Friday, and is accomplished in each of us when we die and rise with him in Baptism, nevertheless it is still necessary that this same redemption be worked out in each of us over time—over the whole course of our lives.

Third, the mystery as it unfolds in the Church's sacred year. The mystery of our redemption is one, and is re-presented in its entirety in every Mass. Yet, historically speaking, a great stream of mysteries both flowed into and flowed out of this single mystery.[15]

The Church celebrates these many mysteries that are but aspects of the single mystery in the course of the liturgical year. Because these many mysteries are but one act in their divine reality, what the Church is really doing is celebrating the single mystery of our redemption from a variety of different aspects.[16] Or perhaps

---

14. Casel, *The Church's Sacred Year*, 66.

15. Casel, *The Church's Sacred Year*, 69.

16. Casel, *The Church's Sacred Year*, 69.

it is more accurate to say that over the course of the Church's sacred year, God brings his faithful into the fullness of the mystery of their redemption through the many mysteries that belong to it.

The Annunciation brings the mystery of Christ's saving death and resurrection to us from the perspective of the Incarnation, and Christmas from that of the Lord's Nativity;[17] likewise the feasts of our Lady, the martyrs and other saints bring us into the same mystery— but from the different perspectives of its myriad saving effects.

We must be clear. The unfolding of the mystery of Christ in the course of the liturgical cycle is *not* the playing out of a historical drama. Rather it is, quite literally, a sacred year ordered to bring the Christian faithful step by step to God.[18] The content of this sacred year is the single divine act that the faithful must appropriate but can only appropriate gradually. Each feast and season is meant to bring us more deeply and fully into the mystery of our salvation.[19] This appropriation takes place principally though spiritual participation in the life communicated to us through these very mysteries, rather than simply through meditation and imitation—for persons without Baptism can meditate and endeavor to imitate.[20]

When we grasp the essential unity of the mystery, of the divine act that saves us, we understand both why the weekly celebration of the Lord's Supper sufficed in the first Christian centuries and why the liturgical calendar developed over time.

PART II: THE ORIGINS OF THE FEAST OF *CORPUS CHRISTI*

The feast of *Corpus Christi* first appeared in the diocese of Liège in 1246, was first placed on the universal calendar in 1264, but only came to be celebrated universally in the fourteenth century—sometime after 1311.

Our discussion of the origins of the feast is divided into two parts. The first considers the remote origins, events that occurred during the three preceding centuries which contributed significantly

---

17. Casel, *The Church's Sacred Year*, 69.

18. Casel, *The Church's Sacred Year*, 67.

19. Casel, *The Church's Sacred Year*, 66–69.

20. Casel, *The Church's Sacred Year*, 66.

to the environment in which the feast arose, and the second traces the thirteenth century events that led directly to the establishment of the feast.

Remote Origins of *Corpus Christi*

The remote origins are found in the spirituality of the Middle Ages, a predominant feature of which was devotion to the sacred humanity of Christ. Clearly devotion to the humanity of our Savior did not originate in medieval times, but for two reasons it did take on a new character and intensity during this period. First, the faithful were reading and discussing the Gospels; second, the Crusades were being preached.[21] As soldiers went off to the Holy Land and returned having walked where Jesus walked, seen where he preached and died, and perhaps even acquired a relic or two in their travels, interest in and devotion to the Lord's humanity increased.

Popular faith focused increasingly on the "mysteries" of Christ's life. Local feasts in honor of the mysteries of his life multiplied; churches and chapels were dedicated to these mysteries; the moral life was described in terms of imitating Christ; art emphasized the Lord's humanity—particularly his sufferings.[22] Most noteworthy, perhaps, is that devotion to the Eucharist was just an aspect, although a very important one, of medieval devotion to the humanity of Christ, for it is in the sacrament of the altar that the sacred humanity of Christ continues to abide in his Church. Medieval eucharistic devotion, however, was deeply colored by the eucharistic controversies of the period.[23]

From the beginning through the eighth century, there was common agreement that the Mass continued the Last Supper and that Christ was truly present on the altar. In the ninth century, Paschasius Radbertus taught that the bread used at Mass literally changes into the real body of Christ. His teaching was contradicted by a contemporary,

---

21. J. Aumann, *Christian Spirituality in the Catholic Tradition* (San Francisco: Ignatius, 2001), 110.

22. Aumann, *Christian Spirituality*, 111. Aumann reports, for example, that "the crucifixes were made more realistic and accentuated the agony of Christ . . . instead of portraying the two feet nailed separately to the cross, one foot was placed over the other and one nail transpierced both feet. As a result the artist or sculptor could portray more intense suffering of Christ crucified."

23. Aumann, *Christian Spirituality*, 110–112.

Ratramnus of Corbie, who said that the bread did not change, but that the body of Christ became present at Mass in a spiritual way. In the eleventh century there was a more public reprise of essentially the same controversy when a schoolman named Berengar of Tours denied, and Lanfranc of Bec defended, the real presence of Christ in the Eucharist.

Berengar found himself accused of heresy. He recanted his errors and then recanted his recantation multiple times before finally dying in communion with the Church. At one point he was required to sign an affirmation that read:

> I believe that the bread and wine which are placed upon the altar are, after the consecration, not only a sacrament but also the true body and blood of our Lord Jesus Christ and are physically taken up and broken in the hands of the priest and crushed by the teeth of the faithful not only sacramentally but in truth.[24]

The raw physically of the statement, if it is taken to mean that Christ himself is crushed by the teeth of the faithful, was never accepted into the Catholic theological tradition. Later theologians endeavored to distinguish the fate of the Lord's body present in the sacrament from the fate of the sacrament itself more satisfactorily. We shall return to this topic below.

As the thirteenth century dawned, then, there was lively interest in, and devotion to, both the humanity of Christ and the Eucharist.[25] And awareness that Christ's humanity remained in his Church only in the Eucharist was so strong and abiding that transubstantiation itself was understood as a way in which the Incarnation is reiterated. Consider the following from Paschasius Radbertus:

> [Christ] wished to make truly in this mystery bread and wine into his flesh and blood by the power of the consecration of the Holy Spirit . . . so that

---

24. *"Profiteor . . . eam fidem tenere ... scilicet panem et vinum quae in altari ponuntur, post consecrationem non solum sacramentum, sed etiam verum corpus et sanguinem domini nostri Iesu Christi esse, et sensualiter non solum sacramento sed in veritate manibus sacerdotum tractari frangi et fidelium dentibus atteri"*; in Lanfranc, *Liber de corpore et sanguine domini*, 2: PL 150,410–411, as quoted in M. Rubin, *Corpus Christi: The Eucharist in Late Medieval Culture* (Cambridge: Cambridge University Press, repr. 2002), 19–20.

25. As a result of the latter, two new practices were introduced around this time: elevating the host at the consecration and reserving the sacrament for adoration. Cf. Aumann, *Christian Spirituality*, 112 and 291, n. 10.

just as real flesh was created from a virgin by the Spirit, without coition, thus from the substance of bread and wine, that same body and blood of Christ is miraculously consecrated.[26]

Proximate origins of *Corpus Christi*

We move now to the events of the thirteenth century which led directly to the institution of the feast. The story of *Corpus Christi* begins with woman named Saint Juliana of Mont Cornillon who is also known as Saint Juliana of Liège.[27] Juliana was born in 1193 near Liège, was sent to live with the canonesses of Saint Augustine when she was orphaned at five, and continued in religious life until her death in 1258. She worked in a leprosarium, served as prioress of her community, was persecuted by the prior of the mixed house, and died in exile from her convent.[28]

A chapter in Juliana's biography speaks of her piety. It describes her devotion to the mysteries of Christ's life one by one, beginning with the Annunciation and ending with his Ascension. The description of the Annunciation compares Juliana's contemplation of the Eucharist to Mary's contemplation of the Word's enfleshment, that of the Ascension ends with the Lord's sacramental presence on the altar where he keeps his promise: "I will not leave you orphans; I will come to you,"[29] not with his definitive physical removal from earth. Juliana's greatest devotion was to the humanity of Christ, above all to

---

26. *"[Christus] uoluit in misterio hunc panem et uinum uere carnem suum et sanguinem consecratione Spiritus Sancti potentialiter creari . . . ut sicut de uirgine per Spiritum uera caro sine coitu creatur, ita per eundem ex substantia panis ac uini mystice idem Christi corpus et sanguis consecretur"*, *De Corpore et Sanguine Domini*, 3: CCM 16,27–28, as quoted in Rubin, *Corpus Christi*, 15.

27. A Latin biography, based on an earlier biography in Walloon and written between 1261 and 1264, survives: *Vita de B. Juliana*, in *Acta Sanctorum X: Aprilis Tomus Primus*, ed. J. Bollandus–G. Henschenius (Paris: Palmé, editio novissima 1866), 435–475; hereafter cited as *VBJ*. See C. Lambot, "Un précieux manuscrit de la vie de sainte Julienne du Mont-Cornillon," in *Miscellanea historica in honorem Alberti de Meyer: Universitatis catholicae in oppido Lovaniensi iam annos XXV professoris*, Université de Louvain. Recueil de travaux d'histoire et de philology, sér. 3, fasc. 22–23, 2 vols. (Louvain: Bibliothèque de l'Université, 1946), vol. I, 603–612; reprinted in *Revue Bénédictine* 79 (1969), 223–231, and R. J. Zawilla, "The *Historiae Corporis Christi* Attributed to Thomas Aquinas: A Theological Study of their Biblical Sources" (Ph.D. diss., University of Toronto, 1985), 1–2.

28. *VBJ*, I.2 (p. 443).

29. *VBJ*, I.4.15–18 (p. 448); cf. John 14:18.

his Passion,[30] and the main focus of both was to his presence in the Eucharist.[31]

From her youth, Juliana had a recurring vision of a moon with a little break in its sphere. In the words of the *Life*:

> In her youth, whenever the virgin of Christ, Juliana, devoted herself to prayer, a great and wondrous sign appeared to her . . . a moon in its splendor, but with a little break in its spherical body, which, the longer she gazed upon it, the more she wondered, not knowing what it might portend.[32]

Thinking at first that she was being tempted, Juliana prayed for the vision to be taken away. When her prayer was not answered, she began to pray for the meaning of the vision to be revealed. After some time Christ answered saying that the "moon symbolized the present-day Church; the little break the absence of a solemnity that he desired to be celebrated here on earth by his faithful."[33] The solemnity would ". . . once a year more solemnly and particularly" celebrate "the institution of the Sacrament of his Body and Blood unto an increase of faith, and the assistance and grace of the elect."[34] According to the *Life*, Christ stated the feast was needed because the Church "is taken up with foot-washing and his Passion" on Holy Thursday, and "a solemnity in commemoration of his Sacrament would attend with greater diligence that which is passed over on other ordinary days with lesser devotion or neglect."[35]

Christ revealed these things to Juliana so she could make his desire for the feast known. Juliana was reluctant to accept the charge

---

30. *VBJ*, I.4.18 (p. 449).

31. Zawilla, *Historiae Corporis Christi*, 3, based on *VBJ*, I.2.10.

32. *VBJ*, II.2.6 (p. 457): "*Tempore juventutis suae, a quotiens Christi Virgo Juliana orationi incumbebat, magnum sibi signum et mirabile apparebat . . . ei luna in suo splendore, cum aliquantula tamen sui sphaerici corporis fractione; quam cum multo tempore conspexisset, mirabatur multum, ignorans quid illa portenderet.*" Zawilla, *Historiae Corporis Christi*, 16, estimates the year to have been around 1208 when Juliana would have been about 15 years old.

33. *VBJ*, II.2.6 (p. 457): "*In luna, presentem Ecclesiam; in lunae autem fractione, defectum unius solennitas in Ecclesia figurari, quam adhuc volebat in terra a suis fidelibus celebrari.*"

34. *VBJ*, II.2.6 (p. 457): "*Hanc autem suam esse voluntatem, ut ad augmentum fidei, in fine seculi debilitandae, nec not et ad profectum et gratiam electorum, institutio Sacramenti Corporis et Sanguinis sui quolibet anno semel solennius ac specialius recoleretur.*"

35. *VBJ*, II.2.6 (p. 457): "*Quam in Cena Domini, quando circa lotionem pedum et memoriam passionis suae Ecclesia generaliter occupatur: in ipsaque solennitate de memoria ipsius Sacramenti supplere dilgentius oportet, quod aliis quotidianis diebus in minori devotiione seu negligentiis fuerit praetermissum.*"

and begged the Lord to use great priests *(magni clerici)* or anyway someone else *(alia persona)* instead. She submitted when she heard a voice saying: "I praise thee, Father, Lord of Heaven and earth, because thou hast hid these things from the wise and prudent, and hast revealed them to little ones."[36] More than 20 years *(plusquam viginti annorum curricula)* elapsed between Juliana's first vision of the moon with the little fissure and her acceptance of the Lord's commission.[37]

She confided her charge to John of Lausanne, canon of the Church of Saint Martin in Liège, that he might tell "many and great clerics and religious persons." John told others, of whom two were the Archdeacon of Liège, a Jacques Pantaléon, who was also known as Jacques of Troyes, and a Dominican provincial named Hugh of Saint Cher.[38] Juliana also arranged for an office to be composed for the feast.[39]

When the liturgy had been completed, her supporters approached the Bishop of Liège, Robert of Torote. Robert issued a letter approving the feast, assigned it to the Thursday after the Octave of Pentecost,[40] and decreed that an extraordinary celebration of *Corpus Christi* be held during October of 1246 in the village of Fosse where he lay gravely ill. But Robert died on October 16, 1246, and the extraordinary celebration did not take place.[41]

A series of interrelated events followed. After the bishop's death, a former prior of Juliana's monastery, an immoral man whom Robert had deposed, returned to his erstwhile post.[42] Juliana and others left the monastery rather than give their obedience to him. With Juliana gone, the cause of the feast was left with her friend and confidant, Eve of Saint Martin—so-called because she was a recluse of that church. The new bishop did not keep the new feast, but an

---

36. *VBJ*, II.2.6 (p. 457).

37. *VBJ*, II.2.7 (p. 457).

38. *VBJ*, II.2.7 (p. 458).

39. Zawilla, *Historiae Corporis Christi*, 17.

40. Robert of Torote [*Robertus Leodiensis episcopus*], "*Inter alia mira,*" in F. Callaey, *L'origine della festa del Corpus Domini*, Arbor vitae: Piccola biblioteca teologica 3 (Rovigo: Istituto Padano di Arti Grafiche, 1958), 78–82.

41. Zawilla, *Historiae Corporis Christi*, 20.

42. *VBJ*, II.2.5 (p.457).

extraordinary celebration of *Corpus Christi* was held at the Church of Saint Martin sometime in the fall of 1251.[43]

Hugh of Saint Cher attended at this extraordinary celebration of *Corpus Christi*. In the years since John of Lausanne told him of Juliana's vision and commission, Hugh had been made a cardinal and appointed papal legate of *Germania*—a region that included present-day Belgium, Poland, Germany, and Holland. The next year, that is a year after the celebration, Hugh decreed that an annual feast of *Corpus Christi* be observed on the Thursday following Trinity Sunday in all the churches of his legature[44]—the same day appointed by Robert, but designated differently.

In 1261, Jacques of Troyes was elected Pope and took the name Urban IV. In August 1264 Urban issued *Transiturus*, a bull ordering that the feast of *Corpus Christi* be celebrated annually on the Thursday following the Octave of Pentecost throughout the whole Church and granting indulgences to the faithful who participated in the Mass and Offices of the feast.[45] The liturgy for the feast was to be sent with the bull.

In a somewhat striking repetition of history, Urban died in October of 1264—before the copies of *Transiturus* and the liturgy that was to accompany it had made their way from the *Scriptorium* to the patriarchal sees whence they would have been sent to lesser dioceses.[46] The universal observance which Urban intended did not come about until almost 50 years later. In 1311, at the General Council of Vienne, Pope Clement V ordered the adoption of the feast by reissuing the bull *Transiturus* with a brief introduction of his own.[47] Clement died three years later and was succeeded in office by John XXII who retained the feast. *Corpus Christi* has been on the universal calendar of the Roman rite ever since.

The history of *Corpus Christi* reflects the age of its institution, its wars, its piety, its theological preoccupations, and includes the

---

43. Zawilla, *Historiae Corporis Christi*, 22.

44. Hugh of Saint Cher (*Hugo, S. Sabinae presbyter cardinalis, apostolicae sedis legatus*), "*Dum humani generis*," in Callaey, *Corpus Domini*, 82–85.

45. Urban IV (*Urbanus Episcopus, servus servorum Dei*), "*Transiturus*," in Callaey, *Corpus Domini*, 87–94.

46. Zawilla, *Historiae Corporis Christi*, 42–43.

47. See Callaey, *Corpus Domini*, 86.

extraordinary story of a devout Augustinian canoness who received a vision and a commission, and, unbeknownst to her, knew someone who knew someone who would one day be Bishop of Rome. It is a moving story of Providence at work in human affairs, and is, perhaps, all the more poignant because none of the principles witnessed the consequences of their efforts to establish the feast. Juliana, who died in exile from her convent three years before Urban IV became Bishop of Rome, did not live to see the moon's fissure filled;[48] neither Robert of Torote nor Urban IV lived to see the feast he decreed observed.

PART III: THEOLOGY OF THE FEAST OF *CORPUS CHRISTI*

In this last part we shall examine the theological reasons for the feast of *Corpus Christi* on the basis of the documents which established it and the texts of the Mass approved by Urban IV, and then consider the feast in the light of the theology of the liturgical calendar articulated in the opening pages of this essay.

There are four foundational documents: *The Life of Blessed Juliana,* which reports Christ's reasons for desiring the feast; Robert of Torote's letter of 1246 mandating the feast for Liège; Hugh of Saint Cher's decree of 1252 establishing the feast in *Germania*; and Pope Urban IV's bull instituting the feast in the Latin Church.[49]

The Lord's reasons for desiring the feast, as these are reported in the *Life [VBJ]* are three: 1) to commemorate the institution of the sacrament of his Body and Blood solemnly and particularly (because the Church is taken up with foot-washing and the Passion on Holy Thursday), 2) for an increase of faith, and the assistance and grace of the elect, and 3) to attend with greater diligence that which is passed over on ordinary days with lesser devotion or neglect.[50]

The ecclesiastical documents echo the *Life* in at least two ways: all refer to the Church's Holy Thursday preoccupations, namely foot-washing and the Passion specifically—Urban adds reconciling

---

48. Juliana died during the Paschal Octave on Friday, April 5, 1258. See J. Cottiaux, *Sainte Julienne de Cornillon Promotrice de la Fête-Dieu: son pays, son temps, son message* (Liège: Carmel de Cornillon, 1991), 232 and *VBJ*, II.8.49 (p. 473).

49. The three ecclesiastical documents are in Callaey, *Corpus Domini*, 79–94.

50. *VBJ*, II.2.6 (p. 457).

penitents and confecting sacred chrism. All speak of the feast supplying for negligence or lapses in devotion on other days.[51]

The three ecclesiastical documents have three other things in common as well: 1) Each appoints the same day for the feast: Thursday after the Octave of Pentecost. This is the first Thursday after Paschaltide. It links the feast to Holy Thursday and establishes its essential character: a solemn commemoration of the institution of the Eucharist. 2) Each names "the confutation of heretics" as the first reason for the feast. The feast is to refute error and clarify truth, a fact that seems to support the view that *Corpus Christi* is a "doctrinal feast." 3) Each expresses a desire that the faithful participate fully in the new feast by receiving Holy Communion after diligent preparation, and instructs the clergy to take measures to promote this.

We turn now to the Mass composed for the feast which Urban ordered to be sent with his bull.[52] The original Mass is identical to that of the first Tridentine Missal (the *Missale Romanum* of 1570) except for the Kyrie,[53] and to that of the 1962 Missal except for the Kyrie and Preface. Besides the usual proper Mass parts, the

---

51. *VBJ*, the extant Latin *Life* of Juliana, is dated between 1261 and 1264 because it mentions Jacques Pantaléon's election to the papacy, but not his establishment of the feast of *Corpus Christi* or his death. The Latin *Life* is based on an earlier life of the saint that was composed in Walloon; see Lambot, *Un précieux manuscrit*, 603. Hence, we cannot say that the letter of Robert of Torote and the decree of Hugh of Saint Cher exhibit literary dependence on *VBJ*. Rather, the 1261–1264 dating invites us to think the dependence is the other way around. But we cannot assume this either as all three documents (*VBJ*, Robert's letter and Hugh's decree) may depend on the no longer extant vernacular *Life*. Three things are noteworthy: 1) the unanimity of the three extant pre-*Transiturus* texts concerning why the feast was needed; 2) the lack of any evidence that the "tradition" of reasons for the feast did not originate in the revelation given to Juliana; and 3) Urban IV's acceptance of the prior tradition and incorporation of the same in *Transiturus*, when it passed to the Church universal. Indeed in *Transiturus*, Pope Urban IV, erstwhile Archdeacon of Liège, writes: "Moreover, some time ago, when we held a lesser office, we understood that it had been divinely revealed to certain Catholics that a feast of this sort ought to be generally celebrated in the Church" (Callaey, *Corpus Domini*, 92: "*Intelleximus autem olim, dum in minori essemus officio constitui, quod fuerat quibusdam catholicis divinitus revelatum festum huiusmodi generaliter in ecclesia celebrandum*").

52. The text presented here is the one posted at the *Corpus Thomisticum* internet site of the University of Navarre: http://www.corpusthomisticum.org/pcx.html, which, in turn, is the text of C. Lambot, "L'Office de la Fête-Dieu. Aperçus nouveaux sur ses origins," in *Revue Bénédictine* 54 (1942), 61–123, authenticated and published on the web page by E. Alarcón. But, as stated in the body of the essay, the very same Mass texts—except for the Kyrie—appear in the Roman Missals published through 1952.

53. Because this troped Kyrie is found already in eleventh century manuscripts it was chosen, not composed, by Saint Thomas, who is generally regarded to be either the author or final editor of the Mass and Office of the feast.

original Mass has an elaborate Kyrie and a long sequence known as *Lauda Sion* or, in English, "Praise, O Zion."

Our examination of the Mass texts is brief and considers only how the Mass 1) commemorates a mystery of salvation, and 2) confutes heretics.

First, the Mass commemorates the institution of the Eucharist—an event which is, in its very essence, a saving mystery. The Epistle lesson is Paul's account of the institution of the Eucharist, a shorter version of the same text used at the Mass of the Lord's Supper on Holy Thursday.[54] The sequence states: "Let praise be full, let it resound; may the rejoicing of mind be happy, be fitting; for a solemn day is celebrated, on which is recalled the first institution of this banquet."[55] The Epistle lesson and sequence show us that *Corpus Christi*, as the *Life* of Blessed Juliana and the ecclesiastical documents state, is a feast devoted to a saving mystery that belongs properly to Holy Thursday—a mystery into which the Church is not able to enter into on that day with the requisite leisure or joy because of the imminence of Christ's death and the other things that attend the same occasion.

Second, "confuting heretics." There are five texts of the Mass which set forth Catholic truth in a clear and profound way: the Kyrie, the sequence, and the three proper prayers: collect, *super oblata*, and post-communion. Here we consider only the sequence.

Lauda Sion is a beautiful poem of twenty-four stanzas whose theme is praise for the "living and life-giving bread." The language of the poem, the Latin, is simple, concise, lovely, and clear. The sequence is truly a hymn of praise, but one which succinctly presents a catechesis on the Eucharist. As the hymn unfolds, it answers the most pressing and disputed medieval questions, or, one might prefer to say, corrects the most troublesome medieval errors concerning the sacrament—but again in language that is, paradoxically, simple, clear, elegant, and praise-filled.

Lauda Sion states six truths of faith concerning the Eucharist:

---

54. Holy Thursday: 1 Corinthians 11:20–32; *Corpus Christi*: 1 Corinthians 11:23–29.

55. *Sit laus plena, sit sonora; sit iucunda, sit decora mentis iubilatio; dies enim solennis agitur, in qua mensae prima recolitur huius institutio.*

1. In the Sacrament bread and wine become the sacrifice of salvation;[56]
2. While bread becomes flesh and wine blood, the whole Christ abides in each form;[57]
3. Those who receive Christ do not consume him;[58]
4. When the good and the wicked receive the sacrament, they receive the same unto different ends;[59]
5. The whole Christ abides equally in both the whole sacrament and any fragment thereof;[60]
6. The sign may be broken, but not the reality,[61] that is, in explicit contradiction to one reading of the statement that Berengar was compelled to affirm, it is the sign or the sacrament that is broken in the hands of the priest and crushed by the teeth of the faithful, not Christ himself.[62]

As stated above, medieval devotion to the Eucharist is an aspect of devotion to the humanity of Christ. And we find that the original Mass of *Corpus Christi* also honors the humanity of the Lord, for the Preface assigned to the Mass from the beginning through at least 1952 is that of the Nativity of the Lord. It reads in part:

Almighty Father . . . through the mystery of the Word made flesh a new day of your glory has dawned upon the eyes of our minds: in order that, as

---

56. *Quod in cena Christus gessit, faciendum hoc expressit in sui memoriam, docti sacris institutis, panem vinum in salutis consecramus hostiam.*

57. *Dogma datur Christianis, quod in carnem transit panis et vinum in sanguinem; quod non capis, quod non vides, animosa firmat fides praeter rerum ordinem. Sub diversis speciebus, signis tantum et non rebus latent res eximiae, caro cibus, sanguis potus, manet tamen Christus totus sub utraque specie.*

58. *A sumente non concisus, non confractus, non divisus, integer accipitur; sumit unus, sumunt mille, quantum isti, tantum ille, nec sumptus consumitur.*

59. *Sumunt boni, sumunt mali, sorte tamen inaequali, vitae vel interitus; mors est malis, vita bonis; vide, paris sumptionis quam sit dispar exitus.*

60. *Fracto demum sacramento, ne vacilles, sed memento tantum esse sub fragmento, quantum toto tegitur.*

61. *Nulla rei fit scissura, signi tantum fit fractura, qua nec status nec statura signati inuitur.*

62. *Summa Theologiae* IIIa, q. 77, a. 7, ad 3 also addresses the point: "What is eaten under its own species, is also broken and masticated under its own species; but Christ's body is eaten not under its proper, but under the sacramental, species. Hence in explaining John 6:64, 'The flesh profiteth nothing,' Augustine (*Tract. xxvii in Joan.*) says that this is to be taken as referring to those who understood carnally: 'for they understood the flesh, thus, as it is divided piecemeal, in a dead body, or as sold in the shambles.'" Consequently, Christ's very body is not broken, except according to its sacramental species. And the confession made by Berengar is to be understood in this sense: what is broken and crushed with the teeth is the sacramental species in which species the body of Christ is truly present; the body of Christ is not broke and crushed in its present risen and glorious form.

we come to know God made visible, we may through him be carried unto love invisible.[63]

In assigning this Preface to the feast, the Church implicitly, as above we saw Paschasius Radbertus do explicitly, presents the Incarnation and transubstantiation as analogous mysteries.[64]

Lastly, we return to the question of *Corpus Christi's* place in the liturgical calendar. In Part I, we explained the absence of feasts on the early liturgical calendars theologically by noting that the entirety of our redemption is mystically re-presented at every Mass. In the strictest sense, then, an annual cycle of feasts is theologically unnecessary. In addition, and without contradiction, we offered an explanation of the liturgical calendars that developed from the fourth century forward by appeal to the givens of Christian anthropology and noted that, just as in the course of salvation history many mysteries flowed into and out of the single mystery of our Lord's dying and rising, so also the cycle of mysteries that the Church celebrates over the course of her sacred year helps each of us, bit by bit, over the whole of our lives, to enter more and more deeply into the Paschal Mystery and thereby, through the grace of Christ, to grow to maturity in him.

The feast of *Corpus Christi* commemorates the institution of the very sacrament that is confected at every Mass—the sacrament in which the sacrifice of Calvary, indeed the whole Paschal Mystery, is re-presented and the Lord gives himself to the faithful as food.

The first and perennial objection to the institution of the feast, lodged already at Liège in Juliana's day, is: "Why appoint a special day to celebrate what is celebrated at every Mass?" But according to Juliana's vision and the explanation given her by the Lord reported in the *Life*, if we accept the truth of the witness, the Church needs the feast of *Corpus Christi*.

We want, therefore, to reconcile the assertion of the *Life* that this feast is necessary or at least to show that such a feast is fitting. That is, we want to explain how the feast of *Corpus Christi* is in no way inconsistent with the theological understanding of the liturgical

---

63. "*Pater Omnipotens . . . per incarnati Verbi mysterium nova mentis nostrae oculis lux caritatis infulsit: ut dum visibiliter Deum cognoscimus, per hunc in invisibilium amorem rapiamur.*"

64. The 1962 Missal assigns the common preface to the feast.

calendar that emerges from consideration of its history and at which
we arrived in the first part of the essay. In service of this end we
consider three questions. First, whether the feast illumines the mystery
(the single mystery) of our salvation from a particular perspective?
This question was partially answered above, but is revisited below.
Second, whether the feast is inappropriately redundant? This is to
address the objection that there is no point in having a special feast to
celebrate what every Mass celebrates. Third, whether the "confutation
of heretics," the first reason for the feast given in all the ecclesiastical
documents that established it, is an unworthy motive that subverts,
or even perverts, the true purpose of liturgical feasts—for here we
have a solemnity that seemingly was founded not to celebrate saving
mystery but to serve doctrinal truth. My response to each of these
questions is very brief.

First, whether *Corpus Christi* illumines the mystery of our
salvation? It is evident from our survey of both the documents establishing the feast and the Mass texts chosen for it that *Corpus Christi*
commemorates one of the mysteries of Christ's own life, namely,
that on the night before he died, he gave his body and blood to the
Twelve under the form of bread and wine and instructed them to
do the same in memory of him. Further, he said and did these things
in a way that established an intimate connection between this new rite
and his death on the morrow, the forgiveness of sins, the new covenant
he was about to establish, and the messianic banquet of the *eschaton*.
Without doubt *Corpus Christi* celebrates a mystery of salvation—one
that is so integrally connected to the Paschal Mystery as to be, in
some ways, indistinguishable from it because the mystery celebrated
is, in a sacramental way, the Paschal Mystery itself whole and entire.

Second, the charge of redundancy. The focus of this feast
is not, to be precise, what is done at every Mass, but the historic event
(the institution of the Eucharist) which makes the Mass possible.
As we have shown, it commemorates an event in salvation history just
as Christmas celebrates the birth of Christ, the Pasch his resurrection
and Pentecost the coming of his Spirit.

Third, the confutation of heretics. In Part I we said that the
single divine act which saves us is presented over the course of the
liturgical year in ways that allow the faithful to appropriate its totality
gradually through its various aspects. This is principally done through

spiritual participation in the various mysteries of salvation which are themselves aspects of the one saving mystery, not through meditation and imitation.

The faithful are human beings, endowed with reason and free choice. And thus, for the faithful to participate in these mysteries fully, they must understand them rightly. The doctrinal aims of *Corpus Christi* are, therefore, intimately attached to the needs of the faithful. Indeed, as the history of Christianity shows clearly, those who do not understand the Eucharist properly do not reverence it rightly and, very frequently, abandon it altogether.

It is important to distinguish the "firsts." The first motive named in the ecclesiastical documents for establishing the feast of *Corpus Christi* is not the first cause for or source of it. The source of the feast is that Christ, on the night before he died, took bread into his hands and said, "This is my body which is given for you. Do this in remembrance of me."[65] Without this saving event, *Corpus Christi* would not and could not exist.

In conclusion, then, the Church's sacred year is the mystery of Christ, and the development of the liturgical calendar over the centuries corresponds to the way in which the Church, in her wisdom, has seen fit to accommodate this mystery to the needs of the faithful so that they may participate in it more deeply, contemplate it more fruitfully, and incarnate it more fully.

---

65. Luke 22:19b (RSV).

Chapter 8

The "Mystical" Meaning of the Ceremonies of the Mass: Liturgical Exegesis in the Middle Ages

Claude Barthe*

There is a longstanding inadequacy that affects not only the spiritual but also the scholarly understanding of the Latin liturgy in general, and the Roman in particular, and that is the neglect of a whole dimension of its meaning, its *spiritual sense*. The misreading of what is commonly called the *allegorical*, or *mystical*, or *spiritual* commentary on the liturgy, predates the reform of Vatican II, the Liturgical Movement, and even the restorations of the nineteenth century. In earlier times, and this is especially true of the Middle Ages, the Christian liturgy, and particularly the Roman liturgy, was formed and lived out of an interpretation of, and commentary and meditation upon the Church, which were fundamental to its understanding. To enter into the Catholic liturgy without this key is like attempting to understand a cathedral by means of architectural instructions accompanied by a catechism. One risks missing those "forests of symbols"[1] evoked by Baudelaire when speaking of the "Temple of Nature," which is itself a metaphor for a religious building.

---

* Translated by a nun of St. Cecilia's Abbey in Ryde, U.K.

1. See, for example, M. Dulaey, "*Des forêts de symboles": L'initiation chrétienne et la Bible Ier–VIe siècles* (Paris: Librairie générale française, 2001); M.-M. Davy, *Initiation à la symbolique romane (XIIe siècle)* (Paris: Flammarion, 1977).

THE LINK BETWEEN SCRIPTURE AND THE LITURGY

When speaking of allegorical, spiritual, or indeed mystical commentaries on the liturgy, one thinks of the analogous commentaries on scripture. William Durandus, Bishop of Mende in the thirteenth century, author of the most famous spiritual commentary on the liturgy, the *Rationale divinorum officiorum* (of which we will discuss more later), introduced his work by recalling the four classic meanings of scriptural interpretation as set out, for example, by Saint Thomas Aquinas in the *Summa Theologiae*:[2] the historical or literal sense (oral history and its theological import),[3] and the three spiritual senses, that is to say the allegorical, by which the Old Testament announces the New (the manna in the desert signifying the Eucharist); the typological or moral sense (Jacob wrestling with the angel signifying that the virtuous gaining of the kingdom of heaven necessitates a struggle) and the analogical sense relating to the things of above (God's rest on the seventh day of creation anticipating the peace of eternal beatitude). The literal or historic sense is fundamental: it is on sacred history as recounted in the biblical text that its interpretation rests. Moreover, in the exegesis of all the Fathers of the Church it is considered as the "the outer layer," the *letter,* covering the deeper spiritual meaning, the *spirit.* Among the spiritual meanings, the most important is the allegorical (the term is Saint Paul's; Galatians 4:24), referring as it does to Christ. The whole of the Old Testament announces Christ,

---

2. Saint Thomas Aquinas, *Summa Theologiae* Ia, q. 1, a. 10: "that first signification whereby words signify things belongs to the first sense, the historical or literal. That signification whereby things signified by words have themselves also a signification is called the spiritual sense, which is based on the literal, and presupposes it. Now this spiritual sense has a threefold division . . . so far as the things of the Old Law signify the things of the New Law, there is the allegorical sense; so far as the things done in Christ, or so far as the things which signify Christ, are types of what we ought to do, there is the moral sense. But so far as they signify what relates to eternal glory, there is the anagogical sense." Translation by the Fathers of the English Dominican Province, *The Summa theologica,* 22 vols. (London: Burns, Oates & Washbourne, 2nd revised edition, 1912–1936).

3. However, the literal sense in traditional exegesis covers a complex reality. This is shown by Gilbert Dahan in his *L'exégèse chrétienne de la Bible en Occident médiéval* (Paris: Cerf, 1999), with special reference to Hugh of St.-Victor. The literal is also tripartite, but in three layers: that of the *littera* in a strict sense, which is textual analysis; that of the *sensus,* which is contextual analysis; and that of the *sententia,* which is philosophical or theological analysis. Because the medievals use a language that evolves constantly, many elements that would later return in the category of "spiritual direction" originated in fact from the search for the "literal sense." The richness and the reach of the "literal sense" were much greater larger than their insistence on the superiority of the "spiritual sense" make would make us believe.

and in the New Testament each text reveals, at the level of the *letter*, the most profound Christological meaning: the Good Samaritan is a figure of Christ, the best wine at Cana "served last" is the Gospel, etc. Because the allegorical meaning is the most important of the spiritual senses, one often speaks of allegorical interpretation to designate the whole range of spiritual interpretations.

For medieval spiritual commentators on the ceremonial of the Church (its architecture, ornaments and sacred vessels), the allegorical meaning of the liturgy remains the same as that of scripture, and like the latter, it remains inexhaustible, that is to say "infinite" (Duns Scotus). It should be noted that Saint Thomas himself in the *Summa Theologiae*, makes a place for the spiritual interpretation of the ceremonies of the Mass.[4] This movement from the *letter* to the *spirit* is, finally, intrinsic to the things of cult, as is shown by that most classic of examples, employed to defend or to attack as "artificial" the mystical sense of the liturgy, the candle: which taken in its literal sense is meant to illuminate (in every sense of the term) the sacred action, while signifying on a spiritual level the light of Christ. The liturgy itself places allegorical interpretation on an even more complex plane in using the word "pillar" to describe the paschal candle in the chant of the *Exsultet*, evoking the pillar of fire which went before the Hebrews at night in the desert.

When searching for examples of spiritual interpretations of the Church's ceremonial, one finds that they are always linked with scriptural references. The search for the spiritual meaning hidden behind the *letter* of the ceremonial, the decoration of the building, the sacred vestments with regard to their color, shape and fabric, is in reality nothing more than a continuation of the search for the *spirit* hidden behind the *letter* of sacred texts: the living water that signifies purification, as well as the assembly of the faithful, as well as humanity as distinct from the wine of the divinity, etc. Holy Scripture itself testifies to this link between spiritual sense, sacred text and liturgy. Thus, Saint Paul evokes the manna and the water in the desert, figures for the Eucharist: "all [our fathers] ate the same supernatural food and all drank of the same supernatural drink" (1 Corinthians 10:3–4), and then he speaks of the eating of the eucharistic bread as a figure of

---

4. F. Quoëx, "Thomas d'Aquin, mystagogue: l'*Expositio missae* de la *Somme de théologie* (IIIa, q. 83, a. 4–5)," in *Revue Thomiste* 105 (2005), 179–225 and 355–409.

the communion of Christians between themselves and with Christ: "the bread that we break, is it not a participation in the body of Christ? Because there is one bread, we who are many are one body, for we all partake of the one bread" (1 Corinthians 10:16).

In fact, this spiritual commentary on the liturgy is already at work in the New Testament, as for example in the Apocalypse (which places the emphasis on the allegories of the Old Testament, for instance, the New Temple in the book of Ezekiel), but also in the Letter to the Hebrews (as in the explanation of the "two tents" of the Old Temple; Hebrews 9:6–8). The Apocalypse moves on to the mystical meaning behind cultic objects which served as a model for the patristic and medieval authors: the seven lamps as the seven spirits of God (Revelation 4:5); the golden cups full of perfumes representing the prayer of the saints (Revelation 5:8; 8:3–4); the fine linen in which the Spouse is dressed signifying the virtue of the saints (Revelation 19:8).

Soundings from History

It is therefore only natural that the typological approach to the interpretation of Scripture should find its way into the catecheses of the Fathers concerning the sacraments, especially when speaking of the Eucharist, which is the focus of this chapter, all the more easily since the sacred species are, as Saint Cyril of Jerusalem noted in the fourth century, the type (*typos*) par excellence, that of the body and blood of Christ, which are the antitype (*antitypos*). Thus in explaining the main ceremonies of the Mass to his neophytes,[5] the washing of the hands, the kiss of peace, the *Sursum corda*, the preface and the *Sanctus*, the epiclesis, the great intercession, the *Memento*, the Lord's Prayer, the *Sancta sanctis* (invitation and warning before communion only to approach if worthy), Saint Cyril gives them a symbolism identical to that which he uses in decoding the words and gestures, the *verba et gesta*, of the Lord.

In the same way Theodore of Mopsuestia, in the fifth century, albeit in reaction against what he thought was the exaggerated allegorization of the Alexandrines, expounds on the symbolic

---

5. Cyril of Jerusalem, *Mystagogicae Catecheses*, V: SCh 126 bis, 146–175.

meaning of each rite described in his catechetical homilies. Thus it is, he explains, that the deacons in the Syrian rite never cease to shake the fans around the altar as soon as the "elements" are placed upon it: this is the same movement, he reports, that accompanies the lowering into the ground, on an open bier, of the body of a great personage. In such a way is shown the reverence and adoration due to the Sacred Body lying incorruptible on the altar.[6] He comments in a similar way on the manner in which honor is paid to the "Royal Body" when communion is received under this same rite.[7]

It is important not to omit in this rapid overview a writer of the fifth and sixth centuries, who had so much influence on the Middle Ages, known as Dionysius. He favored an interpretation of the liturgy that in his case could be described as particularly mystical, forming the support for the loftiest of spiritual edifices. For example, when referring to the incensing of the church by the bishop, "one sees the high priest distancing himself from the sanctuary, wafting the delicious odor right into the least sacred corners of the temple, then returning to his point of departure, to signify that the divine gifts are communicated to all the saints according to the merits of each, without succumbing to any diminution nor any modification, whilst maintaining the abundance of the qualities which are theirs within the Divine Immutable One."[8]

The Greek commentaries that followed on from the patristic catecheses accompanied the evolution of the Byzantine liturgy from late antiquity. The expression "heaven on earth," which became a sort of cliché to define the atmosphere that this liturgy wished to convey, came precisely from the opening chapter of one of these allegorical liturgical commentaries, that of Germanus I, Patriarch of Constantinople in the eighth century.[9] This fundamental typology of

---

6. Theodor of Mopsuestia, *Homiliae catecheticae*, XV,26–29: ed. R. Tonneau–R. Devreesse, Studi e Testi 145 (Città del Vaticano: Biblioteca Apostolica Vaticana, 1949), 505–511.

7. Theodor of Mopsuestia, *Homiliae catecheticae*, XVI, 27:577.

8. Ps.-Dionysius the Areopagite, *De Ecclesiastica Hierarchia*, IV, 3: ed. G. Heil, Patristische Texte und Studien 36 (Berlin: de Gruyter, 1991), 97 (PG 3,476D).

9. See R. F. Taft, *The Byzantine Rite: A Short History* (Collegeville, Minnesota: The Liturgical Press, 1992). This understanding of the liturgy was developed in a systematic way by Maximus the Confessor (580–662) in his *Mystagogia*: PG 91,657–707. The *Mystagogia*, which was translated into Latin at an early stage, has had some influence on those writing in the golden age of liturgical commentary, the thirteenth century.

liturgical interpretation found in the East, but also in the West, which sees the earthly liturgy as a "concelebration" with the worship exercised by the angelic choirs before the Throne of the Lamb, underlines the fact that the liturgical commentaries see themselves as continuing the cultic allegories of the New Testament.[10]

As for Isidore of Seville (560–636), whose principal work, the *Etymologies*, nourished the Christian intellect for a millennium, it should be noted that he was a real "technician" of the liturgy, having an in-depth experience of the sacred chant and the training of the professionals of the *schola cantorum*, while being a theoretician when it came to the modes of execution. The link between liturgical creation and interpretation must be kept in mind when discussing the history of spiritual commentary on the liturgy. There is much discussion about the likely connections between his *De ecclesiasticis officiis* and this or that piece of the liturgy known as Mozarabic (liturgy belonging to the Iberian Peninsula, adopted and slightly expanded by the Visigoths, who had encountered the Moorish occupation). Even if considered modest, Isidore's contributions to compositions of the Visigothic period are not in doubt. Indeed it is he who discourses on the hymns, the prayers, the blessings, and the various parts of the liturgy, and gives their mystical meaning: for example, alluding to Lot's wife, the salt of baptismal exorcism, is a warning given to catechumens not to look backward.

One should also recall, a century later, two letters falsely attributed to Saint Germanus of Paris (d. 576) and published by an anonymous cleric in the final years of the eighth century.[11] They contain an allegorical commentary on the *Ordo missae* of the Old Gallican rite, which evokes the somewhat earlier *Mystagogia* of Maximus the Confessor.[12]

---

10. The Eastern tradition speaks of "heaven on earth," the Western tradition of earthly participation in the heavenly liturgy. This is one of the commonplaces employed in spiritual literature about the chanting of the psalms: "He who carries out faithfully and attentively this task that is given to him joins in with the singing of the angels"; Saint Isidore of Seville, as cited by P. Cazier, *Isidore de Séville et la naissance de l'Espagne catholique*, Théologie historique 96 (Paris: Beauchesne, 1994), 141.

11. A critical edition of the Latin text will be published by Philippe Bernard in the CCM series. See also the forthcoming volume *Transitions liturgiques en Gaule carolingienne*, traduction et commentaires par P. Bernard (Paris: Hora Decima, 2007).

12. P. Bernard, "La christianisation de l'espace et du temps: le temps de la liturgie," in J.-M. Mayeur *et al.* (ed.), *Histoire du christianisme des origines à nos jours, tome III: Les églises d'Orient et*

THE *EXPOSITIONES MISSAE*

It seems that with Amalarius of Metz,[13] in the ninth century, confidant of Charlemagne and of Louis the Pious, liturgical commentaries, known as the *Expositiones missae,* became a distinct genre. Amalarius used fragments chosen from Saint Augustine and Saint Gregory the Great and developed and enlarged the symbolic interpretations that they had sketched out. One of their main ideas, taken from a well-established tradition and found among the majority of their successors, is that there exists a rapport between the Mass and the history of salvation.[14] The Mass is thus the representation of the life of Christ, from his Incarnation (the entry procession corresponding to the entry of Christ into the world, the choir singing the Introit being the chorus of prophets who announced his arrival), right up to his Ascension (corresponding to the *Ita missa est*).[15] Much later Saint Francis de Sales adopts this schema, as though it were self-evident, when he explains in *L'introduction a la vie devote,* "how one must hear" Holy Mass while thinking all the while of the entry of Christ into the world, etc.[16]

Without going into greater detail over the meanings that Amalarius draws from the ceremonial, one should note that with regard to one of the most classical—the uniting of the water to the wine at the offertory representing the union of the faithful with Christ—he is simply recalling the allegorical interpretation of the patristic age,[17] an interpretation that has a scriptural significance: ". . . and these waters . . . are the people the crowds, the nations, and the languages" (Revelation 17:15). This is moreover a perfect example

---

d'Occident (432–610) (Paris: Desclée, 1998), 1015–1047, at 1031.

13. Amalarius, *Opera liturgica omnia,* ed. J.-M. Hanssens, Studi e Testi, 138–140 (Città del Vaticano: Biblioteca Apostolica Vaticana, 1949–1950).

14. According to this idea of the order of Mass as a *mimesis* of the history of salvation, the canticle of Zacharias, father of John the Baptist, the precursor of Christ, came before the readings in the Old Gallican liturgies; see Bernard, *La christianisation de l'espace et du temps,* 1039.

15. See E. Mazza, *The Celebration of the Eucharist: The Origin of the Rite and the Development of its Interpretation,* trans. M. J. O'Connell (Collegeville, Minnesota: The Liturgical Press, 1999), 162–173.

16. Saint Francis de Sales, *Introduction à la vie dévote,* ed. E.-M. Lajeunie (Paris: Seuil, 1995), part II, chapter 14.

17. Cyprian, *Ep. 63,*13,1: CCL 3C,407: "When the wine in the chalice is mingled with wine, the people are united with Christ."

of allegory explaining the choice of texts that traditionally accompany a particular action, and not the other way around: in the Roman Mass, the prayer *Deus qui humanae substantiae*, an ancient prayer given in the Sacramentaries for the feast of Christmas, refers to this very interpretation (the union of the faithful to Christ); in the Ambrosian and Carthusian rites, it alludes to the water that issues from the opened side of Christ.

From Amalarius in the ninth century, to the *Rationale* at the end of the thirteenth century, this genre saw its greatest expansion. The four-part division of the meanings was fixed, identical to those that were applied at the time to scripture. It was both the great period of biblical spiritual exegesis and of the spiritual commentaries on the liturgy: Rupert of Deutz and his *De divinis officiis*;[18] Honorius of Autun and his *Gemma animae*;[19] Yvo of Chartres in the *Sermones de ecclesiasticis sacramentis*;[20] and many others, such as John Beleth of the University of Paris.[21] Everything that had gone before was brought together in that supreme *expositio missae*, William Durandus' *Rationale*.

Timothy M. Thibodeau, the main specialist on Durandus of Mende, identifies four predecessors to Durandus,[22] as the representatives of the *expositio missae* at the start of the thirteenth century, in the great age of the cathedrals: Prevostinus of Cremona (c. 1150–1210), at the end of his life chancellor of the University of Paris with his *Tractatus de officiis*;[23] William of Auxerre, (d. 1231), archdeacon of Beauvais and celebrated Parisian master who appears to be the first to have used the terms "matter" and "form" in the theology of the sacraments, with his *Summa de officiis ecclesiasticis* (no printed edition exists); Sicardo of Cremona (c. 1150–1215), professor of Law,

---

18. Rupert of Deutz, *De divinis officiis*, ed. H. Haacke, CCM 7 (Turnhout: Brepols, 1967).

19. Honorius of Autun, *Gemma animae*: PL 172,541–738.

20. Yvo of Chartres, *Sermones de ecclesiasticis sacramentis*: PL 162, 505–610.

21. John Beleth, *Summa de ecclesiasticis officiis* ed. H. Douteil, CCM 41, 41A (Turnhout: Brepols, 1976).

22. T. M. Thibodeau, "Les sources du *Rationale* de Guillaume Durand," in P. Gy (ed.), *Guillaume Durand, évêque de Mende (v. 1230-1296), canoniste, liturgiste et homme politique: actes de la Table ronde du C.N.R.S., Mende, 24-27 mai 1990* (Paris: CNRS, 1992), 143–153, at 152.

23. *Praepositini Cremonensis Tractatus de officiis*, ed. J. A. Corbett, Publications in mediaeval studies 21 (Notre Dame, Indiana: University of Notre Dame Press, 1969).

papal legate to Frederick II, Bishop of Cremona, with his *Mitrale*,[24]
a liturgical summa that had a similar significance for Durandus
as the *Sentences* of Peter Lombard had for Saint Thomas; and above
all Lothar of Segni (c. 1160–1216), later Pope Innocent III, whose
De missarum mysteriis was adopted and expanded in William
Durandus's *Rationale*.[25]

THE LITURGICAL *SUMMA* OF WILLIAM DURANDUS OF MENDE

William Durandus, named "the Elder" to distinguish him from a
nephew of the same name who succeeded him in the see of Mende,
was born about 1230 at Puimisson in the Narbonnaise. He studied
canon law at Bologna—*ius decretorum* as it was known, based upon
the *Decretals*. He went on to teach, seemingly at Bologna and certainly
at Modena. Swiftly taken up by the curia, he assisted at the Second
Council of Lyon in 1274, the one toward which Saint Thomas Aquinas
was heading when he died. As a close collaborator of the popes of the
last third of the thirteenth century, he undertook various judiciary
charges, administrative and diplomatic, under the patronage of Saint
Peter. An austere man, he was appointed Bishop of Mende in 1285,
then returned to Italy in 1295, dying in Rome on November 1, 1296
(his tomb is in the Dominican church of Santa Maria sopra Minerva).[26]

Durandus, a representative of the high ecclesiastical administration of his day, is the author of a *Repertorium* or *Breviarium*, a
systematic exposé of the essential points of canon law, and of a "mirror"
of canonical procedure, a *Speculum iudiciale*, republished many times,
which earned him the title of "the Speculator." He is, more than
anything, a compiler, understood in the strict sense of the title as used

24. Sicardo of Cremona, *Mitrale seu de officiis ecclesiasticis summa*: PL 213, 13–436.

25. Lothar of Segni, *De sacro altaris mysterio*: PL 217, 775–916; a Latin edition with an
Italian translation was published by S. Fioramonti, *Il sacrosanto mistero dell'altare*, Monumenta
studia instrumenta liturgica, 15 (Città del Vaticano: Libreria Editrice Vaticana, 2002).

26. In addition to private penance, Durandus tried to restore the custom of public penance,
which had fallen into disuse for a long time. Both in the *Rationale* (IV, 22 and 68) and in the
Pontificale, he discusses the dismissal of penitents on Ash Wednesday and their reconciliation on
Maundy Thursday; both practices had disappeared from the liturgical books of its time. His
nephew, the younger William Durandus, collected his spiritual heritage and took side with the
bishops who at the time of the Council of Vienne (1311–1312) asked for a reform of the Church
tam in capite quam in membris.

in the Middle Ages. The compilation, along with the gloss, and closely related to the *catenae* of the patristic commentaries on Scripture, consisted in collecting all that previous authors, whose works were accessible, had to say on a matter. One's own stamp was placed on it by such things as the organization of the material—and it is certainly to this that William Durandus, with his genius for presentation, owes much of his success—and adding one's own reflections, forming a seamless whole with the quotations from previous authors.

His liturgical work consists essentially of the *Rationale* and the *Liber ordinis pontificalis* or *Pontificale* (as well as pastoral works, the *Instructions* and the *Constitutions*, which he composed for use in his diocese and which contain numerous directions for the liturgy).

The *Pontificale*, written around 1292, sufficed to make William Durandus one of the great figures in the history of the Latin liturgy. It is a compilation of the ceremonial ordinances normally reserved to the bishop, conforming essentially to the Roman usage. It is, properly speaking, the first true Pontifical and was not slow to replace the Curial Pontifical, which was the successor to the Romano-Germanic Pontifical. Durandus' *Pontificale* served as the basis for that of Innocent VIII of 1485, produced by Patrizi and Burckard, this last edition being practically identical to the Tridentine Pontifical of 1595, and remaining in use until the reforms of Vatican II.[27]

The *Rationale divinorum officiorum* is a liturgical commentary.[28] Written some fifteen years after the death of Saint Thomas, it represents the most complete medieval summary, designed, according to the plan laid out by the author in his prologue, to instruct those who used it in "the mysteries hidden in the divine office." Its influence was huge: more that 200 extant manuscripts testify to its diffusion throughout the Middle Ages, followed by 111 editions, in Latin or in

---

27. An anastatic reprint of the 1595/1596 *editio princeps* of the *Pontificale Romanum* was published by M. Sodi, A. M. Triacca and G. M. Foti, Monumenta liturgica Concilii Tridentini 1 (Città del Vaticano: Libreria Editrice Vaticana, 1997).

28. *Guillelmi Duranti Rationale divinorum officiorum*, ed. A. Davril, T. M. Thibodeau, B. G. Guyot, CCM 140, 140A, 140B (Turnhout: Brepols, 1995–2000). The Latin text of books I and III was published with an Italian translation by S. della Torre, M. Marinelli and G. F. Freguglia, Monumenta studia instrumenta liturgica, 14 (Città del Vaticano: Libreria Editrice Vaticana, 2001). There is a French translation of the complete work by C. Barthélémy, *Rational ou manuel des Divins Offices de Guillaume Durand*, 5 vols. (Paris: Vivès, Paris, 1854). A French translation of book IV on the Mass was done by C. Barthe and D. Millet-Gérard, *Le sens spirituel de la liturgie: Guillaume Durand, Rational des divins offices, livre IV de la messe* (Genève: Ad Solem, 2003).

translation. These are essentially spread over the period from 1459 to 1672: over the centuries the *Rationale* has been one of the books most often found in ecclesiastical libraries.

William Durandus completed a first revision of his work in 1286, the year of his episcopal consecration. A second revision, undertaken during the course of his episcopate came to an end around 1296, due to his return to Italy. The title *Rationale* was inspired by one of the most renowned cultic objects in the Old Testament, a pouch in rich material, associated with the ephod, which the high priest wore on his chest (also known as the breast piece).[29] On this "rational" the high priest had written, according to the Vulgate, two words: *doctrina et veritas*, which Durandus translated, interpreting them after the fashion of his day, as "revelation and truth." It is the finishing touch given to his work of unveiling the hidden meanings of the Divine Office (*Rationale*, Prologue, 18).

Like the Pontifical, the *Rationale* deals with the "common and most often used rites" (Prologue, 14), in other words the rites of the Roman liturgy. This was for Dom Guéranger its principal advantage and the one which he acknowledged gratefully.[30] William Durandus was Roman in his broad declarations on the principles of the rights of the pope ("everything belongs to him"; *Rationale*, IV, 30, 41), but also in always conceding to the Roman Rite down to the last little detail (the host being placed next to the chalice and both being blessed; cf. *Rationale*, IV, 30, 22 and *Rationale*, IV, 53, 6).

He divided the *Rationale* into eight books:
- Book I: On the Church and its dependent premises, its ornamentation and likewise;
- Book II: On the ministers of the Church ordained and un-ordained (cantor, psalmist, porter, reader, exorcist, acolyte, sub-deacon, deacon, priest, and bishop);

---

29. Two liturgical vestments of particular importance are inspired by the *rationale* of the High Priest, the stole and the pallium; cf. Bernard, *La christianisation de l'espace et du temps*, 1026. In various diocesan liturgies (Eichstätt, Paderborn, Krakow), the *rationale* is a vestment reserved to the bishop, but Durandus makes no mention of this.

30. Dom Prosper Guéranger acknowledges Durand as a great compiler: "On peut considérer ce livre comme le dernier mot du moyen-âge sur la Mystique du culte divin"; *Institutions liturgiques*, 4 vols. (Paris: Société Générale de Librairie Catholique, 2nd edn, 1878–1885), vol. I, 341. However, he also writes with much condescension that "dans la partie de son travail qui lui appartient en propre, il n'est pas toujours sûr de prendre, pour le génie de l'Église, les explications qu'il donne"; *Institutions liturgiques*, vol. I, 342.

- Book III: On liturgical vestments;
- Book IV: On the Mass;
- Book V: On the Divine Office (Matins, Lauds, etc.)
- Book VI: On Sundays and feasts of the Lord;
- Book VII: On the feasts of the saints;
- Book VIII: On the *computus* and the calendar.[31]

Everything written before him is reprinted and classified, with precision added where necessary. There is moreover, beneath the appearance of abundance, a strong coherence: this is not simply due to the arrangement of the material under headings, but corresponds to a theological-spiritual ordering that is very clear and satisfying to the soul. This approach stems from the medieval tradition with its concern for orthodoxy, and therefore unity and unification, most notably by means of the repetition and harmonization of what is said by the authorities, and the many and varied explanatory insights, which attempt to grasp as best they can an inexhaustible material. Thus, when he speaks of the thurible, depending on whether it has one, two, three or four chains, different symbolic meanings are attributed to them, or rather, to be exact, different shades of meaning along the same lines (it being understood that the thurible essentially represents Christ). For William Durandus, as for Innocent III, the literal meaning of prayers was the object of a theological development of some significance.[32] It was as though the urgency over debates and controversies, especially over the Eucharist, at times relegated allegorical meditation to second place. For the rest, references to the history of the liturgy, if at times rather brief, are not uncommon in the *Rationale*.

The Great Decline in Allegorical Meaning

Ad litteram commentaries were not previously unknown in the Middle Ages. Florus of Lyon (d. about 860), an adversary of Amalarius,

---

31. The original French reads "Du comput" here. *Computus* is a technical term for the calculation of the date of Easter in the Christian calendar.

32. See, for instance, an extraordinary passage about the three elements of a sacrament (*sacramentum tantum, res et sacramentum, res tantum*) in *Rationale* IV, 20–28, which reaches its climax with a reflection on the sign that signifies in a certain sense by emptying itself: bread and wine become *sacramentum*, that is, the sign of the body and blood of Christ, at the precise moment when they really cease to be bread and wine.

published a commentary on the Canon of the Mass completely free
of allegory.[33] However, for want of historical knowledge and of a sense
of history, this type of interpretation was not able to establish itself
during these centuries. From the end of the fifteenth century, when
humanist erudition began to make headway, it was to be to the
detriment of the rich mystical tradition in interpreting both Scripture
and the liturgy (although there was still a strong allegorizing tendency
in Christian humanism).

After Durandus, one of the spiritual commentaries most often
cited is *Sacri Canonis Missae expositio resolutissima literalis et mystica*
by Gabriel Biel (1425–1495), professor at Tübingen. There had been
others during the fifteenth century, like the *Expositio missae* of the
Carthusian, Nicolas Kempht. The sixteenth century is the age of the
collectors and editors of ancient liturgical commentaries, notably in
Germany, proving the interest of the ecclesiastical public. One still
finds compositions on the *Expositions of the Mysteries of the Mass*,
but descriptions of the rites and ceremonial are proportionally more
numerous, such as the learned *Défences* with its anti-Lutheran
aims (*De l'Antiquité et de la Solennité de la Messe* by Jean du Tillet,
Bishop of St-Brieuc).

Since that time, allegorical interpretation was still employed,
but without being sufficiently important to give rise to specific treatises; it appeared more and more "gothic." After the Protestant crisis,
the wellspring seemed forever dried up, but it was not completely so.
Just as the middle of the seventeenth century brought forth composers
of plain-chant (Du Mont, Nivers) and builders of gothic cathedrals
(Auch, Orléans), so it produced the author of a very medieval *expositio
missae*: Jean-Jacques Olier, *curé* de Saint-Sulpice. The creator of the
major seminaries in France, aimed at the formation of candidates to
the priesthood, he published in 1657 an *Explication des cérémonies de la
grand messe de paroisse selon l'usage romain*. The original manuscript
consists of notes from classes given by Olier to the clerics of Saint-
Sulpice, although formation in carrying out the rites was provided by
other professors.[34] The fact that there seem to be only two new

---

33. Florus of Lyon, *De actione missae*: PL 119, 15–70.

34. J.-J. Olier, *L'esprit des cérémonies de la messe: Explication des cérémonies de la grand'messe de
paroisse selon l'usage romain*, ed. C. Barthe, with M. Debaecker (Paris: Le Forum, 2004). The
original title to Olier's manuscript is "L'esprit des cérémonies de la messe."

editions of the *Explication* after the seventeenth century[35] arousing little interest is evidence of the decline of mystical commentaries on the liturgy.[36] Olier makes use of those images employed a thousand times over but never exhausted. For example, Durandus explains: "The angel—that is to say Christ—has arrived; he is standing before the altar, that is in the presence of the Church; with a golden thurible, that is his immaculate body; filled with fire, that is to say love; and he receives from the faithful many gifts of incense, that is prayers, in order to offer them, that is to present them to the Father together with the prayers of the angels" (*Rationale*, IV, 8, 1). Compare this with the commentary of Olier: "The grains of the incense, cast three times on the fire, signify the faithful of the Church cast into the burning furnace of the heart of God, where they pour out praises and are consumed in him by Jesus Christ . . . . The body of the thurible, which contains the burning coals, represents the humanity [of Jesus Christ], whose depths are in glory and consumed in the divine fire."[37]

However, those commentaries on the Mass more or less contemporary with that of Olier are noticeably less allegorical than his. Gilbert Grimaud's *La liturgie sacrée, où toutes les Parties et Cérémonies de la Sainte Messe sont expliquées, leurs Mystères et Antiquités* is essentially an historical explanation followed by sparse and merely token notes. Among these contemporary works, it is perhaps in an *Auto* by Pedro Calderón de la Barca (1600–1681), *Los misterios de la misa*,[38] that one finds the most traditional allegorical inspiration.

The decline of spiritual interpretations of the liturgy parallels the rise in biblical criticism. Of course, the new methods of editing and the research into original texts in the humanist period, the application of historical scholarship to the sacred texts from the seventeenth century onward, and the use of the archaeological,

---

35. The work was published in Clermont-Ferrand: Thibaud-Landriot, 1835, and in *Oeuvres complètes de M. Olier*, ed. J. P. Migne (Paris: Ateliers Catholiques, 1856), 281–456.

36. However, he is mentioned very favorably by Dom Guéranger: "Ce saint prêtre [Jean-Jacques Olier], l'un des derniers écrivains mystiques de France, avait reçu d'en haut l'intelligence des mystères de la Liturgie, à un degré rare avant lui, nous dirions presque inconnu depuis"; *Institutions liturgiques*, vol. II, 96. It should be noted that Olier discusses the Roman rite (which would have been a matter of course to him since the new Parisian Missal had not yet come into existence); for Prosper Guéranger, this was an outstanding quality of his work.

37. Olier, *Explication*, ed. Migne, 341 and 346.

38. P. Calderón de la Barca, *Obras completas III. Autos sacramentales* (Madrid: Aguilar, 1991), 299–314.

philological and historical advances of the nineteenth and twentieth centuries have improved our understanding of the literal sense of Holy Scripture. However, we also know that rationality is often confused with rationalism and that the errors of Loisy, Bultmann, and their like cannot simply be accounted for by fearful and suspicious ecclesiastical authorities, slow in approving scholarly breakthroughs. In any case, the application of the historical-critical method to the Bible gradually exhausted all straightforward interest in researching its spiritual meaning. The latter, bearing as it did the patristic stamp, kept a place midway between spirituality and the academic discipline of patrology. But neither the name nor the extraordinary erudition of Henri de Lubac[39] has been sufficient to rehabilitate medieval spiritual exegesis, at least until very recently.[40]

All the same, it would be absurd to find fault with the academic progress that the study of the "literal sense" of the liturgy has made over this time. The critical method applied to historical research into the liturgy has stimulated many scholars in the modern age: Dom Martène with his *De antiquis ecclesiae ritibus*;[41] the very learned Cardinal Bona,[42] although he deliberately discards all allusions to any mystical meaning, be it to the whiteness of the dawn or the light of candles. One could also mention here Pierre Le Brun, an Oratorian and professor at the seminary of Saint-Magloire, who is not hostile to the principle of allegory but the title of whose major work, published in 1716, expresses his main preoccupation: *Explication littérale, historique et dogmatique des prières et des cérémonies de la messe*.[43] Certainly one of the reasons given, altogether praiseworthy, was apologetic in tone: it was only right, so they said, not to lay oneself open to a charge of obscurantism that might have been expressed by scholars and intellectuals, and moreover not to offend the sensibilities of

39. Above all in his *Histoire et esprit: l'intelligence de l'Écriture d'après Origène*, Théologie, 16 (Paris: Aubier, 1950), then in his *Exégèse médiévale: les quatre sens de l'Écriture*, 4 vols. (Paris: Aubier, 1959–1964).

40. Among other signs for a return of this method of exegesis, there is the abovementioned book by Dahan, *L'exégèse chrétienne de la Bible en Occident médiéval*, and, in a more general way, the plaidoyer for a new balance between searching for the "literal sense" and for the "spritiual sense" in I. de la Potterie (ed.), *L'exégèse chrétienne aujourd'hui*, (Paris: Fayard, 2000).

41. E. Martène, *De antiquis ecclesiae ritibus quatuor* (Rothomagi: Behourt, 1700–1706).

42. G. Bona, *De sacrificio missae* (Rothomagi: Billaine, 1668).

43. P. Le Brun, *Explication littérale, historique et dogmatique des prières et des cérémonies de la messe*, 4 vols. (Paris: Delaulne, 1716–1726); reprinted Farnborough: Gregg, 1970.

"new converts" or of Protestants ready to engage in controversy with Catholics.

Pierre Le Brun, who professes to be as distanced from the excesses of the allegorists as from those of the anti-allegorists, nevertheless devotes a large part of his preface to refuting the rational principles of an anti-allegorist, Dom Claude de Vert, treasurer of Cluny. The latter was considered to be one of the fiercest and most systematic opponents to the mystical interpretation of the liturgy, following his publication of an *Explication simple, littérale et historique des cérémonies de l'Église pour l'instruction des nouveaux convertis.*[44] It should be said that Claude de Vert was not one for nuance: "Having it on hearsay from an educated man, well-versed moreover in antiquity, that originally candles were only ever in a church to illuminate it, I was struck by this notion and set myself on the trail of the natural and historical meanings of ceremonies, and in that moment I understood that it must be the case that all the other practices of the Church will have had their early, material causes and reasons for being instituted."[45] To this Le Brun replied decisively: "The true literal and historical sense of a written word or ceremony is that which the author or institutor had in mind; and it is often a figurative sense that has to do with symbol or mystery."[46] Thus, for example, the liturgy of Holy Saturday employs the paschal candle to proclaim the "Light of Christ," rather than to illuminate the church (particularly since up to the reforms of Pius XII, the *Exsultet* was sung in broad daylight).

Nonetheless, condescension toward the "allegorists" became *de rigeur.* The liturgists of the twentieth century are generally contemptuous of this type of interpretation "designed to satisfy, under the pretext of devotion, a naive and ill-educated clergy."[47] Dom Cabrol writes: "[Durandus] gives symbolic explanations a very exaggerated

---

44. C. de Vert, *Explication simple, littérale et historique des cérémonies de l'Église pour l'instruction des nouveaux convertis,* 4 vols. (Paris: Delaulne, 1706–1713).

45. Cited in Le Brun, *Explication littérale,* XVIII.

46. Le Brun, *Explication littérale,* XXIV.

47. A. Wilmart, "*Expositio missae,*" in *Dictionnaire d'archéologie chrétienne et de liturgie,* vol. V, pt. 1 (Paris: Letouzey et Ané, 1922), 1014–1027. These are the typical comments of an eminent Church historian: "la lettre ne suffit plus; on l'enveloppe de mystère, pour s'édifier à tout prix, avec un zèle que les réalités directes ne satisfont pas et qui, dans ce pieux dérèglement, n'a plus d'autre sauvegarde que la pureté de la foi," ibid., 1022. Amalarius was the first one to blame, because he has "réussi à infester de ces rêveries presque toute la littérature du moyen âge"; ibid., 1024.

prominence. Its principles, which have led certain nineteenth century authors astray, ought only to be accepted with reservations."[48] George Martimort will admit that in one instance and "for once, Durandus avoided falling into artificial allegory": when he makes a parallel between the processional march and the march of the Church Militant toward its heavenly home.[49] One could marshal hundreds of similar citations, which perhaps reveal a reaction against excess, but which fundamentally express a misunderstanding of a whole tradition, which, like it or not, forms an integral part of the history of the liturgy.

Allegory has, as a result, been excluded from academic research and from treatises and textbooks of the 1950s and 1960s; until then it had been popularized for use in seminaries. For them, the *expositiones missae* of Durandus or of Rupert of Deutz were part of the history of medieval thought, but definitely not part of the history of the liturgy, broadly understood as liturgical life and devotions. The blindness of scholars! It is significant that it was J. A. Jungmann who penned the following assertion: "Liturgical commentators of the Middle Ages discovered symbolic meanings in all sorts of details of the church structure; but these were practically all extrinsically attributed meanings—that is, allegory."[50] As though the conception, construction and decoration of abbeys and cathedrals were not caught up in the stream of allegory which bathed a whole society: "thus the peasant knew that his plough was an image of the cross, that the furrows that it traced were the ploughed hearts of the saints; he was not ignorant of the fact that sheaves of wheat were the fruits of contrition; that flour was the multitude of the faithful; that the barn was the kingdom of heaven; and it was the same for most other occupations and trades; in short this method of analogy was for each person a constant invitation to better self-awareness and to pray better."[51]

---

48. Cited in R. Aigrin (ed.), *Liturgia* (Paris: Bloud et Gay, 1930), 1054.

49. A.-G. Martimort (ed.), *L'Église en prière: introduction à la liturgie* (Paris: Desclée, 1961), 635, no. 4. Martimort in fact draws attention to a fine piece of rhetoric (*Rationale* IV, 6); such examples of Durandus' eloquence are rare in his work.

50. J. A. Jungmann, *Public Worship*, trans. C. Howell (London: Challoner Publications, 1957), 69.

51. J.-K. Huysmans, *La Cathédrale* (Paris: Éditions du Rocher, 1992), 438. Huysmans largely draws on the riches of the *Rationale*.

Conclusion

It is appropriate at this point to highlight an unobtrusive but altogether exceptional event, that is to say the publication in 2001 in
France by Cerf and Fleurus, of a reference edition of the Jerusalem
Bible, consisting of notes and key reading referring largely to the
spiritual meaning of Scripture (essentially the allegorical meaning by
which the Old Testament in *types* and *figures* announced the New
Testament). It was revolutionary: notes such as these, relating to the
spiritual sense, were unknown or at any rate did not appear in such
great numbers in the previous editions of the Jerusalem Bible, or in
Canon Osty's bible, nor that of the Pléiade edition of Edouard
Dhorme, or indeed in that of Canon Crampon. The publication of
this Bible by Cerf/Fleurus, fruit of the *lectio divina* of the ancients and
a tool offered to contemporary Christians, confirms that in spite of
everything a real corner has been turned in the biblical world. We
may hope that in the area of the liturgy a similar movement will begin
to show itself and that, for example, missals will be produced that
devote a considerable part of their introductions and commentaries to
a spiritual explanation of the ceremonial of the Church (the symbolism surrounding the sacred vestments, the gestures, implicit and
explicit references to scriptural typology, etc.) by way of a simple and
educative initiation.

The study of spiritual commentaries on scripture, notably
from patristic and medieval sources, also requires a scholarly invest-
ment (to which the works of Père de Lubac and the publications
of *Sources Chrétiennes* have given a serious impetus) as significant as
that of critical exegesis, which would in no way devalue the impact
of the latter.

The *spiritual* commentaries on the divine worship—whether
they are patristic, medieval, or later—are, all things being equal,
worthy of as in-depth an academic study as those relating to the history,
pure and simple, of texts and ceremonies. All the more so, since this
history itself cannot but be a "history of mentalities," within which
mystical exegesis on the one hand and the "creation" of texts and rites
or their customary enactment on the other, are intertwined. Durandus
of Mende, prince of the liturgists, is, like Isidore of Seville and so
many others, at one and the same time annotator and shaper. The

"mystical" side of his work influences the "creative" side, a fact borne
out in the development of his Pontifical: the choice or composition of
the "monitions," prayers, gestures, refer, sometimes deliberately, to
that universe of symbols that his *Rationale*, and the decorative art of
contemporary gothic cathedrals bear witness to. To be true to the
mediaeval world, one cannot ignore the parallel developments and
reciprocal relationships between the symbols encountered in the
rituals of royalty and those in the consecration of bishops or abbots
(or between the chivalric rituals and some of the body language
of the sacraments and sacramentals).

It is important that scholarly interest in allegorical commentaries of the liturgy not only continues the lead that it has begun,
but that it becomes integrated into the history of divine worship
(at least on a level with the history of spirituality and the history of
institutions, among others). It is appropriate that popular works on
the liturgy and its history should make a place for *expositiones missae*
so as to take more account of the liturgical life and piety of the various
eras in history.

Chapter 9

Sacrosanctum Concilium and the Organic Development of the Liturgy

Alcuin Reid

INTRODUCTION

Those who support the continued and extended celebration of the *usus antiquior*, the more ancient liturgical use of the Roman rite, in the Church today have sometimes been portrayed by some as people wanting to go back in time, as people who reject the Second Vatican Council, as people who somehow do not belong in the modern Church. There are no doubt some whose reactions to what followed the Council may have provoked such retorts, but we must never forget the real suffering that lay beneath these reactions. And indeed we must not overlook the obedience and loyalty to the Church that frequently motivated those seeking to "move on" in the "spirit of the Council" as it was called.

Today, however, it is time to say that these somewhat dated and uncritical stances need to be abandoned. Both those promoting the *usus antiquior* and those committed to the rites promulgated after the Council need to look again, and more critically, at the liturgical and historical issues involved in the question of the liturgy after the Council and in our day. Taking an a-historical stance and claiming that no liturgical development is possible, desirable or legitimate beyond October 1962, or claiming that the apex of liturgical enlightenment in Christian history is to be found in the reforms of Pope Paul VI, are, quite frankly, historically and theologically untenable positions.

It is in this context that we need to look again at the Council's call for liturgical development. For development—*organic development*—is part of the reality of Catholic liturgy in the tradition of the Church.[1] To be committed to the Church's liturgical tradition one must accept the possibility of the organic development of the liturgy, indeed at times its desirability.

Accordingly, I wish to examine what the Second Vatican Council's Constitution on the Sacred Liturgy intended when it spoke of the organic development of the liturgy, to look at what authoritative commentators made of this at the time, to look at one key example of its later interpretation and at two related questions. In doing so it is my hope to facilitate further critical discussion of the issue of the historical legitimacy within Catholic liturgical tradition of the post-conciliar rites. In no way am I questioning their validity, nor am I in any way seeking to undermine the real pastoral value and efficacy of the continued use of the pre-conciliar rites today. I am simply seeking a better historical understanding of these critical issues in order better to inform our discussions of what is or is not to be done with the Catholic liturgy today and in the future.

SACROSANCTUM CONCILIUM

Chapter I of *Sacrosanctum Concilium* lays down "general principles for the restoration and promotion of the sacred liturgy." These principles were approved by the Council Fathers on December 7, 1962, at the end of the Council's first session. They constitute, therefore, the keys that unlock the meaning of the Constitution's call for specific reforms called for in its later articles which were finally approved by the Fathers in the second session in 1963.

The Council's fundamental principle for the reform of liturgical rites is without doubt found in article 14's insistence "that all the faithful may be brought to take that full, intelligent, active part in liturgical celebrations which the nature of the liturgy itself requires, and which in virtue of their baptism, is the right and duty of the

---

1. Cf. A. Reid, *The Organic Development of the Liturgy* (San Francisco: Ignatius Press, 2nd edition, 2005).

Christian people." This was no innovation: the Liturgical Movement, itself drawing upon many earlier efforts, had promoted this partici- pation assiduously for the preceding half century.[2] Of course we know that, in English, the word "active" poorly translates the meaning of the Latin *actuosa*, which speaks primarily of that internal and contemplative participation of mind and heart in the liturgical rites rather than an activist concern for everyone to be doing externally observable things as frequently as possible.[3] One can find nothing other than sound, traditional Catholic spirituality—endorsed by many pre-conciliar popes—in the Council's call for actual participation in the liturgy.

Sacrosanctum Concilium envisaged that this reform was pri- marily to be achieved by means of the improvement of the liturgical education and formation of the clergy and the laity: articles 15-19 call for liturgical education for all according to their particular state in life, most particularly the clergy.

These calls for actual participation and for widespread liturgical formation are the first liturgical "decisions" of the Council and, I submit, we shall read the rest of *Sacrosanctum Concilium* cor- rectly only if we give them this primacy. Thus formation in "the spirit and power of the liturgy" (as this phrase was understood in 1962)[4] to bring about actual, contemplative participation in the sacred liturgy is fundamental to the liturgical renewal of the Church as desired by the Council. To loose sight of these aims could not be without severe consequences and indeed, any ritual reform not underpinned by the desired formation might well be said to risk being built on sand (cf. Matthew 7:26–27), just as an activist interpretation of *participatio actuosa* risks the adopting the error of Martha to the exclusion of the indispensable contemplative role of her sister Mary (cf. Luke 10:48–32).[5]

---

2. Cf. Reid, *The Organic Development*, 359 for a list of references. See also: *Liturgy, Participation and Sacred Music: The Proceedings of the Ninth International Colloquium of Historical, Canonical and Theological Studies on the Roman Catholic Liturgy, Paris 2003* (London: CIEL UK, 2006).

3. Cf. J. Ratzinger, *The Spirit of the Liturgy*, trans. J. Saward (San Francisco: Ignatius Press, 2000), 171–177.

4. Cf. SC, 14: *spiritu et virtute Liturgiae*. One wonders whether the allusion to Romano Guardini's seminal work *The Spirit of the Liturgy*, trans. A. Lane (London: Sheed & Ward, 1935), is more than coincidental.

5. Cf. Joseph Cardinal Ratzinger's homily "Mary and Martha" in A. Reid (ed.), *Looking Again at the Question of the Liturgy with Cardinal Ratzinger: Proceedings of the 2001 Fontgombault*

Of course, *Sacrosanctum Concilium* did call for specific ritual reforms. It did so in the context of the desired renewal of liturgical formation. And it did so having enunciated the fundamental principle for such ritual reform in article 23:

> That sound tradition may be retained, and yet the way remain open to legitimate progress, careful investigation is always to be made into each part of the liturgy which is to be revised. This investigation should be theological, historical, and pastoral. Also the general laws governing the structure and meaning of the liturgy must be studied in conjunction with the experience derived from recent liturgical reforms and from the indults conceded to various places. Finally, there must be no innovations unless the good of the Church genuinely and certainly requires them; and care must be taken that any new forms adopted should in some way grow organically from forms already existing.
>
> As far as possible, notable differences between the rites used in adjacent regions must be carefully avoided.

How are we to interpret the intention of this article with regard to liturgical reform?

We should observe that before and during the Council this article attracted no controversy: the text is identical in the draft schema on the liturgy drawn up in late 1961 or early 1962 for the Preparatory Commission and in the schema approved by Pope John XXIII and submitted for the examination of the Council Fathers in October of 1962.

At the Council only one emendation was proposed, by the German Bishop of Essen, Franz Hengsbach, which sought to ensure that the text was sufficiently open to the possibility of new ritual forms. Bishop Hengsbach cited an expression of the Jesuit Cardinal Bea—that no other door be shut (in this context, on liturgical development)—as a justifying principle for his proposal.[6] However the Conciliar Liturgical Commission (let us remember that Father Bugnini was not a member of this) replied:

Liturgical Conference (Farnborough: St. Michael's Abbey Press, 2003), 13–15.

6. Cited by Bishop Hengsbach: *Ne aliqua porta claudatur.* The full text of his written intervention may be found in F. Gil Hellín, *Concilii Vaticani II Synopsis: Constitutio de Sacra Liturgia Sacrosanctum Concilium* (Vatican City: Liberia Editrice Vaticana, 2003), 593–594.

We considered an emendation proposed by one of the Fathers, which went like this: "that [the] new forms which arise, be organically joined to those which already exist." We decided that this change was useless, because the text of the schema is sufficient to suggest that new rites can be produced, when [since] it says "innovations" and "new forms"; and it [the schema] does not close any door, but better inculcates the fact that continuity must be preserved in evolution, and does not prevent skillfully inventing things.[7]

The Latin *inventis* used here refers more to recovering things as article 50 would say of reinstating certain practices that had fallen into disuse, rather than innovating *ex nihilo*.

The Council's Liturgical Commission did, however, in response to Bishop Hengsbach's proposal, tighten up the text of the Constitution with the addition of the words *et certa* ("and certainly") so that the crucial phrase of article 23 read "there must be no innovations unless the good of the Church genuinely *and certainly* requires them." The Commission stated that "genuinely" (or "truly"—the Latin is *vera*) did not suffice on its own.[8] Thus amended, it formed part of the text of chapter one voted on and approved in December of 1962 and duly promulgated on December 4, 1963.

I do not think that we should underestimate the importance of article 23 or indeed of the fact that it attracted no controversy on the Council floor, for while article 14 states the overall aim of the reform (actual participation), while articles 15-19 indicate the means by which this reform is to be effected (liturgical participation), and while other later articles speak about specific reforms, article 23 presents the parameters within which specific reforms must remain. That these parameters were utterly uncontroversial and were in fact tightened as a result of their consideration at the Council is a testament to the Council Fathers' understanding that, yes, the liturgy is capable of reform, but that such reform must be an organic development and not a radical innovation.

---

7. "*Praeterea a nobis expensa est aliqua emendatio ab uno Patre proposita, quae sic sonabat:* ' *ut novae formae, quae oriuntur, cum iam extantibus organice coniungantur.' Censuimus inutilem esse hanc mutationem, quia textus schematis sufficit ad suggerendam [sic] novos ritus produci posse, dicendo 'innovationes' et 'novae formae,' nec ullam portam claudit, sed melius continuitatem in evolutione inculcat servandam et ab artificiosis inventis non praecavet*"; Gil Hellín, *Constitutio de Sacra Liturgia*, 77. Translation: G. Di Pippo.

8. "*Post verbum* vera *addatur* et certa *quia non sufficeret* vera"; Gil Hellín, *Constitutio de Sacra Liturgia*, 77.

A closer look at the whole text of article 23 will illustrate this. The article firstly states its aim: of "sound tradition" being maintained while enabling "legitimate progress." These utterly acceptable intentions form the purpose (as the *ut* clause of the Latin indicates) for the "theological, historical, and pastoral" investigation of "each part of the liturgy which is to be revised," for which the article calls. Such investigations and any possible consequent revisions are, therefore, to maintain sound tradition and be open to legitimate progress.

Furthermore, such reforms are to take account of the laws of the structure and the spirit of the liturgy, and the "experience derived from recent liturgical reforms and from the indults conceded to various places," namely, the reforms of the 1950s and early 1960s. This places talk of ritual reform in a clear historical context. While some liturgical reforms of the previous decade may well have been infected with questionable principles, and while it is true that no two liturgists are ever likely to agree on the best way to develop or reform the liturgy, overall, the reforms of the decade prior to the Council cannot be said to have constituted a substantial rupture in Catholic Western liturgical tradition.[9] Therefore one may assert that when article 23 imposes the condition of taking this specific historical context into account, it does not envisage itself as authorizing anything more than the continuation of gradual and organic development of the liturgy as begun by Pope Pius XII.

This sentiment is made perfectly clear in the conclusion of the article which, as we have seen, is clearly restrictive in its requirement that there be "no innovations unless the good of the Church genuinely and certainly requires them" and that "any new forms adopted should in some way grow organically from forms already existing."

Article 23 is, then, a carefully balanced and nuanced text. Read in context it does not write a blank check for radical liturgical reform. The Fathers of the Council simply did not intend to do this and, whatever of any later interpretations of the Constitution, it is not possible historically to assert that this article as approved by the Fathers in 1962 and 1963 is capable of authorizing anything other than a moderate, prudent, and traditional liturgical reform.

9. Cf. Reid, *The Organic Development*, 145–301.

COMMENTARIES ON *SACROSANCTUM CONCILIUM*

This becomes even clearer when we look at expert commentaries on *Sacrosanctum Concilium* published in the wake of its promulgation.

An authoritative commentary on the Constitution published in 1964, the English edition of which credits Father Bugnini as one its editors, confirms the essentially conservative intention of this article. In it Msgr. Salvator Famoso, Chancellor of the diocese of Catania and a consulter to the Preparatory Conciliar Commission and to the post-conciliar *Consilium*, writes:

> Reforms should correspond to the traditional laws of the structure and mind of the Liturgy. They should flow organically from the forms or rites which already exist, lest they be so different from present forms that they resemble new creations. There is, then, to be a true progress from what has gone before. This rule is of the greatest importance, particularly lest an adaptation to the genius and traditions of various peoples should result in the institution or creation of new liturgical families independently of the Roman rite. . . .
>
> Innovations should be such as required by a true and certain usefulness for the Church lest, from mere love of novelty, sacred rites venerated and used for centuries by our forefathers be needlessly rejected or the Sacred Liturgy be treated as if it were merely a field for experimentation.[10]

Also writing in 1964, the French liturgist Pierre Jounel, a member of the Preparatory Conciliar Commission for the Liturgy and later a dedicated protagonist of the rites promulgated by Pope Paul VI, commented:

> The Church today does not have to invent the forms of its rites. This rite was born in the apostolic community and it developed itself continuously until our days. Any progress should therefore consist in enriching the tradition. It is to assure the compliance of the liturgical restoration to this essential law that the Constitution describes the process to be followed in the works that have to be undertaken. . . .
>
> The present rites have been in use for at least four centuries, for the Tridentine books have not been substantially modified. Therefore, one

---

10. *Constitutio de Sacra Liturgia Cum Commentario*, Biblioteca "Ephemerides liturgicae," sectio pastoralis 2 (Rome: Edizioni Liturgiche, 2nd edition, 1964), 254–255. The English is taken from A. Bugnini–C. Braga (ed.), *The Commentary on the Constitution and on the Instruction on the Sacred Liturgy*, trans. V. P. Mallon (New York: Benziger Brothers, 1965), 87–88.

should not modify them just for pleasure of changing them, but only if such a modification is really and certainly useful. In any case, never should this reform appear as a break with the past. It consists of a "somewhat organic development" which gives birth to new forms from forms that already exist. This is very important from a pastoral point of view. It is essential for the Christian people that the transition between the past and the future should be smooth. The new liturgical forms should never appear as a revolution of the rites, but as a realization of a more perfect form of the public prayer of the Church. This is no less important from the perspective of the very nature of the liturgy. The liturgy is life, and life does not ordinarily propagate itself by abrupt mutations.[11]

In May of 1964, the American canonist, Frederick McManus, a member of both the Preparatory and the Conciliar Liturgical Commissions, wrote in the North American journal *Worship:*

To a certain extent, the limitations set down in Article 23 affect the norm of pastoral usefulness set elsewhere as the chief determining factor in liturgical reform. In other words, the reform does not envision the creation of entirely new rites merely because they seem to satisfy the needs of the present time, but rather an organic development of existing forms. On the one hand, such a rule is justified by respect for the goodness of past devel-

---

11. "L'Eglise n'a pas à inventer aujourd'hui les formes de son culte. Celui-ci a pris naissance dans la communauté apostolique et il s'est développé sans rupture jusqu'à nous. Tout progrès doit donc consister dans un approfondissement de la tradition. C'est pour assurer la fidélité de la restauration liturgique à cette loi essentielle que la Constitution expose le processus à suivre dans les travaux que l'on doit entreprendre. . . . Les rites actuels sont en usage depuis au moins quatre siècles, car les livres tridentins n'ont pas subi de modifications substantielles. On ne les modifiera donc pas pour le plaisir de changer, mais seulement si la révision de tel ou tel est vraiment et certainement utile. En tout cas, jamais la réforme ne devra apparaître comme une rupture avec le passé. Il s'agit d'un *développement en quelque sort organique*, qui fait jaillir les formes nouvelles de formes déjà existantes. Cela est très important du point de vue pastoral. Il est indispensable que le passage entre le passé et l'avenir se fasse sans heurt pour le peuple chrétien. Les formes liturgiques nouvelles ne doivent pas apparaître comme une révolution dans le culte, mais comme l'épanouissement d'une forme plus parfaite de la prière publique de l'Eglise. Cela est non moins important du point du vue de la nature même de la liturgie. Celle-ci est vie, et la vie ne se propage pas d'ordinaire pas mutations brusques." P. Jounel, "Commentaire complet de la Constitution conciliaire sur la Liturgie," in *La Maison-Dieu*, 77 (1964), 3–221, at 47–48. See also M.-D. Bouyer, "La Réforme de la Liturgie: La Constitution de Vatican II sur la Liturgie," in *Notes de Pastorale Liturgique* 48 (January 1964), 1–6, at 2: "Mais surtout—précision de la plus haute importance quant à l'esprit de la réforme—toute adaptation doit savoir conjuguer deux exigences différents: un progrès, mais aussi une fidélité à la tradition."

opments. On the other hand, it guarantees a better evolution of the Liturgy for the future.[12]

Let us repeat a key sentence from Msgr. McManus: ". . . to a certain extent, the limitations set down in article 23 affect the norm of pastoral usefulness set elsewhere as the chief determining factor in liturgical reform." In other words, the stipulations of article 23 are clearly seen as imposing limits to reforms that might otherwise be desired or thought to be pastorally expedient.

In the same year the French Oratorian, Louis Bouyer, who held no official role in the reform until he was appointed to the post-conciliar *Consilium* in 1966, explained the authority the Fathers of the Council had in respect of the reform of the liturgy:

> The apostolic authority of the bishops has been given them, not to destroy, not to alter in any way what has been done by the Apostles once and for all, but to keep it and to keep it alive. In other words, they only have authority to alter those things which, through a secular evolution, no longer express and achieve what the Apostles intended. They can modify the Liturgy only to maintain its living authenticity under altered circumstances.[13]

However, Bouyer also explains how the Council intended this authority to be used:

> Tradition is not opposed to progress, but is the living principle of a development faithful to the seed, however altered may be the soil where it has to rise, flower and fructify. And the Council is careful to make it perfectly clear, in opposition to all false reforms—which start only from abstract ideas—that tradition cannot be maintained either by unprecedented innovations or by artificial archaisms. All healthy progress, as well as all true reformations, can only be effected by an organic process. One can neither add wholly foreign elements to the Liturgy from the outside, nor make it regress to some idealized vision of the past. One can, and sometimes should, either prune or enrich the Liturgy, but he should always keep in

---

12. F. R. McManus, "The Constitution on the Liturgy Commentary, Part One" in *Worship* 38 (1964), 314–74, at 339; also in his *Sacramental Liturgy* (New York: Herder and Herder, 1967), 33. In the previous year he had written: "Of course, to be sound and fruitful, both liturgical education/promotion and liturgical reform must be gradual, prudent, and careful. But the twentieth-century liturgical movement is too old and too wise to indulge in half measures or compromise proposals"; "The Future: Its Hope and Difficulties," in F. R. McManus (ed.), *The Revival of the Liturgy* (New York: Herder and Herder, 1963), 203–24, at 211.

13. L. Bouyer, *The Liturgy Revived: A Doctrinal Commentary of the Conciliar Constitution on the Liturgy* (London: Libra, 1965), 54.

touch with the living organism which has been transmitted to us by our forefathers, and he should always respect the laws of its structure and of its growth. No innovation, therefore, can be accepted simply for the purpose of doing something new, and no restoration can be the product of a yen for romantic escape into a dead past. The continuity, the homogeneity of Tradition in this case must be retained by authority as the *sine qua non* condition for the perpetuated life of a reality which is not merely immensely sacred but even the life of the mystical body.[14]

The commentary on article 23 by the renowned Jesuit liturgist, Father Josef Andreas Jungmann, originally published in 1966, is similarly clear and insists on the conservation of liturgical tradition. Father Jungmann was a *peritus* on the Conciliar liturgical commission, a consulter to the *Consilium* and a member of the *Consilium*'s "study group" number 10 charged with examining the reform of the *Ordo Missae*. Of article 23 he writes:

> In article 23 the ideals which must serve as a norm for the reform of the Liturgy were described. They are the same which had been held by all prudent supporters of the cause of liturgical revival. The reform of the Liturgy cannot be a revolution. It must try to grasp the real meaning and the basic structure of the traditional rites and, making prudent use of existing deposits, build on them organically in the direction indicated by the pastoral needs of a living liturgy. The [Conciliar Liturgical] Commission further strengthened the demand of the Schema, that in each case there should be the prospect of real good for the Church, by adding "and certainly."[15]

I must add a reservation here: Jungmann's desire to "grasp the real meaning and the basic structure" of the rites and his willingness to give weight to the "pastoral needs of a living liturgy" are, if given disproportionate weight, capable of underpinning a reconstruction of the liturgy on antiquarian or pastorally expedient lines. Nevertheless, writing here in 1966, he is writing of development, not "revolution."[16]

---

14. Bouyer, *The Liturgy Revived*, 54–55.

15. J. A. Jungmann, "Constitution on the Sacred Liturgy," in H. Vorgrimler (ed.), *Commentary on the Documents of Vatican II*, vol. I, trans. L. Adolphus (London–New York: Burns & Oates Herder and Herder, 1967), 1–87, at 20.

16. For a critique of Jungmann's principles of liturgical reform cf. Reid, *The Organic Development*, 164–172.

What do these five contemporary and authoritative commentaries teach us about the Council's intention for liturgical reform?[17] I think the answer is perfectly clear: there may be enrichment, there may be growth, there may even be some prudent pruning, but, the living organism that is the sacred liturgy received from tradition is not to become the cut-and-paste plaything of scholars, pastors or other experts.

They also teach us how to read *Sacrosanctum Concilium*'s later calls for specific liturgical reforms. More importantly, they furnish criteria with which we can judge the implementation of these reforms. Yes, the Council wanted an increase in the use of the vernacular for pastoral benefit (cf. article 34) but in no way did it want the vernacularization of the liturgy. But as we know, with very, very few exceptions, the liturgy of the Roman rite today labors under a worldwide vernacularization which eclipses the sacred language that is an integral part of its tradition.

Yes, the Council called for a reform of the *Ordo Missae* (cf. articles 50 ff.). But before voting on this article of the Constitution the Fathers Council were assured by the Council's Liturgical Commission in the following words: "*Hodiernus Ordo Missae, qui decursu saeculorum succrevit, retinendus est.*"[18] I translate: "The current *Ordo Missae*, which has grown up in the course of the centuries, is to be retained." What honest historian who puts the pre-conciliar *Ordo Missae* beside that promulgated in 1969 can say that this seemingly incredible assurance was honored?

Certainly, Chapter V of the Constitution called for a renewal of the liturgical year and of the calendar of saints. It did not, however, call for abolition of the season of Septuagesima or of the most ancient octave of Pentecost. Nor did it authorize the radical and grossly pastorally insensitive de- and re-construction of the calendar of saints that in fact took place.

We could go on and look at other reforms called for by the Council—and indeed much scholarly work remains to be done in carefully studying each element of the post-conciliar reform. Nevertheless, I submit, that if we use the criteria given us by

---

17. Curiously, the commentary edited by Austin Flannery, OP, passes over article 23; cf. *Vatican II: The Liturgy Constitution* (Dublin: Scepter, 1964).

18. Gil Hellín, *Constitutio de Sacra Liturgia*, 150.

Sacrosanctum Concilium in article 23, we cannot but come to see that there are clear indications that the reform that followed the Council exceeded the legitimate and traditional boundaries of organic development it itself imposed.

Some Opinions from Fathers of the Council

This is not simply the judgment of traditional liturgists. Ten years ago, I sought the opinions on this matter of some of the then remaining Fathers of the Council. Asked what he thought of the Council's discussion of the sacred liturgy, the Australian-born Bishop Ignatius Doggett, a Friar Minor and Emeritus Bishop of Aitape, New Guinea, spoke plainly. He recalled the conciliar debate on the sacred Liturgy as:

> Horrible: if we judge the debate on the liturgy as we have it today. Very few bishops would be proud to say they had a hand in it. Communion in the hand was never mentioned in the debate, neither was the word Table (MENSA) to take the place of ALTAR—place of sacrifice . . . . In my opinion the Debate on the Liturgy has been hijacked. The Council was . . . to *reform*, not to *change completely*.[19]

Another Father of the Council, Bishop Nicola Maria Agnozzi, a Conventual Franciscan and auxiliary of the diocese of Ndola in Zambia at the time of the Council recalled that "changes were asked if necessary but nothing drastic: they came later in the commissions from pressure groups."[20] He continued:

> There are reasons to believe that the *Consilium* went beyond what was contained in the decree. The determinate presence of some Cardinals and/ or their men in the *Consilium* is believed to be behind some of the changes brought about. . . .
>
> I presume they thought they were faithful even when they interpreted the principles not taking into consideration the established traditions— some of them very popular—of the Church. It is significant that the competent Congregation had to issue three Instructions on how the S.C. Constitution was to be applied and observed. . . .

---

19. Sic. Bishop Ignatius Doggett, ofm, manuscript response to questionnaire: received June 1, 1996.

20. Typescript response to questionnaire: received June 19, 1996. It should be noted that Bishop Agnozzi attended the first, third, and fourth sessions of the Council, but not the second. He therefore did not vote on *Sacrosanctum Concilium* on December 4, 1963.

I don't think the *Consilium* did always take into consideration the wishes of the Council in their decisions; there were some decisions introduced in the final reports that had not been discussed in the plenary assemblies according to what I have been told.[21]

No less than the recently deceased Argentinian Archbishop of Cordoba, Raúl Francisco Cardinal Primatesta, Bishop of San Rafael during the Council, recalled:

I think that the post-conciliar *Consilium* for liturgical reform was looking to keep to the decreed conciliar line, but . . . *in various places* they permitted or made or introduced experiences of the *time* or went further away from the decree and spirit of the Council.

I think that the *Consilium* suffered from the influence of partial tendencies or interpretations and division amongst themselves about the conciliar decree.[22]

Even the liberal Franz Cardinal König, Emeritus Archbishop of Vienna, articulated a reservation:

It was the concern and the intention of the Council to give a "right of domicile" to the native tongue beside the Latin language. This led the way that Latin was abandoned in many countries and the native language only was used. At present Latin should be stressed and be more used in the Western world. I personally find it important that Latin must not be eliminated completely from the liturgy, but that as a sign of international solidarity and for reasons of tradition—Latin should be granted a special place particularly at festive occasions.[23]

The centenarian Emeritus Bishop of Grand Island, Nebraska, Bishop John L. Paschang, argued:

Altogether too much time was spent on the discussion of the sacred liturgy. The desired reforms could have been made by the Holy See. Pius XII made some changes in the liturgy. Other changes could have been made

---

21. Ibid.

22. Typescript response to questionnaire: dated February 22, 1996. "Creo que el Consejo Postconciliar para la Reforma Litúrgica buscó mantenerse en la linea del Decreto Conciliar, pero reitero que *en diversos lugares* se permitieron, o se hicieron o se introdujeron experiencias al *margen* o más allá del Decreto y espiritu Conciliar. Creo que el Consejo padeció la influencia de tendencias o interpretaciones parciales, y contrarias entre si, del Decreto Conciliar."

23. Typescript letter: February 1996.

with the debates in the council. The present ferment and confusion in matters liturgical could have been avoided.[24]

He continued:

In my opinion the innovations were a mistake. We should have retained the substance of the former Mass. "By their fruits you shall know them." Church attendance has declined. Few people . . . go to the sacrament of Reconciliation. People are losing their faith. Almost 50 percent of the faithful no longer believe in the Real Presence, etc. etc.[25]

Of course, these are anecdotal opinions, but they are the opinions of Fathers of the Council.[26] Academically, we must say that they are by no means conclusive: unfortunately, bishops tending to be older men, most Fathers of the Council had gone to their particular judgment by the time scholars became interested in asking such questions. So while we cannot assert that these opinions are historically conclusive, I think we can say that it is true that some Fathers were concerned that the post-conciliar reform went beyond their intentions.

AN EXAMPLE

By way of example I would like to look briefly at one key example of the implementation of the liturgical reform: the introduction of three (and indeed subsequently many more) new Eucharistic Prayers into the Roman rite. The issues involved here are immense and again deserve a thorough study (here, as in many areas of the post-conciliar reform there is an enormous scope for doctoral research). But before entering into this minefield I must repeat my clarification that whatever their historical or traditional caliber, the new Eucharistic prayers authorized by Pope Paul VI are valid.

But this is not enough. For article 23 of *Sacrosanctum Concilium* does not read "that sound tradition may be retained, and

---

24. Typescript response to questionnaire: received February 2, 1996.

25. Sic. Ibid.

26. For a further discussion see my paper "The Fathers of Vatican II and the Revised Mass: Results of a Survey," delivered at the Research Institute for Catholic Liturgy Conference at The Inn at St. John's in Plymouth, Michigan, U.S.A., June 4, 2006, published in *Antiphon* 10 (2006), 171–190.

yet the way remain open to legitimate progress, *including substantial innovation.*" And no matter what one thinks of the texts of these prayers themselves, there is simply no way that one can argue that the Council intended this reform, that the good of the Church genuinely and certainly required them or that the texts promulgated by Pope Paul VI grew organically from forms already existing. Furthermore, this reform effectively placed a number of cuckoo eggs in the midst of the Roman liturgy which have, as the years have passed, all but displaced that anchor of substantial unity in the Roman rite, that monument of liturgical tradition that is the Roman Canon.

Having said this, it will come as no surprise to say that I disagree with Archbishop Bugnini's belief, stated in his memoirs, that:

> In the new anaphoras, more than elsewhere, care has been taken to be true to article 23 of the Constitution on the Sacred Liturgy, which urges that "sound tradition" and "legitimate progress" be combined.[27]

At the root of my disagreement with Archbishop Bugnini is his concept of liturgical tradition. He does not regard the sacred liturgy as an objective organism handed on in tradition and only modified with the profound respect for the tradition according to that principle we term organic development. He regards liturgical tradition as something to be rediscovered through historical scholarship, edited according to current pastoral exigencies and posited juridically by authority regardless of what has been handed down in history. And this is precisely what we have in the juridical positing of the new Eucharistic Prayers.

LITURGICAL POSITIVISM

This liturgical positivism is a crucial factor in understanding the reform following the Council. For while article 23 of *Sacrosanctum Concilium* gave clear parameters for future reform, once it became clear that the Supreme Pontiff was prepared juridically to posit reforms that were neither called for by the Council nor that respected the limits laid down in article 23, there were very few limits to what Archbishop Bugnini and his experts could and did indeed bring about.

27. A. Bugnini, *The Reform of the Liturgy 1948–1975*, trans. M. J. O'Connell (Collegeville, Minnesota: The Liturgical Press, 1990), 455.

Thus, the virtue of obedience, particularly the practice of its uncritical exercise, meant that questionable prudential reforms posited by legitimate authority were accepted by the Church. John Carmel Cardinal Heenan, the only cardinal or bishop worldwide successfully to gain an indult from Pope Paul VI for the continued use of the traditional missal in his diocese, illustrates the depth of this obedience in a letter to a distressed laywoman in 1970:

> I thoroughly understand how you feel about the new Mass. There are thousands that feel bitter that the old beauty has faded. . . .
>
> I probably suffer more than you because for forty years I have offered Mass in the old rite every day but I must not pretend to know better than the Holy Father. It is he who has authorized the new rite.[28]

When we have a Father of the Council writing thus, I think we may say that we have travelled a long way from the reform envisaged by article 23 of the Constitution on the Sacred Liturgy.

Professor Duffy reminds us in his contribution to this volume that we are blessed indeed to live in the pontificate of a pope who understands acutely the problem of this liturgical positivism. We must pray earnestly that His Holiness continues to be given light and strength further to address it.

ORGANIC PROGRESSION

Post-conciliar liturgical positivism has itself given birth to an alarming principle of liturgical reform called "organic progression." Father Anscar Chupungco, its principal exponent, explained in 1990:

> The organic progression of the liturgy may be described as the work of supplementing and completing, when necessary, the shape of the liturgy established by the Liturgy Constitution and the *editio typica* of the liturgical books. It accomplishes this by rereading these documents, with the purpose of supplying what they lack or putting to completion what they only partially and imperfectly state.
>
> Organic progression is what its component words say: it is both organic and progressive. It is progressive because it operates through two dynamics that bring about a development in the shape of the liturgy. These dynamics are supplementation, whereby new elements are inserted into the liturgy,

---

28. March 19, 1970: Archive of the Archdiocese of Westminster.

and continuance, which is a sequel to the work begun by the council and the Holy See. It is organic because it results in a new shape that is coherent with the basic intention of the liturgical documents and, on a wider breadth, with the nature and tradition of Christian worship. Such coherence guarantees the correct or proper use of the dynamics of supplementation and continuance. It serves as an assurance that the new forms adopted are not extraneous or foreign to the spirit of the conciliar reform or at least to a longstanding liturgical tradition.

In short, organic progression is a way of saying that the new liturgical reforms should have been there all along, and that if the liturgical rite were drawn up today, they would surely be part of it.[29]

Notice that Father Chupungco speaks of such developments being coherent with *Christian* worship and not extraneous at least to the *spirit* of the conciliar reform or at least to *a* longstanding liturgical tradition. The Roman rite as handed on in tradition does not have priority here. It is but one resource amongst many from which one may draw.

Father Chupungco goes so far as to claim that this concept of organic progression was "present not only in the . . . text of SC 23 but also on the mind of the conciliar commission which drafted it."[30] I beg to differ. While there is a great deal that could and should be said about this principle of organic progression, let it suffice to say that *Sacrosanctum Concilium* did not intend to provide employment to generations of liturgists engaged in reconstructing the liturgy according to the desires of passing generations. No, *Sacrosanctum Concilium* authorized a limited reform within the context outlined above, and we have the testimony of Bouyer, Jungmann, Jounel, McManus, Famosa, as well as that of others, to assure us of the probity of this interpretation.[31]

Conclusion

It is in understanding that context, it is by identifying and defending the true nature of *Sacrosanctum Concilium*'s call for an organic

---

29. A. Chupungco, "Inculturation and the Organic Progression of the Liturgy," in *Ecclesia Orans* 7 (1990), 7–21, at 9–10.

30. Chupungco, *Inculturation,* 11.

31. Preeminently the later writings of the Council *peritus* Father Joseph Ratzinger.

development of the liturgy, and in recognizing that this was substantially exceeded, that we underline our insistence that the liturgical reform be looked at again and with some urgency. For the Roman rite has suffered severe damage and its repair is urgently required.

None of us, not even our beloved Holy Father, can know with absolute certainty the best way of carrying out that repair. But as the years go on and more people seek to celebrate the new rites in a manner consistent with Catholic worship, while others talk of reforming the reform, and others still come to savor the splendor and value of the more ancient use of the liturgy of the Roman rite, a solution, please God, draws nearer.

History will record the answer to our malaise. We, in daring to do as much as we are able in response to this crisis, through our studies and most importantly by our worthy celebration of the sacred liturgy, may be privileged to be part of that answer.

Chapter 10

Roman Liturgy and Popular Piety: The "Devotional Revolution" in Irish Catholicism

Sheridan Gilley

Most Catholics in the British Isles in the modern period, indeed many Catholics in the English-speaking world, have been of Irish birth or descent, and so I wish to begin with some reflections on the recent historiography of the Catholic Church in nineteenth-century Ireland. In 1972, the veteran historian of Irish Catholicism, Emmet Larkin, wrote an iconoclastic article in the *American Historical Review*, advancing *inter alia* two important ideas.[1] The first, which drew upon the then unpublished research of another scholar, David Miller,[2] was that the norm of religious practice for Ireland for most of the twentieth century, in which over 90 percent of the Catholic population attended Mass every Sunday, was a comparatively modern phenomenon, and that as recently as the 1830s and 1840s, the percentage of Catholics who went to Mass every week had been much lower, perhaps as little as 30 percent in much of northern and western Ireland, where parishes were large and priests were few. The more recent state of things had been partly the consequence of the Irish Famine of 1846–1849, in which more than a million people had died and more than a million had emigrated, largely to North America.

---

1. E. Larkin, "The Devotional Revolution in Ireland, 1850–75," in *The American Historical Review* 77 (1972), 625–652.

2. D. W. Miller, "Irish Catholicism and the Great Famine," in *The Journal of Social History* 9 (1975), 81–98.

The Famine bore most lightly upon the prosperous middling farmer class in eastern Ireland which sent its sons and daughters into the Church; it bore most heavily on the poorest, the rural laborers and smallholders or cottiers of Connaught and Ulster, among whom regular church attendance was weakest. Because of the Famine, there was a state of things in Ireland which was rare elsewhere in Europe: a still burgeoning population in 1840 entered upon more than a century of decline, converting a low ratio of priests and religious to an expanding population before 1840, into an improving ratio of clergy to a declining population after it.

Larkin's second principle was just as startling as the first, and this was the transformation of the character of Irish Catholicism itself, a point made in other ways by historians like Sean Connolly.[3] Irish Catholics were undoubtedly Catholics by conviction before the Famine, but they were Catholics of a particular kind. The religion of much of the Irish-speaking population was more based upon prayer in the home and upon such extra-ecclesiastical foci as holy wells and patterns or pilgrimages to ancient shrines in a sacred landscape, as upon the Mass and devotions in the chapel. Weddings and wakes were religious occasions, but could erupt into an indecency or violence beyond the reach of the clergy. At the pilgrimage to Glendalough, an ancient Irish holy site near Dublin, immense crowds assembled around tents and booths: there was "Dancing, drinking, thimble-rigging, prick-o'-the-loop, and other amusements," and the massed ranks of devout young and aged penitents walked their rounds saying their prayers, before the faction fighting between rival groups and villages began in the afternoon.[4] In short, bar a few broken heads, a good time was had by all. In the west especially there was still the custom of stations, of Masses said in private houses, while popular folklore retained pre-Christian elements untouched by the Reformation or Counter-Reformation. The trauma of the Famine, however, showed that this folk magic did not work, and delivered the *coup-de-grace* to the older native culture, as to the language which embodied it, and what then occurred was a "Devotional Revolution."

---

3. S. J. Connolly, *Priests and People in Pre-Famine Ireland 1780–1845* (Dublin: Gill and Macmillan, 1982).

4. See M. P. Carroll, *Irish Pilgrimage: Holy Wells and Popular Catholic Devotion* (Baltimore and London: Johns Hopkins University Press, 1999), 115.

This was built round Sunday Mass attendance and centered on ever more lavishly decorated shrine chapels that were under clerical control. David Miller has recently suggested that the cycle of occasional sacramental conformity common before the Famine fitted in with the seasonal patterns of, for example, the movements of herds between highland and lowland pastures; regular Sunday Mass attendance harmonized with the new weekly commercial rituals of the market town.[5] In a more directly historical explanation, Larkin especially associated the "Devotional Revolution" with the long archiepiscopate at Armagh and then Dublin of the neo-Ultramontane Paul Cardinal Cullen, Rome's man in Ireland, the first Irish cardinal, between 1850 and 1878, and with his imposition of a firmer Ultramontane discipline on the Irish Church, and his exorcism of the elusive shadow of Irish Gallicanism.

Change there was, and perhaps the most dramatic aspect of Larkin's richly illustrated article was his descriptive account of the "Devotional Revolution," drawing on practices which would be still familiar to any old-fashioned Catholic. "The new devotions," he wrote,

> were mainly of Roman origin and included the rosary, 40 hours, perpetual adoration, novenas, blessed altars, *Via Crucis*, benediction, vespers, devotion to the Sacred Heart and to the Immaculate Conception, jubilees, triduums, pilgrimages, shrines, processions, and retreats. These devotional exercises, moreover, were organized in order to communalize and regularize practice under a spiritual director and included sodalities, confraternities such as the various purgatorian societies, the Society of St. Vincent de Paul, and Peter's Pence as well as temperance and altar societies. These public exercises were also reinforced by the use of devotional tools and aids: beads, scapulars, missals, prayer books, catechisms, holy pictures, and *Agnus Dei*, all blessed by priests who had recently acquired that privilege from Rome [while], the whole world of the senses was explored in these devotional exercises, and especially in the Mass, through music, singing, candles, vestments, and incense.[6]

---

5. D. W. Miller, "Mass Attendance in Ireland in 1834," in S. J. Brown–D. Miller (ed.), *Piety and Power in Ireland 1760–1960: Essays in Honor of Emmet Larkin* (Belfast / Notre Dame, Indiana: University of Notre Dame Press, 2000), 158–179.

6. Larkin, *Devotional Revolution*, 644–645.

There are other elements to this argument. Improving standards of living and of popular education in the second half of the nineteenth century brought Ireland nearer to a Victorian moral and church-going norm, making the devotional life with its disciplines a vehicle of modernization. Dr. Gerard Connolly has argued that much of the Irish Famine influx into Britain, with its low standard of canonical practice, was an embarrassment to English Catholics, whose levels of practice were generally high ones.[7] But the new Anglo-Irish Romanized religious culture could be transplanted to the urban slums of the Irish Diaspora, in Britain as in North America and Australasia, where the new shrine church was the one holy place, with no surrounding ancient sacred landscape to sustain it. There was, of course, something of a similar "Devotional Revolution" among Catholics in England, and as I am going to draw on English material, I would especially point out the Englishness of, for example, the new vernacular hymnody, in Ireland as well as England, preeminently the work of the English Oratorians, Frederick William Faber, Edward Caswall and John Henry Newman, which bore fruit in the Arundel, Westminster and Parish hymnals in the twentieth century. In Ireland, English was the language of modernity and improvement, and of "getting on," and the Irish "Devotional Revolution" was a largely Anglophone affair, reflecting the general indifference in the Irish Catholic Church to the dying culture and language of the Gael. Most Catholics in England were of Irish birth or descent, and popular Catholicism in the two islands developed on similar lines, encouraged by Cullen's English counterpart, the Ultramontane Cardinal Wiseman, in a process in which the much smaller English Catholic Church played an important part.

Larkin's picture has been modified to show that the "Devotional Revolution" was well and truly under way, at least among the better off, among English speakers in Ireland, and in the eastern and southern towns, especially in Dublin; among the farming communities of east Munster and south Leinster; and in the chapels of the religious orders, long before the advent of Cullen. Thus as early as the era of Archbishop Troy, in Dublin, between 1786 and 1823, the

---

7. G. Connolly, "Irish and Catholic: Myth or Reality? Another Sort of Irish and the Renewal of the Clerical Profession among Catholics in England, 1791–1918," in R. Swift–S. Gilley (ed.), *The Irish in the Victorian City* (London: Croom Helm, 1985), 226–254.

Denmark Street Dominicans sponsored a Confraternity of the
Holy Rosary, the Carmelites a Confraternity of the Scapular, and the
Franciscans Sodalities of the Sacred Cord, while various convents
were homes to Sodalities of the Sacred Heart. Elsewhere in the city,
the Rosary, Stations of the Cross and purgatorian societies flourished,
and where they led, the rest of Ireland eventually followed.[8] Much
of the church building in Ireland took place before 1840, expenditure
afterward consisting largely in the enrichment of existing structures
with new shrines and sanctuaries. And again, as Desmond Keenan
has emphasized,[9] Irish Catholicism had the particular advantage over
its English counterpart, that while it had lost its cathedrals and parish
churches to the Protestant Church of Ireland, it retained the full
medieval hierarchy of 22 archbishops and bishops and its own paro-
chial system, so that it was well-placed to reassert itself by the
mid-nineteenth century as the church of the great majority of the
Irish people.

   Larkin points out the importance of prayer books in this
"Devotional Revolution," and here, as in hymnody, English devotional
works were of primary importance, and the "Devotional Revolution"
was not so much the Romanization of the Irish Church as part
of the Anglicisation of Ireland. The extra-liturgical diet of English
Catholicism centered, according to Dr. Mary Heimann, in her classic
work on Victorian Catholic devotion, on the Rosary and Benediction,
which held prominent places in the standard English devotional work,
the eighteenth-century Bishop Richard Challoner's *Garden of the
Soul*,[10] and these devotions, with Vespers, remained central to
Catholic life in both England and Ireland.

   As to the contents of *The Garden of the Soul*, there is an
excellent summary of the book in its edition of 1755 by Dr. Heimann:

> The work opens with a summary of Christian doctrine, followed by "a
> morning exercise" which includes the Lord's Prayer, Hail Mary, Apostles'

---

   8. D. Keogh, "The Pattern of the Flock': John Thomas Troy, 1786–1823," in J. Kelly–
D. Keogh (ed.), *History of the Catholic Diocese of Dublin* (Dublin: Four Courts, 2000), 215–237,
at 228.

   9. D. Keenan, *The Catholic Church in Nineteenth-Century Ireland: A Sociological Study* (Dublin:
Gill & MacMillan, 1983).

   10. R. Challoner, *The Garden of the Soul, or, A Manual of Spiritual Exercises and Instructions for
Christians, Who, Living in the World, Aspire to Devotion* (London: s.n., 1741).

Creed, and *Confiteor*, as well as "acts" of faith, hope, and charity. Ten meditations of St Francis de Sales and instructions and devotions for hearing
Mass are followed by various psalms; more acts of faith, hope, love, and
contrition are given, along with "an universal prayer for all things necessary
for salvation". The Lord's Prayer is explicated and the Athanasian Creed
given. Rubrics and prayers for "Vespers, or Even-song" are included, as are
those for "Complin" and "Benediction of the Blessed Sacrament". Evening
prayers, complementing the "morning exercise", incorporate an examination of conscience . . . further "devotional flowers" . . . include the rosary,
St Bernard's hymn "Jesus, the only thought of thee . . .", *Ave Maris Stella*,
various aspirations and ejaculations, "affections", resolutions and meditations, instructions and devotions for confession, mental exercises to prepare for death, prayers for the dead, and litanies of Jesus and of Our Lady
of Loreto. The Manual . . . closes with the Jesus Psalter.[11]

Dr. Heimann points out that after 1850, *The Garden of the
Soul* kept its popularity, and the greater part of it remained perfectly
intact, even down to the original wording, not least of which were the
meditations on that "most devotional of acts" of hearing Mass. Rather,
the editions after 1850 add a good deal of extra material, including
"Stations of the Cross," "Visits to the Blessed Sacrament," "Devotions
to the Sacred Heart," and prayers for the conversion of England.
Dr. Heimann therefore downplays, to some degree, the effect of the
Devotional Revolution in English Catholicism, pointing out the
controversialist and thoroughly papistical character of Challoner's own
outlook, in a manner which was not much behind that of the new
nineteenth-century Ultramontanes themselves.

Something of the pattern of both change and continuity in
the new prayer books occurs in a compact little English volume of
a thousand pages, *The Path to Heaven*, published by Burns & Oates in
1866, in London, with the *imprimatur* of Archbishop Manning, and
the strong commendation of Archbishop Cullen.[12] *The Path to Heaven*
opens with a summary of what every Christian must do and believe,
and as in Challoner, there are extensive vernacular forms of morning
and evening prayer; all the common Catholic prayers, like the *Salve
Regina* and the *Memorare*, in English and Latin; and prayers for every

---

11. M. Heimann, *Catholic Devotion in Victorian England* (Oxford: Clarendon, 1995), 79.

12. *The Path to Heaven: A Complete Collection of All the Public and Private Devotions in General
Use* (London: Burns, Oates & Co., 1866).

worldly occasion. Then there are methods prescribed for hearing
Mass, of which more anon, and prayers before and during Mass; no
fewer than 44 litanies, beginning with the Litany of the Saints, and
including a few young Jesuit exotics like Saint Aloysius Gonzaga
and Saint Stanislas Kostka, and Vespers, Compline and Benediction
in Latin and English. The litanies are a study in themselves. Nine
or ten of them bear the name of Jesus, and they are packed with solid
theological reflection as well as preaching an ardent piety. Then
follow various common canticles and hymns, like the *Magnificat*,
Te Deum and *De Profundis*, in Latin and English; the Little Office of
the Immaculate Conception; the Jesus Psalter, consisting of "150 invocations of the Name of Jesus, interspersed with verses in imitation of
the psalms";[13] the common Latin hymns, also in metrical translation;
then 12 sets of devotions, by months of the year, beginning with
the Holy Child, Epiphany and Holy Name in January, each section
including vernacular hymns; the *bona mors*; prayers to do with the
seven sacraments, in the vernacular; meditations for every day of the
month, in the vernacular; all the principal epistles and gospels in
translation, for Sundays and festivals; and a hymnal with 293 hymns,
mostly new, nearly all in the vernacular. There is a great deal of direct
or incidental doctrinal instruction, touching on every aspect of the
faith, from the metaphysical to the practical. The Mass is firmly placed
in the context of a much wider daily round of prayer and devotion.
Here, then, is God's plenty, and some one knowing no or little Latin
had any amount of matter on which to feed his soul.

Challoner's *Garden of the Soul* was popular in English-speaking
Ireland, where the commonest native prayer book was *The Key of
Heaven; or, a Manual of Prayer*, with 33 Dublin editions by 1839.[14]
Much of it is centered on the Mass in relation to the Christian Year,
on the rules of the Church for attending it and with prayers for before,
during and after it, and with an explanation of its ornaments and
ceremonies, including a disquisition on the colors of the seasons.
There are common prayers for morning and evening in the vernacular,
with the Angelus, the *Confiteor*, "devout prayers" for many occasions

---

13. *The New Catholic Dictionary*, ed. C. B. Pallen and J. J. Wynne (London: The Universal
Knowledge Foundation, 1929), 507.

14. *The Key of Heaven; or, a Manual of Prayer*. Thirty-third edition (Dublin: Richard Grace,
1839).

and states of life, some from the Holy Week liturgy, the Litanies
of the Holy Name of Jesus, of the Saints, of Loreto, of the Blessed
Sacrament and Sacred Heart, reflecting the early advance of the
Devotional Revolution, fifteen meditations on the passion, the Jesus
Psalter, prayers for the dying and for the departed soul, and the
Rosaries of Jesus and the Blessed Virgin. I am not sure of the point,
but there seems to be nothing specifically Irish: "The Prayers of
Saint Brigid," "To be said in honor of the sacred wounds of our blessed
Savior," are attributed to Saint Brigid of Sweden, not Saint Brigid
of Kildare, although it should be stressed that in the Jesuit Diarmuid
Ó Laoghaire's great collection of Gaelic prayers and blessings, no
fewer than 88 are concerned with serving at Mass.[15] In *The Key of
Heaven*, a few hymns and canticles like the *Salve Regina, Te Deum*,
and *Veni Sancte Spiritus* are given in translation. The Marian content
is already high, though lower than in the edition of nearly half
a century later: in 1884, *The Key of Heaven: A Manual of Catholic
Devotion*,[16] now included the Ordinary of the Mass, Vespers
and Benediction in Latin and English, "Devotions for Mass in Union
with the Blessed Virgin Mary," and the principal epistles and gospels
in English. The prayers of Saint Brigid survive. There is a section
of common Latin hymns, also in translation. With its Gothic decora-
tions and capitals it is more obviously a prayer book for public use
in church. This is quite a different volume, which is more directly
liturgical, with less in the way of private prayer.

Some modern liturgists take a dim view of a great deal of this,
but in fact this devotional world answers to the modern criteria of
accessibility and comprehensibility. Above all, there is the solid historical fact, and this is my major point, that the radically improved
rates of Mass attendance in Ireland by the end of the nineteenth century had complicated historical and social causes, but they were also
the product of the "Devotional Revolution." In short, the Mass did
not stand or fall by itself; it was part and parcel of a wider movement
of prayer, and of other so-called extra-liturgical devotions. Together,
with the many devotional foci of statues and altars, they made the

---

15. See *Ár bpaidreacha dúchais: cnuasach de phaidreacha agus de Beannachtaí ár ainsear* ("Our
native prayers: a collection of our ancestors' prayers and blessings") (Dublin: Foilseacháin Ábhair
Spioradálta, 1975). I am grateful to the Rev. Gerard Deighan for this information.
16. *The Key of Heaven: A Manual of Catholic Devotion* (M. Gladbach: A. Riffarth, 1884).

church a place of frequent public prayer; the decline of the whole devotional ethos and atmosphere which they fostered in the churches, the "Catholic atmosphere," in the second half of the twentieth century coincided with a drop in Mass attendance. Of course, like the Devotional Revolution itself, the new cultural currents had complicated social causes; the trouble was that some local churches abetted them by stripping their sanctuaries of the devotional iconography. In defense of the old devotions, I would note that many of them could be used in either Latin or English. They were, moreover, as much communal as individual, and I would stress the public and objective character of a great deal of this prayer, in the face of the sort of criticism that rejects it as privatized and individualist and emotive.

In the older world, the leading role in collective public prayer often was taken by the confraternities and sodalities, whose members seem to have formed the core or cadre of enthusiastic and fervent Mass-goers in many parishes. There was, in short, a sort of sliding scale among parishioners from ardor to indifference, or a set of concentric circles, from an inner one in which Catholicism meant a life centered on the Church, to one marked by the official minimum of practice, fading to an outer circle in which Catholicism was chiefly a badge of cultural identity, among people who might be reclaimed by a mission. In his study of Irish Catholicism in England, Steven Fielding has suggested that at a sensible guess, in the Catholic paishes of twentieth-century Manchester, "the devout accounted for 5 per cent of Catholics, those who frequently attended to their devotions amounted to 35 per cent, those who infrequently did so, 40 per cent, whilst those who rarely if ever attended mass came to 20 per cent."[17]

I am not sure what is meant by "attended to their devotions," but Dr. Fielding usefully draws attention to the variety of religious practice among Catholics in England. The figures for practice were obviously higher for Ireland, and here I draw on a recent essay by Dr. Maurice Hartigan on religious practice in the diocese of Dublin. In 1931, the Society of St Vincent de Paul made 70,000 visits to Catholic households in Dublin, and found only one persistent

---

17. S. Fielding, *Class and Ethnicity: Irish Catholics in England, 1880–1939,* Themes in the Twentieth Century (Buckingham: Open University Press, 1993), 55.

non-attender.[18] Poor man, he must have felt lonely. The first half of
the twentieth century was the golden age of the Irish laity. In 1928,
there were 450,000 Communions at the Jesuit Church of St. Francis
Xavier, Lower Gardiner Street, where the Workingmen's Sodality,
founded in 1872, could claim nine hundred members in 1939. Other
churches could boast nearly as many. At the Dominican Church,
St. Savior's, the exclusively male Holy Name Sodality had 1,800
members by the 1920s, reaching 3,000 at its Golden Jubilee in 1934.
The same church had a Rosary Confraternity for women, the
St. Savior's Chapter of Brothers, affiliated to the Dominican Third
Order, the Imeldist Sodality for girls and the Angelic Warfare
Sodality for boys. The Vincentian church of St Peter's, Phibsborough,
operated the Archconfraternity of the Sacred Heart, founded in 1874,
specifically designed to secure attendance at the sacrament, with
4,000 members in 1924. There were no fewer than forty sodality guilds
for women, with thirty members each, in the 1950s, at the Carmelite
church in Whitefriar Street. The Augustinians at St. John's Lane,
the Franciscans at Merchant's Quay, and the parishes of St. Michan's
and St. James, had similarly strong lay followings.

One needs to multiply such memberships throughout Ireland.
Between August 1927 and July 1928, the *Irish Messenger of the Sacred
Heart* received the promise of 644,750 visits to the Blessed Sacrament.
In this statistical list, promises of attendance at weekday Mass over
the same period came third, after an undertaking to keep an hour of
silence, at 379,670, and the reception of Holy Communion came
eighth, at 197,025. Dr. Hartigan suggests on this basis that the Irish
preferred to visit the Blessed Sacrament than to receive it, a plausible
conclusion in the light of the seriousness with which reception was
regarded, as requiring Confession beforehand and fasting from the
previous midnight.[19] Yet even here, the statistics for the reception of
Communion are impressive, as in the 10,000 Communions during
the missions in the Dublin pro-Cathedral in 1933. The Eucharistic
Congress of 1932 appeared to show Dublin as the most practising
Catholic city in the world. It seems to me that the pitch of piety

18. M. Hartigan, "The Religious Life of the Catholic Laity of Dublin, 1920–40," in J.
Kelly–D. Keogh (ed.), *History of the Catholic Diocese of Dublin* (Dublin: Four Courts, 2000),
331–348.

19. Hartigan, *Religious Life*, 336.

attained with other cultuses—to St. Brigid, at Killester, and to such local holy men as Matt Talbot, Fr. Charles of Mount Argus, and the Jesuits John Sullivan and Willie Doyle—secured a level of ordinary religious practice hardly attained elsewhere, with the numbers of Communions rising during and after the frequent parish missions and retreats, and with the strict policing of the Church's rules on weekly Mass attendance and annual Confession and Communion by the laity themselves.

Unfortunately, Dr. Hartigan does not discuss the rules and books of guidance of the confraternities, and we need to know much more about these and their internal organization, and how far they operated independently of the clergy, under some kind of lay control. It would be also useful to discover if they were more popular with women, and whether they supplied church choirs and the lay servants of the sanctuary, as a semi-professional religious elite. Certainly these must have known their religion extremely well. Above all, the rules of the confraternities urged the frequent reception of Communion, partly no doubt as a result of the background of Tridentine teaching, the powerful Jesuit influence, the clergy's pride in the statistics for overall Communions, in the rivalry of parishes with one another, and in line with the decree on frequent Communion by Pope Saint Pius X in 1905.

Then there is the issue of the cult of Mary, sometimes alleged to have superseded the Mass itself. The modern Marian revival has been studied largely in terms of the strong papal support which it received, especially from the time of Pius IX's definition of the dogma of the Immaculate Conception in 1854. The doctrine was indeed the lynch-pin of his long pontificate of 32 years, the longest in the history of the Church, as the pope found in the figure of the perfect woman his succor and defense against the modern liberal heresies. The other two landmarks of his period of rule, the *Syllabus of Errors* of 1864 and the opening of the Vatican Council in 1869 were both dated by the feast, December 8, on the tenth and fifteenth anniversaries of the proclamation of the dogma. Yet the Pope appears, from another perspective, to have been only the most significant contributor to a much wider current of Marian piety, stimulated by the numerous appearances of the Virgin to child visionaries, most famously at Lourdes in 1858 and at Fatima in 1917. Marian devotion was encouraged from Rome, but Rome clearly did not create it, and even without papal patronage and approval, it would have happened anyway.

Did Marianism, however, outshine the Mass? Not so, I think, in England or Ireland. Irish devotion to Mary had always been strong.[20] But the expatriate Irish Catholics of New York were scandalized by the saint-based devotions of the equally expatriate Italians, who seemed to practice a religion built upon the Madonnas of their rival homeland villages. The only Marian appearance in Ireland, at Knock, combined the Blessed Virgin and Saint Joseph with the Mass through their appearance with the sacred host in the form of the *Agnus Dei* above an altar dedicated to the Sacred Heart, and with Saint John the Evangelist, the main New Testament origin of the Eucharistic teaching of the Church. The high point of Marian devotion in modern Ireland was between 1930 and 1960, beginning in 1930 with the creation of the shrine of Our Lady of Lourdes at Inchicore, by the Oblates of Mary Immaculate, which claimed to have received a million pilgrims during its first two years. The climax of Irish Marianism was the solemn dedication of the Irish Armed Services to the Queen of the Most Holy Rosary in 1951. It has been suggested that the intensity of Irish Marian devotion showed the inadequacy of the parish-based sacramental system to meet the growing hunger of the Irish for spiritual sustenance, with the claim that the cults of Lourdes and Fatima eclipsed the sacraments themselves. Take, however, one of the more significant expressions of modern Irish Marian piety, the Legion of Mary, founded in 1921 by Frank Duff, a Dublin member of the Society of Saint Vincent de Paul doing good works among the destitute, as in founding hostels for homeless men and women. Duff was inspired by the Marianism of Saint Louis-Marie Grignion de Montfort, and took the devotion of Mary into the Mass, but this, if possible, was designed to raise the level of Mass attendance, as it urged and implored all its members "to assist frequently—every day if at all possible—at Mass, and at that Mass to receive Holy Communion,"[21] and required daily Mass attendance and the daily reception of Communion from its "Praetorian" elite.

---

20. See P. O'Dwyer, *Mary: A History of Devotion in Ireland* (Dublin: Four Courts, 1988).

21. *The Official Handbook of the Legion of Mary* (Dublin: Concilium Legionis Mariae, 1962), 170.

Indeed it could be said that the Latin liturgical tradition was never so well-known as by the English-speaking laity in Ireland on the eve of its virtual disappearance. Professor Duffy has emphasized the accessibility of the medieval rite in an age of illiteracy. The Irish were now literate, and Mass was no longer a distant mystery to anyone who could read an English text and could afford a bilingual Missal, with Latin in one column and the English translation in another. I am not sure when these became widely available, but the English translation of the Holy Week services into English goes back to *The Compleat Office of the Holy Week* translated from a French version by two members of the Blount family in 1687,[22] and I possess *The Office of the Holy Week according to the Latin Missal and Breviary*, which is dated 1738, and had belonged to the Vaughan family of Courtfield, with all the services in English translation, in parallel columns with the Latin.[23] John Gother's *Instructions and Devotions for Hearing Mass* (1699) expressed a preference for accompanying the priest "almost in all he says"[24] over the recitation of the Rosary and *Particular Devotions*, although he reluctantly recognized that this was not possible to every one, and he divided his methods of hearing Mass into three, the third and highest method involving the attendant in following the priest in every word and action. There appeared in 1708 *The Vespers, or, Even-Song: with the Holy Mass, in Latin and English together, with the Antiphons, Hymns and Prayers.*[25] I have been unable to consult the British Library copy of *The Roman Missal in Latin and English* (1737), said to have been destroyed by wartime bombing.[26] *The Divine Office for the Use of the Laity (The Mass for every day of the year, Vespers and Complin)* appeared in four volumes in 1763. This declares that the reader "will find the *Mass* for every day in the year: *Vespers* and *Complin* for all *Doubles* and *Sundays*, with *Commemorations* of the *Semidoubles*, *Singles*, and *Ferias*: The administration of the sacraments of *Baptism*, *Confirmation*, *Matrimony*, and *Extreme*

---

22. *The Compleat Office of the Holy Week. With Notes and Explications. Translated from the Latin and French* (London: Matthew Turner, 1687).

23. *The Office of the Holy Week According to the Latin Missal and Breviary.* The third edition, corrected (London: T. Meighan, 1738).

24. J. Gother, *Instructions and Devotions for Hearing Mass* (London: s.n., 1699), 88.

25. *The Vespers, or, Even-Song: with the Holy Mass in Latin and English Together, with the Antiphons, Hymns and Prayers* (s.n., 1708).

26. *The Roman Missal in Latin and English*, 4 vols. (s.n., 1737).

Unction: The *Visitation* of the *Sick*, the *Burial-Service*, the *Office* for the *Dead*, the *Penitential Psalms*, the *Litany, etc.*"[27] The *Roman Missal for the Use of the Laity*, published by R. Keating, Brown and Co., appeared in 1806.[28]

By 1800, the Ordinary of the Mass, in parallel columns of Latin and English, was printed in editions of *The Garden of the Soul*. I own and used at Mass for a number of years, until it fell to pieces, F. C. Husenbeth's edition of *The Missal for the Use of the Laity*,[29] with the Proper and Ordinary in Latin and English, for all the Sunday and Holy Week Masses, as well as the Sanctoral. The collects, epistles and gospels are in English only; the book was inscribed by the future Cardinal Wiseman. Ambrose Lisle Phillipps' *The Catholick Christian's Complete Manual* also contains a great deal of material from the Missal, including the propers, epistles and gospels in English, though it is less well arranged.[30] Such translations, like Dom Gaspar Lefebvre's *Saint Andrew Daily Missal*, became common in the twentieth century. Ecclesiastical authority in both kingdoms during more than two centuries seems to have given them every encouragement, in the interests of accessibility and intelligibility. This is a remarkable fact, given the high value placed on the very letter of the Latin text, and the (wholly unavailing) ban by the Sacred Congregation of Rites on translations of the Ordinary, "renewed as late as 1857."[31] For the true aficionado of the prayer of the Church, there was also the whole the three thousand page translation of the Roman Breviary by John, Third Marquess of Bute, though it seems that this was largely for use in religious communities needing to check the Latin.[32]

---

27. *The Divine Office for the Use of the Laity (The Mass for Every Day of the Year, Vespers and Complin)* 4 vols. (s.n., 1763), vol. I, 6–7.

28. *The Roman Missal for the Use of the Laity* (London: P. Keating, Brown & Co., 1806). I have not seen this edition. Cf. A. Reid, *The Organic Development of the Liturgy* (Farnborough: St. Michael's Abbey, 2004), 52, and 53 for other examples.

29. F. C., *The Missal for the Use of the Laity*. This edition is a bit of a mishmash. It contains a Preface of January 1847, *imprimaturs* of 1848 and title pages of 1849 and 1850. Reid, *The Organic Development*, 53 dates the original edition to 1845, but the edition seems to be London: Joseph Booker, 1831.

30. A. L. Phillipps, *The Catholick Christian's Complete Manual* (London: Thomas Richardson and Son, 1847).

31. Reid, *The Organic Development*, 52.

32. John, Marquess of Bute, *The Roman Breviary*, 2 vols. (Edinburgh: W. Blackwood, 1879).

I have referred to Challoner's devotions, suggesting that not all the pious simply said their Rosaries during Mass. My *Path to Heaven* of 1862 recommends that one profitable method of hearing or assisting at Mass "is to follow the Priest in the Ordinary of the Mass as contained in the Missal; joining with him, as far as the laity may, in the very words of the service, and uniting our intention with him in what he does as Priest for the people." *The Path to Heaven* argues that the Ordinary and Canon "have been made into almost all languages, and circulated by authority," but it requires a certain mastery of the book to get to the Mass in its separate parts. The *Path* also recommends that one can follow the Mass by "not using or not confining ourselves to the words of the Ordinary," by reading the Scriptural Sentences supplied for each part, or by a sustained meditation on Our Lord's life or Passion.[33] One complete form of meditation on the Mass is by way of union with the Sacred Heart; another follows some lengthy prayers by Blessed (now Saint) Leonard of Port Maurice. There are special devotions given for use before Mass, at the time and after Communion, as well as a particular set of "Meditations for the Mass" for an intending communicant. Given the speed at which Low Masses were often said, there seems a good deal of printed prayer matter to get through as well as a need to keep one eye on the book and another on the priest, to know where one is, and this is a much more complicated method than just saying the Rosary. But it seems to me to be also a great deal more devout than the manner in which the Mass is often heard nowadays, and certainly the piety reflected is an affective one, ensuring that the liturgy was a prayerful experience and the congregation a devout one, with an overall mood which might be called Evangelical or Romantic, but was one supplied with a great deal of doctrinal instruction as well.

Indeed by the twentieth century, there was a flood of writing about the meaning of the Mass, from highly sophisticated works like those by Adrian Fortescue[34] or Maurice Zundel's *Splendor of the Liturgy*,[35] to the *Thirty Ways of Hearing Mass*, compiled by the

---

33. *The Path to Heaven*, 71–72.

34. E.g. A. Fortescue, *The Ceremonies of the Roman Rite Described* (London: Burns & Oates, 1917).

35. M. Zundel, *Splendor of the Liturgy*, trans. E. I. Watkin (London: Sheed & Ward, 1939).

Redemptorist George Stebbing.[36] In short, there was only one way for the clergy to say Mass; but excepting the well-drilled server, the laity at a Low Mass could hear it in any way they chose. In Cardinal Newman's words, "There is the gentleman with his missal, the old woman with her beads, the pious handmaiden with her crucifix, the child with its pictures."[37] Newman himself rejoiced in this diversity, reflecting on the variety of lay practice, "This is a *popular* religion."[38] The Church wisely allowed for the variety of human nature and culture, and for varying degrees of enthusiasm and commitment. This means that the testimony of older Catholics is bound to be greatly varied, from "I said my Rosary," to "I belonged to a confraternity which went to Communion together," to "I was a server," to my favorite, "like my father before me, I always carried the ombrellino on Maundy Thursday and Corpus Christi," to "I just used occasionally to slip in at the back," with a welcome anonymity, now alas also unavailable.

This abundance also seems to have produced a certain permissiveness about how to hear Mass among some of the clergy, but there was also a movement against this. "There are many methods of assisting properly at Mass," wrote Father Tanquerey, adroitly facing both ways at once, in his *Doctrine and Devotion*, translated from French in 1933. "The one which yields the best results to the individual is evidently the best for him. But the method which is more in conformity with the spirit of the Church and which in itself is the most efficacious of all, is that of uniting with the Celebrant of the Mass by reciting devoutly at least some of the time-honored prayers of the Missal."[39]

There were, no doubt, always those like Gother who held that this was the highest way, but there was also a tendency for apologists for the older use of the Roman Rite to emphasize its accessibility and intelligibility, even for those without Latin. "As for the people," wrote Bishop Hedley of Newport,

it is abundantly possible for them to understand and follow the Mass without either knowing Latin or possessing minute knowledge of the

---

36. G. Stebbing, *Thirty Ways of Hearing Mass* (London: Sands & Co., 1913).

37. Cited in Stebbing, *Thirty Ways*, 14.

38. J. H. Newman, *Loss and Gain: The Story of a Convert* (London/New York: Longmans, Green, tenth edition, 1891), 426.

39. A. Tanquerey, *Doctrine and Devotion*, trans. L. A. Arand (Tournai: Desclée, 1933), 209.

ceremonies. The Mass has broad features, which are easily brought within the comprehension of the least cultivated minds. It is easy to make the faithful realize what is the central point of the Mass—the consecration of our Lord's Body and Blood. It is easy to point out how certain actions lead up to this, and certain others follow it. The preparation or Confession, the reading of prayers and of Holy Scripture, the bringing on and oblation of the Bread and Wine, the Preface, the Sanctus and the Canon—these features, with preliminary explanation, can easily be followed with or without a book. After the Consecration, there is no difficulty in recognizing the 'Our Father', the *Agnus Dei*, and the Communion. Every Catholic is carefully taught these things from childhood. . . . The whole office and rite of the Mass is translated and explained in books of every degree of simplicity or elaborateness. There can be no question, therefore, that the most uninstructed Catholics may, and do, find it perfectly easy to follow the Mass with discernment and devotion.[40]

No one, as far as I know, has analyzed the kind of Mass-based meditations which existed before the Second Vatican Council in lavish overabundance, or what is just as important, their integration with other forms of devotion. There also seems to me to be no doubt that the growth of so-called extra-liturgical devotional societies was extraordinary, providing a solid core of ardent Mass-goers, some at least of whom practiced their religion almost as lay religious. Of course, there were other forms of lay participation in the rite, by acolytes and servers, who knew the Mass extremely well, but also, in larger parishes with a *Missa Cantata* or even a High Mass, by choirs singing normally from the west gallery, and by the congregations at such Masses, who had to know at least when to cross themselves and to stand and sit and kneel. The flourishing musical subculture, much encouraged in convents, appeared with startling rapidity: the Oratorian hymns seem to have spread almost as soon as they appeared in the 1850s, and appear in the *Crown of Jesus Music*, edited by a teacher at Ushaw College, Henry Frederick Hemy, and published by Thomas Richardson and Son in 1864. This contains no fewer than 20 settings for Benediction, as well as numerous settings for litanies, as well as a large vernacular hymnody.[41]

---

40. J. C. Hedley, *The Holy Eucharist*, The Westminster Library (London: Longmans, 1907), 201–202.

41. H. F. Hemy, *Crown of Jesus Music* (London: T. Richardson, 1864).

The tendency of what writing there is about this subject stresses that the "Devotional Revolution" marked the increasing control of religion by the clergy, but I can find nothing compulsory about so-called "extra-liturgical devotion," unless one joined a confraternity to say one's prayers with other people, in which case they can hardly be called private. The Mass remained the one mandatory service for every Catholic, but no one, to my knowledge, apart from Mary Heimann, has suggested, in the manner of Eamon Duffy's analysis of late medieval religion,[42] that devotions spread not primarily because the Pope or even prelates like Cardinal Cullen pushed them, as Larkin argued, but because in part for local and social as well as spiritual reasons, they were intrinsically popular with laymen and women who had control of them themselves.[43] A very good, if older, example is Benediction, in origin a late medieval lay copy of the monastic offices, at first centered not on the Sacrament but on the Virgin Mary.[44]

One last consideration is that belief needs practice to become ingrained. But what sort of practice? The Mass is primarily an action, not a form of words, with holy silences punctuated by bells. It seems to me a rather Protestant notion that one can only understand a thing by following a text. On the one hand, the blessed silences of the older use of the Roman Rite, a silence so lamentably lacking in many contemporary liturgical celebrations, reminds us that devotion is more than words, but is the heart's offering. Newman asserts that the gentleman following the priest's words in his Missal is in no way superior to the old Neapolitan woman who chatters to her crucifix, or to the French peasant who said of the sacrament, "I look at him and he looks at me."

Yet words are important. To know a prayer, a collect, a litany by heart, with its associations of times of joy and gladness, and to repeat it in moments of sorrow or weariness or stress, is to find the

---

42. E. Duffy, *The Stripping of the Altars: Traditional Religion in England c. 1400–c. 1580* (New Haven, CT/London: Yale University Press, 1992).

43. M. Heimann, "Catholic Revivalism in Worship and Devotion," in S. Gilley–B. Stanley (ed.), *World Christianities c. 1815–c. 1914*, The Cambridge History of Christianity 8 (Cambridge: Cambridge University Press, 2006), 70–83, at 83.

44. H. Thurston, "Benediction of the Blessed Sacrament," in *Report of the Nineteenth Eucharistic Congress, held at Westminster from 9th to 13th September 1908* (London: Sands, 1909), 452–464.

consolation of the faith when it is felt most needed. Indeed this is possibly especially the case for people whose culture is more oral than written, and who relate more easily to the simple repetitions of a litany and to the rhythmic pattern of versicle and response than to anything more challengingly literary or intellectual. It may be otherwise on the higher slopes of mystical experience, but at a lower altitude, if there is nothing in the mind but a void, without familiar images or well-known forms of words, the person praying may well pray in vain.

This world of the Devotional Revolution now seems as lost as the city of Lyonesse beneath the sea, although it was flourishing in the lifetime of many still living. It still awaits its Eamon Duffy,[45] to bring it back to life.

---

45. Duffy, *The Stripping of the Altars*.

Chapter 11

The Liturgy and Theology

Laurence Paul Hemming

There is no more vexed or difficult place in the life of the contemporary Catholic Church than in the question of her worship, the meaning and place of the sacred liturgy, and, it seems to me, that is how it should be. And if that statement surprises you, I hope to explain why, for it is a statement made in hope. I am not the first person to stand at a lectern and say that the contemporary world is still living the effects of an upheaval visited on it in the North, since the Reformation; in the South, since Napoleon and the French Revolution; in the West, since the American Independence; and everywhere else, since this busy, tiny and interfering corner called Europe began busily deploying and exporting the intellectual, moral, and physical engines of its internal combustion across the globe. If the Church is a redemption from this combustion, and if the sacred liturgy *is* the Church at its work of redemption, then there is every reason why the Church, of all the places in the world, should *not* be free of an upheaval that is now a planetary phenomenon. Above all, that this upheaval—of thought, of morals (and I do *not* mean ethics), of being itself—should both sting, and seek its diagnosis *in* the very moment and action of redemption (which means in the most sacred actions a man may know in his life) seems right. Actions that are shared in by man, and which make of man what he really is to be (and so which are constitutive of his being), but which are never *his* actions. Above all, liturgical actions spring from and have their origins in God himself.

Those of us who love the sacred liturgy are confronted with this question of the place and meaning of the sacred liturgy. The

Constitution *Sacrosanctum Concilium*, the first documentary act of the Second Vatican Council, stated that:

> The study of sacred liturgy is to be ranked among the compulsory and major courses in seminaries and religious houses of studies. In theological faculties it is to rank among the principal courses. It is to be taught under its theological, historical, spiritual, pastoral, and juridical aspects. In addition, those who teach other subjects, especially dogmatic theology, sacred scripture, spiritual and pastoral theology, should—each of them submitting to the exigencies of his own discipline—expound the mystery of Christ and the history of salvation in a manner that will clearly set forth the connection between their subjects and the liturgy.[1]

If any statement of the documents of the Council exposes the unfulfilled and—I hesitate to say unfinished, since I actually mean not even begun—work of that Council, and even I would say, work of Holy Mother Church herself, it is exactly this one.

The order indicated by the statement makes explicit its interior force: the sacred liturgy is the *fons et culmen*, source and summit, of the very training of those to whom themselves the sacred liturgy is most entrusted: in seminaries, and next to those who have most given their lives to its practice and effects, those in religious houses—these are the ones who, drawn from the ranks of the faithful, are those to be made most familiar with the practice of faith. To practice faith means to become a liturgical practitioner. Next in order are those most entrusted with the work of reflecting on what faith makes known: those concerned with *sacra doctrina*, holy teaching, the teaching that itself makes saints of those both teaching and taught.

First in rank, even before priests, seminarians, and religious, and mentioned two paragraphs before, are those apostolically responsible for the Church in her very being: "pastors of souls"—which means the bishops, the hierarchy of the Church herself—"[must]

---

1. SC, 16: "*Disciplina de sacra Liturgia in seminariis et studiorum domibus religiosis inter disciplinas necessarias et potiores, in facultatibus autem theologicis inter disciplinas principales est habenda, et sub aspectu cum theologico et historico, tum spirituali, pastorali, et iuridico tradenda. Current insuper aliarum disciplinarum magistri, imprimis theologiae dogmaticae, sacrae Scripturae, theologiae spiritualis et pastoralis ita, ex intrinsecis exigentiis proprii uniuscuiusque obiecti, mysterium Christi et historiam salutis excolere, ut exinde earum connexio cum Liturgia et unitas sacerdotalis institutionis aperte clarescant.*"

become fully imbued with the spirit and power of the liturgy and capable of giving instruction about it."[2] What actually took place in liturgical study in the wake of the Council? In fact, much contemporary liturgical theology is mired in so-called "pastoral concerns," which seems to mean at best an anodyne sense of common purpose represented by those who seek membership of the "parish liturgy committee," and at worst a conversion of the worship of the Church into social work.[3] Where liturgical theology escapes being "pastoral" it is often relegated to historiography— a study of the texts and their historical relations, but with only tangential concern (if at all) for their theological meaning. Of course, I do not in the least denigrate the historical questions, indeed, I stand taught by and exulting in their fruits, but this historiographical concern is not liturgical study as such. Liturgical theology comprises— let me repeat *Sacrosanctum Concilium*—"theological, historical, spiritual, pastoral, and juridical aspects." It is the referent of, I repeat again, "dogmatic theology, sacred scripture, spiritual and pastoral theology." What this means is that the document understands the place of liturgy in theology in a way entirely consistent with the most ancient theological texts. Liturgy, and the study of the meaning of the liturgical texts, is the *inner unity* and *possibility* of every *other* subject in the theological curriculum.[4] I assure you, in *no Catholic institute anywhere that I know of* has this been put into practice in the way envisaged. Liturgical theology means: theology *as such*, and *from whence* every other theological discipline must take its license, and

---

2. SC, 14: "*Sed quia, ut hoc evenire possit, nulla spes effulget nisi prius ipsi animarum pastores spiritu et virtute Liturgiae penitus imbuantur in eaque efficiantur magistri, ideo pernecesse est ut institutioni liturgicae cleri apprime consulatur. Quapropter Sacrosanctum Concilium ea quae sequuntur statuere decrevit.*"

3. The diocese of Clifton, for just one example, advertised its course for a "Certificate in Pastoral Liturgy," as "informational, formational and inspirational. Its goal is to educate the Sunday assembly and to deepen its appreciation of the ministry of all the baptised within the liturgy of the Church. Such an appreciation will enhance the celebration of the liturgy in every parish community" (http://www.cliftondiocese.com/Articles/478/). In other words, the *community* and its goods are the goal of liturgy.

4. Cf. Prosper of Aquitaine, *Capitula Coelestini*, 8: PL 51,209–10: "*obsecrationem quoque sacerdotalium sacramenta respiciamus, quae ab apostolis tradita, in toto mundo atque in omni catholica Ecclesia uniformiter clebrantur, ut legem credendi lex statuat supplicandi*": "let us consider equally the rites of the priestly supplications which, transmitted by the apostles, are celebrated in the same manner in the entire world and in the whole catholic Church, in such a way that the law of prayer determine the law of belief." This is often, and quite incorrectly, truncated to the tag *lex orandi, lex credendi*.

to which every other theological discipline is subordinate. In this
is a most important insight, taken for granted by the Fathers of the
Council but completely overlooked, even when lip-service is paid to it:
theology which is not *prayed* by the one theologizing is *not theology*;
it is, at best, religious studies. Prayer is not "belief in," which simply
reduces what is done to an intention. "I believe in God" means nothing,
with respect to God—even the devil can say that. But: "I pray to
God," "I live a life of prayer in God" means: "I am available to be
addressed by God"; "God makes himself known to me;" "my life is a
life ordered toward and within the hope of God's own divine promise
to include me in it."[5] All prayer is first and foremost and only liturgical: every para-liturgical practice is dependent for its meaning
on the sacred liturgy. Even the 150 beads of the Rosary represent the
recitation of the one hundred and fifty psalms in the offices of the
Church, contained in the breviary.[6] Theology requires the unity of an
interior disposition with respect to what is to be learned. Theology
begins in prayer, and prayer is first and foremost the prayer of the
Church: the sacred liturgy. Theology has no other home.

I want in this essay to do only two things. I want first, to
elicit how difficult any genuine theology of the sacred liturgy is, by
naming and unfolding just some of those difficulties. And second,
I want to point out from where a future theology of the sacred liturgy
must arise. I want to look out to the "wherefrom" and "whence" of
a future for the Roman rite that is different from the future that we
as men have prepared for it not only in the last 40 years, but perhaps
right back to when liturgical reform in the West first began to be

---

5. The more common formula in Latin for *credo in Deum* is *confiteor Deo*—literally, "I am
confessed to God," which retains a relic in English in the notion of making a "confession of
faith." This grammatical structure of the deponent verb (*confiteri*) followed by the dative is best
translated as "believing in . . . ."

6. The Rosary is perhaps the best example of a genuinely paraliturgical practice (taking the
prefix *para* here in its Greek sense of "alongside and together with"). If the Lord discloses himself
through the unfolding of the meaning of the recitation of the hours of the Church, in which the
entire Psalter is recited week by week, and which conforms the heart of the one praying the hours
to receive God's self-disclosure, then the combination of the recitation of the prayer *Ave Maria*
on each bead of the Rosary (each of which represents one of the psalms) with the central
mysteries of redemption wrought in Christ also corresponds to the actual activity and action of
the liturgy on the Christian soul. The Rosary is, therefore, more than a merely pious exercise in
meditation (which is how it is usually explained, "psychologically"): rather it is the patter of
prayer which an individual lay member of the faithful may share in which is exactly *parallel* to the
religious and clerical obligation to the hours.

discussed and implemented, under Pope Saint Pius X. In this I want to draw attention to the work of Professor László Dobszay, who more than anyone has discussed the issue of what liturgical reform could mean for the future, and who has drawn attention to what has been lost since 1911.[7]

I want to begin, therefore, with the simple philosophical observation that what does not change nevertheless does not remain the same. What I mean by this is that "preserving" the Roman rite must mean that we come to a far greater understanding of its history by understanding the world in which it arose and came to fruition. This is not, however, a merely historiographical exercise, but requires a *philosophical* understanding that takes adequate account of the historical character of the being of being human. Let me give just a simple example. The upheavals of the sixteenth to the nineteenth centuries destroyed the feudal relation of the Roman rite to the land almost everywhere in Europe except to a certain extent in two places—in England, insofar as many of those relations were preserved in the establishment of the Church of England (and much of which holds to this day, although in process of erosion), and in those areas of Germany where not even Bismarck tampered with the specific rights of canonries and chapters.[8] These latter were not done away with until the future Pope Pius XII, then Papal Nuncio in Munich, signed the concordat of the Catholic Church with the Hitler regime in 1933, precisely ushering in the possibility for the full introduction of the 1917 *Code of Canon Law* into Germany, which many of the German bishops and canonical chapters had up to that point resisted. At that point centuries of local territorial and feudal customs and conventual rights of chapters of canonries and cathedral churches were brought to a final close. The 1917 code, a necessity elsewhere in Europe in that it put in place a legal framework that codified the chaos left after the

---

7. Cf. L. Dobszay, *The Bugnini-Liturgy and the Reform of the Reform*, Musicae Sacrae Meletemata 5 (Front Royal, VA: Church Music Association of America, 2003), especially 56–63, for discussion of the 1911 reform of the Office.

8. To understand the wider philosophical issues in the transformation of land, especially around the 1648 treaty known as the Peace of Westphalia see, for instance, S. Elden, "The Place of Geometry: Heidegger's Mathematical Excursus on Aristotle," in *The Heythrop Journal* 42 (2001), 311–28.

Reformation and the Napoleonization of southern Europe,[9] represented a step forward in many places, but in Germany was at times the backward destruction of ancient customs and practices (many of which had liturgical consequences) in significant regions of a nation where it was not needed in the same way. The legacy of Eugenio Pacelli, Pope Pius XII, can at times be ambiguous, despite his very best intentions.

To take one aspect of medieval *feudal* life that the 1917 code marked as having finally collapsed, namely the practice of benefices (still legally the basis for the appointment of Anglican ministers as rectors or vicars to English parishes), we have to understand that it was not in itself a church practice, but was a feudal practice which the Church took over and made its own. Many public officials and their offices were beneficed. In fact the conferral of certain rights on individuals in virtue of their public status would have been taken as self-evident to the medieval mind. Relics remain even outside England: in Germany today you can still see journeymen, who have rights to be fed and receive certain standards of payment from anyone who contracts them, and rights from certain townships—in return for which they must for a specified period of time be registered with certain authorities and wear a very specific uniform—testifies to the fact that rights which are still to some extent present even in the 1983 Code of Canon Law are not ecclesiastical in origin but were universal across society and so were adopted by the Church because they were immediately intelligible to anyone. They are—if they come from anywhere specific—(philosophically) Greek in their explanation, if not their origin. You act and are treated in a particular way because of something—some "being" or property (essence)—that you already *are*. This is the very opposite of Nietzsche's claim that abolishes all essences—his protestation that there is no doer to be inferred as prior to the deed—the deed performs, and so produces, the doer and the deed *constitutes* the doer (what is now called performativity) from out of the deed.[10]

---

9. Many of these countries—France, Portugal, Belgium, even Spain and Austria—are countries we in England continue to regard as Catholic despite their clear laicist constitutional status.

10. F. Nietzsche (ed. P. Gast–E. Förster-Nietzsche), *Der Wille zur Macht: Versuch einer Umwertung aller Werte* (Stuttgart: Kröner, 1996), no. 550.

To the European mind until very recently it would have been self-evident not that what you do makes you what you are, but rather what you are makes possible for you to do what you do. How else are we to understand the ceremonies of the sacred liturgy? The priest and his sacred ministers act in the way they act because they are constituted in their respective ministries through ordination and in Christ, they act in accordance with what they already are (and so exhibit the beings that they are), because of an *essential* transformation in their proper being through ordination. Were I to act in an order I do not possess the actions would not be true, they could not make manifest what it is they are meant to do. To a Christian of 1300 this would have been self-evident, and drawn from his understanding of the *world*, and so precisely not the *Church*, he inhabited. It would be an understanding he took *to* church when he went, not one he would have to learn when he got there. Every human being was constituted by their being ordered to a wider whole—to be outside this ordering would constitute destitution, and would make of the human person something indeterminate, to the point of invisibility. Conversely, contemporary man celebrates precisely that indeterminacy *as* a freedom (from which we can infer immediately the extreme poverty of the modern "celebration" of freedom: if you know what you are you already are much freer to become something else: if you are indeterminate, and have no idea who or what you are you are driven by a desperation, a drive, to become something, *anything*). To be anything I want to be, and in every action to *make something of myself* is precisely the modern mentality. Anyone for whom the sacred ceremonies are familiar is already far in advance of the man who would walk off the street and see them unfold for the first time, and yet we still have had to *learn* what to our predecessors would have been a self-evidence.

It becomes clear, by extension, that the need for an historical sense in setting out to make explicit the interior meaning of the sacred liturgy is indispensable. However, what historical study of the sacred liturgy has all too often overlooked is precisely the philosophical aspect—or substituted the most fundamental philosophical aspect for a metaphysics or rationalism (this is how the "historical critical method" works, and what work it is supposed to do). That missing aspect is precisely what we might call the surrounding world— the place from out of which man emerges, needing to be redeemed.

It is this surrounding world, place as such, which the sacred liturgy addresses. This sensitive subject of the Church's sacred liturgy came to the fore—in the liturgical movement preceding Vatican II and in the confusion in some places that has succeeded the reform—in the same century that has seen the rise (and fall) of the description of and debate concerning the philosophical subject–subjectivity, the so-called "modern man" and the needs of his age implied by the Constitution *Sacrosanctum Concilium.* The inability properly to elucidate what I have called the "surrounding world" which the sacred liturgy addresses was marked in that document by the reference to the "requirements of the age,"[11] also a quote from *Sacrosanctum Concilium,* which supposedly necessitated an adaptation of the sacred rites.

The confusion that arose—of who should be at the center of that adaptation—can now exactly be seen when we take the history of philosophy as one in which a transition over *from* a philosophical understanding of being as the disclosure of the meaning of the being of the surrounding world *to* the disclosure of the meaning of the being of God. This may seem a surprising thing to say, since Catholic thinking, especially since just before and then especially following Leo XII's *Aeterni Patris,* has been so shaped by what has often been called "Thomistic philosophy," which has concentrated with great fervor on questions arising from the being of God.[12] But we must not lose sight of the fact that Saint Thomas borrowed the language of philosophy to give form to an understanding of God which he believed was authenticated from an entirely different, and indeed higher, place. That higher place was God himself, in the form of his self-disclosure through all that is concerned with the epiphany, life, death and resurrection of his divine Son. The *place* of that self-disclosure was for Saint Thomas, however, not philosophy—the practice of argumentation, disputation, and the extent and limits of *human* science—but the knowledge (science) imparted by God through the sacred liturgy itself: theology is a divinely authorized science, higher in its order and in its truth than any human science.

---

11. Cf. SC, 1, when it speaks of those aspects of the liturgy capable of being changed *ad nostrae aetatis necessitates.*

12. And also, self-evident to the medieval mind, that our being, the being of creation, flows from and is dependent on God's own being.

You will note from my earlier citation of *Sacrosanctum Concilium* that the list of the subordinate disciplines which had to be referred to the sacred liturgy did not include philosophy, despite the fact that a vicious philosophical rationalism (from whose vice none of the other subordinate disciplines escaped) drove the post-conciliar liturgical reform. Saint Thomas could *borrow* the language of philosophy so freely because all truth—the truth made available and revealed in the *cursus* of the liturgy—is consonant with divine truth, and so insofar as philosophy speaks truly, it speaks adequately but incompletely of what *in faith* has been more completely revealed in Christ. Even what faith knows (and prayer—and this means the liturgy—is how faith comes to know what faith knows) will be completely revealed not just to faith but directly to the intellect of the blessed at the end of time. Faith will be confirmed, after the last things, by the divine gift of the certain knowledge of the truth: at this point, faith ceases. Faith is not faith where certainty reigns. Certainty, the goal of rationalism is the enemy of faith. But faith's enemy is to triumph, not in this life, where rationalistic certainty is sought, but following death, after all has been completed (the purification of purgatory), and after the last things, when faith is no longer needed, because it gives way to certain knowledge imparted directly by the divine mind.

"Thomistic philosophy," insomuch as there is such a thing (and Saint Thomas himself *never* said there was), is only possible because of faith: it seeks no rationalistic certainty. This concentration on the meaning of the being of God in all subsequent philosophy (this even lies at the roots and initial impulses of Cartesian rationalism) found its eclipse in rationalism's declaration of God's death, and resulted in an emphasis solely on being of the human subject, now deprived not only of his surrounding world, but also of his relation to the divine, once given in faith, but which the pursuit of certainty had destroyed. In the absence of any more profound philosophical insight, this isolated figure of the modern philosophical subject, the so-called "human person" revealed in his truth (now certainly, that is, by reason and not in faith), was almost explosively propelled forth to become the very center of liturgical action.

Is modern man—the man for the sake of whom our liturgy became a vexation (if this is what was meant by that man at whom the drive to adapt the sacred liturgy was aimed)—the subject of the liturgy because the "subject" is that one by whom, and against whom, everything is measured? Or is the real subject of the liturgy—the one underpinning it and making it possible, none other than Christ himself, as the tradition itself has from ancient times taught and held, in faith? In 2000, in a work translated into English as *The Spirit of the Liturgy*, the future Benedict XVI spoke of "the boundless superiority of the subject" which characterizes contemporary liturgical life.[13] Few theologians, let alone liturgical experts, have addressed the question put here, of what unfolds—and what clash is unleashed— in the interrelationship of modern humanity with the liturgical life of the Church and with Christological reflection: in other words few contemporary *liturgical* theologians have thought it their business to ask what the impact of their surrounding world has been on their methods, their assumptions, and their work. Few enough theologians have been philosophically self-reflexive or self-aware. The theologians, especially those who drove the liturgical reform but ignored these philosophical questions, were all too often prey to the very thing they thought irrelevant to their work and so ignored.

The absence of any serious elucidation of the surrounding world—of being itself—has in part arisen because since the Middle Ages, and since the eclipse of the ancient insight into being—" being insofar as it is being," as Aristotle thematized it—has been preoccupied with the being, not of man in his surrounding world, but of (the theistic, and precisely in relation to the European Schools, the Christian) God. The degeneration of philosophy into both rationalism and nihilism, noted by Pope John Paul II in his Encyclical Letter *Fides et Ratio* precisely resulted in the call for a return to a "philosophy of being." Without this necessary philosophical corrective, a theology which is genuinely a reflection on faith and so a genuine liturgical theology will never extract itself from mere historiography to become what it should be (and what *Sacrosanctum Concilium* called for it to be): as we have seen, the very ground and center, the very *possibility*, of theology itself. Why should this be so, and why should we want to find ourselves so in accord with this clear and decisive implication of the first Constitution of the Second Vatican Council? Because liturgical theology, and theology in general—precisely as Saint Thomas

---

13. J. Ratzinger, *Der Geist der Liturgie: Eine Einführung* (Freiburg: Herder, 2000), 133: "Die maßlose Übersteigerung des Subjekts."

himself held—can *never* be grounded in the practices or results of any of the human sciences, but *precisely and only because* the liturgy is the continued means of God's continued self-disclosure of himself to the world, every other science and branch of human wisdom is itself already grounded in the meaning of the liturgy, by connections which, although trusted now in faith, will actually be revealed in their proper character not now but at the end of time. Theology is the queen of the sciences because the liturgy is the summit of human life as it is lived on earth: in death, something greater (the heavenly liturgy attested to in the book of Revelation) will be given.

Before we proceed to how and from where we could elicit an adequate theology, a truly *liturgical* theology, we need to consider one clear and important aspect of the eschatological character of the sacred liturgy itself. It is a clear corollary from what I have already said that, when at the end of time the blessed are deified, their minds will be flooded with the divine light, insofar as God chooses to flood their minds.[14] This is precisely what Saint Thomas says, both in the *Prima Pars* and in the *Supplement* to the *Summa Theologiae*, and in the *Commentary on the Sentences*. Redemption will mean that our minds will be perfected, and able to see *as* God sees and see *what* God sees (insofar as God chooses).[15] Indeed, Saint Thomas goes so far as to say that this is the real meaning of the passage from the Epistle of Saint John, "we shall be like him, for we shall see him as he is" (1 John 3:2). Because God has no body, Saint Thomas says, you will not see God, but what you do see will be seen as God himself sees it.

This is the moment at which faith ends, for all that faith has hoped for will now be confirmed in a knowledge that can be said genuinely to be certain. But the most important part of this—a perspective which has been completely lost since the quest for certainty and the transparency of knowledge as such—since the triumph of what we would call rationalism—is that *first* what faith knows is incomplete and provisional, in a knowledge that is yet to be completed

---

14. I examined this question in detail in L. P. Hemming, "The Experience of God: Aquinas on the Identity and Difference of Divine and Human Knowledge," in L. P. Hemming–L. Boeve (ed.), *Divinising Experience: Essays in the History of Religious Experience from Origen to Ricoeur*, Studies in Philosophical Theology, 23 (Leuven: Peeters, 2004), 58–74.

15. This divine permission is how St Thomas explains the possibility of full deification of the human soul, while at the same preserving the essential difference between Creator and created beings.

at the end of time, and *second*, that the knowledge itself sought is eschatological in its structure. What you know now in faith is constituted by the full truth which you will *come* to know with certainty at the end of time: knowing is directed not to what you can remember as having been, but to when you will *yet* perfectly know.

This has fundamental consequences for the liturgy. For contrary to the belief that the liturgy must be immediately accessible and intelligible to all, the liturgy is the *work* of the becoming-intelligible of God. It is the *means* of intelligibility. It is the *sacred instrument* by which God *comes to be* known. More precisely: the liturgy is, both in every particular sacred action, and in the whole life of each baptized man and woman, the means by which faith increases in what it knows. A further consequence: it is not only permitted, it is *necessary* to undertake some actions, to be present at some sacred actions, whose full meaning is yet to be available to you. Incomprehension is part of the character of worship, which discloses the distance the soul has yet to travel in its thirst for deification.

When we have understood this, we can begin to understand from where a genuinely liturgical theology can arise. This source is the end of time, the place from where the Holy Spirit is poured out, when we will be made perfect in Christ (and we are given a present share in that future perfection). Here, I simply want to present a sketch of the liturgical theology I am trying to indicate.

The liturgy—first, foremost, and only—is oriented around the body of Christ. In this sense its proper expression is normatively with respect to a consecrated altar (the symbolic presence of the Lord's body in our midst), and even when that altar is absent it is presumed. Sacramentally (which here means symbolically and mysteriously) understood, the life, death, and resurrection of the sacred body of our Blessed Lord is unfolded with respect to the altar. The altar authorizes and makes possible every sacred action of the Liturgy, which shows who the author and subject is of every sacred action, and the embodied means by which those sacred actions are made available to us. All sacred actions are drawn from and return to the altar.

The meaning of this is disclosed for us in scripture—it is the apostolic activity par excellence which is explained by Saint Paul in the Acts of the Apostles in the following way: "For passing by and seeing your idols, I found an altar also, on which was written: To the

Unknown God. What therefore you worship without knowing it, that I preach to you."[16] The verb here translated as "I preach" is in Greek καταγγέλλω. Saint Paul, when he speaks of preaching, much more frequently uses the verbs κηρύσσω. (I proclaim), or εὐαγγελίζω (I bring good news). Καταγγέλλω is a word less commonly used by the apostle, and does not really mean preach or announce as such, but rather that the message to be laid out is κατά, "with respect to some which." Precisely in this passage of Saint Paul, the "with respect to" is the altar. The apostles and their successors lay out the meaning of the God who is unknown to us. We are moved by the message the apostles bring from the unknown to what of God is to be known (in faith, with respect to the altar and to what it brings, do we take knowledge that is knowledge of God). The meaning of an altar by which the unknown God is made known is through knowledge of the sacrifice of Christ, and as it is offered on any altar now, the sacrifice of the Mass. What is sent (the *missa* of "it has been sent," *Ite, missa est*) effects what it signifies, exactly the theology of signification which we understand to be at work in sacramental theology.

The liturgy is even more basic than scripture, since it is the means by which the Word of God is uttered, "with respect to some which," that is, the altar, which has the power to make available the hiddenness and knowledge of the unknown God. Symbolically the activity of the liturgy as undertaken by the apostles and their successors and their cooperators, the ranks of the clergy, is how the altar "speaks" and how it enters human conversation. The conversation is double: it is the means by which the conversation between the first and second persons of the Divine Trinity is made available to the understanding of the baptized, and so how the baptized are inserted into the eternal conversation between the Father and the Son *through* the work of the Spirit, and it is the means by which mere human conversation is fully taken up into the divine life so that it can disclose, and so be, what it signifies. Speaking here does not just mean words: it means every symbolic or ritual gesture, every silence, which the liturgy employs in its divinely authorized activity.

The altar makes available a site or place, but a place with three specificities, not one. It allows several places to become visible

---

16. Cf. Acts 17:23.

and be seen all at once: it is itself *not* a place in that it is precisely what *makes places* (in this sense it exactly corresponds to Aristotle's ἔσχατον and περιέχον, the altar—symbolically—has to indicate what is outermost to our world: the altar is the place where the outermost of the heavens regulates and unfolds—gives order to—the living cosmos). It makes place with respect to its origin: it gives a place to the sacrifices of the pagans and to what Saint Thomas calls the sacraments of the old covenant—the sacrifices of Melchizedek and of the Aaronic priesthood and the means by which God (in his second person) manifested his hiddenness before the Incarnation; it gives *us* a place, or rather we can now find a place with respect to the altar: as sinner; as baptized, and so as one made available to the means of salvation, and as ones receiving from the altar the means of our salvation. Finally, the altar is the goal of the end time: it is the heavenly altar where the Lamb is worshipped in the New Jerusalem. As such the altar is the *center* of the *Civitas Dei*, the New Jerusalem, the pole around which the redeemed become visible to one another in their (we hope our) entirety. It is—to paraphrase a philosophical text—the πόλος, the pole of the πόλις, the people that God has redeemed through his Son. The altar *establishes* these relations and lets them be known, so that the liturgy can be undertaken, both now and for all eternity. The altar therefore encompasses what is before us, what is to come, and the present (our present worship before it). The altar is a sign of how time, and so history, is to be understood. As such it represents fully the different ways in which God has approached man historically: both before, and now, and how God will accomplish the end of time.

In this, the sacred liturgy is even more basic than the sacraments, since it is the "means by which," the conditioning *possibility*, of the sacraments at all. Here the liturgy disappears in our consideration as some kind of a unified object (a "thing"), and appears *only* as the form—*forma*—of Christ himself, since it is through the liturgy that the body of Christ becomes available to us. The form of Christ is unfolded through the liturgical cycle which makes available the form in its specificities, its specific moments (the pre- and post-resurrection life of our Lord on earth), and in his eternal identity and unity.

As more basic than the sacraments themselves, the liturgy *as* the activity of Christ is—to steal the words of *Lumen Gentium* and to

give them the ecclesiological significance that they really deserve—
veluti sacramentum "like a sacrament,"[17] since the proper subject
of the liturgy is Christ (who alone is the sacrament of the Father), and
insofar as we insert ourselves into the what the sacred liturgy inserts
us into, we are inserted into the body of Christ. Only with respect
to the liturgy and in its activity can the Church ever be genuinely said
to be in the manner of a sacrament.[18]

The liturgy is sacred. We are not free with respect to its
activity—these actions are divinely ordained and should be entrusted
only to those who have both an aptitude for them and a training in
their inner life, because they are the sanctifying power of God. Every
sanctification takes place *with respect to the actions of the liturgy*, which
means, with respect to the altar and thus to the body of Christ
through the way in which its meaning becomes manifest in human
life and history. Even those who have both aptitude and training for
the activity of the liturgy are not adequate for it (and so must abandon
themselves ever more to the mercy and grace of God), which is why
the closer to the activity of the liturgy—and this means the closer to
the altar—one comes the more holiness is both demanded of us and
made available to us. Abandoning oneself to the mercy of God means
abandoning oneself in perfect trust and faith to the sacraments which
will effect what they promise, and so make possible what they effect.
In this sense above all is the Blessed Sacrament the sacrament of the
altar (*sacramentum altaris*). Here we abandon every pretence that grace
is in some sense "invisible" like radiation, as the reformers supposed or
claimed, or that it is granted "subjectively." Grace is objectively
communicated through and by means of the significatory activity of
the sacraments, with respect to the altar. This means that *how* the
sacraments are done affects, and has the capacity to alter, their
effectivity. A sin of omission before the altar of God is more serious
than a sin of the same rank committed in some other place. And yet

---

17. *Lumen Gentium*, 1.

18. This is important, lest anyone read into my remarks too much the liturgy as some kind of
"realized eschatology," or as some authors have suggested that life "in the Church" is tantamount
to being already redeemed, already in heaven. From and with respect to the altar our present
being and identity is referred to the being and identity we will receive at the end of time. Who
we are now will from now on be referred to who we will be, but does not bring heaven to earth
now, but refers everything we are now to the end of time and the new earth and new heaven we
hope in faith to inhabit.

even here, and above all here (before and with respect to) the altar, mercy is given.

To conclude: every genuine liturgical theology begins there-fore καταγγέλλων—announcing an understanding with respect to some which, and so *Introibo ad altare Dei* . . . .

Contributors

Claude Barthe, a priest of the *Société des Prêtres auxiliaires* resident in Paris, is the religious chronicler for the French periodical *Catholica*. His publications include *Le ciel sur la terre* (François-Xavier de Guibert, 2003) on the Roman liturgy, and *Propositions pour une "Paix de l'Église"* (Hora Decima, 2006). He has overseen the edition of *Le sens spirituel de la liturgie: Guillaume Durand, Rational des divins offices, livre IV de la messe* (Ad Solem, 2003) and of *Poésie et mystique* (Éditions de Paris, 2006), a collection of Catholic literature.

Nicola Bux is a priest of the archdiocese of Bari and professor of liturgy and sacramental theology at the *Facoltà Teologica Pugliese*. He is a consulter to the Congregation for the Doctrine of the Faith, the Congregation for the Causes of the Saints and the Office for the Liturgical Celebrations of the Supreme Pontiff; he was also a *peritus* at the Synod of Bishops on the Eucharist, held in October 2005. His latest book is *La riforma di Benedetto XVI: La liturgia tra innovazione e tradizione* (Piemme, 2008).

Gabriel Díaz Patri was ordained a priest of the diocese of San Luis in Argentina and served as a liturgical advisor to Bishop J. R. Laise. He is currently head of the section for the study of medieval liturgy at the Centre for Medieval Philosophy (National University of Cuyo, Argentina). He has been resident in Paris since 2001. His publications include various articles on Greek and Latin hymnology and a course on ecclesiastical Latin, published in Buenos Aires in 1996.

László Dobszay is a member of the Musicological Institute of the Hungarian Academy of Sciences and a leading scholar in the fields of ethno-musicology, medieval music history, and history of chant. He is professor emeritus in musicology and analysis, founder and former head of the Church Music Department of the Liszt Ferenc Music University Budapest, and co-conductor of the chant ensemble Schola Hungarica (50 records).

Cristina Dondi was Lyell Research Fellow in the History of the Early Modern Printed Book, University of Oxford, 2002–2005 and is one of the editors of *A Catalogue of Books Printed in the Fifteenth Century now in the Bodleian Library* (Oxford University Press, 2005). Her research focuses on the history of printing in Italy in the fifteenth century and on liturgical texts, both manuscript and printed.

Eamon Duffy is Professor of the History of Christianity and Fellow of Magdalene College, University of Cambridge. His work *The Stripping of the Altars: Traditional Religion in England 1400–1570* (Yale University Press, 1992) received wide acclaim. His latest book is *Fires of Faith: Catholic England under Mary Tudor* (Yale University Press, 2009). He is a Fellow of the British Academy and a frequent broadcaster on radio and television.

Sheridan Gilley is Emeritus Reader in Theology, University of Durham. He is the author of *Newman and His Age* (London: Darton, Longman & Todd, 1990, republished 2003) and of numerous articles on modern religious history. He co-edited *The Cambridge History of Christianity. Volume VIII: World Christianities, c. 1815–c. 1914* (Cambridge University Press, 2006).

Laurence Paul Hemming is a co-founder of the Society of Saint Catherine of Siena and the author of *Postmodernity's Transcending: Devaluing God* (SCM Press–University of Notre Dame Press, 2005), *Benedict XVI: Fellow Labourer for Truth* (Burns & Oates, 2005), and *Heidegger's Atheism: The Refusal of a Theological Voice* (University of Notre Dame Press, 2002). His latest book is *Worship as a Revelation: The Past, Present, and Future of Catholic Liturgy* (Continuum, 2008).

Uwe Michael Lang, a priest of the Congregation of the Oratory of St Philip Neri in London, is a staff member of the Congregation for Divine Worship and a consulter to the Office for the Liturgical Celebrations of the Supreme Pontiff; he also teaches at the Università Europea di Roma. He has published on Patristic and liturgical studies, including his book *Turning Towards the Lord: Orientation in Liturgical Prayer* (San Francisco: Ignatius Press, Second Edition, 2009), which came out first in German in 2003 with a preface by then-Cardinal Joseph Ratzinger and has since been translated into several languages.

Lauren Pristas is Professor of Theology at Caldwell College, New Jersey. She has worked on liturgical translations and has published a series of essays examining the orations of the 1970 Roman Missal in the light of their respective sources in *The Thomist, Communio, New Blackfriars, Nova et Vetera*, and in *Ever Directed Towards the Lord: The Love of God in the Liturgy of the Eucharist Past, Present and Hoped For* (T & T Clark, 2007).

Alcuin Reid has edited and published a number of books on the liturgy, including *Looking Again at the Question of the Liturgy with Cardinal Ratzinger* (St. Michael's Abbey Press, 2003) and *The Monastic Diurnal* (St. Michael's Abbey Press, 2004). The second edition of his principal work *The Organic Development of the Liturgy* (Ignatius Press, 2005) carries a preface by Joseph Cardinal Ratzinger. His international speaking on liturgical topics has included the CIEL Colloquium in Paris (2003) and Rome (2005).

About the Liturgical Institute

The Liturgical Institute, founded in 2000 by His Eminence Francis Cardinal George of Chicago, offers a variety of options for education in liturgical studies. A unified, rites-based core curriculum constitutes the foundation of the program, providing integrated and balanced studies toward the advancement of the renewal promoted by the Second Vatican Council. The musical, artistic, and architectural dimensions of worship are given particular emphasis in the curriculum. Institute students are encouraged to participate in its "liturgical heart" of daily Mass and Morning and Evening Prayer. The academic program of the Institute serves a diverse, international student population—laity, religious, and clergy—who are preparing for service in parishes, dioceses, and religious communities. Personalized mentoring is provided in view of each student's ministerial and professional goals. The Institute is housed on the campus of the University of St. Mary of the Lake/Mundelein Seminary, which offers the largest priestly formation program in the United States and is the center of the permanent diaconate and lay ministry training programs of the Archdiocese of Chicago. In addition, the University has the distinction of being the first chartered institution of higher learning in Chicago (1844), and one of only seven pontifical faculties in North America.

For more information about the Liturgical Institute and its programs, contact: usml.edu/liturgicalinstitute. Phone: 847-837-4542. E-mail: litinst@usml.edu.

Msgr. Reynold Hillenbrand
1904-1979

Monsignor Reynold Hillenbrand, ordained a priest by Cardinal George Mundelein in 1929, was Rector of St. Mary of the Lake Seminary from 1936 to 1944.

He was a leading figure in the liturgical and social action movement in the United States during the 1930s and worked to promote active, intelligent, and informed participation in the Church's liturgy.

He believed that a reconstruction of society would occur as a result of the renewal of the Christian spirit, whose source and center is the liturgy.

Hillenbrand taught that, since the ultimate purpose of Catholic action is to Christianize society, the renewal of the liturgy must undoubtedly play the key role in achieving this goal.

Hillenbrand Books strives to reflect the spirit of Monsignor Reynold Hillenbrand's pioneering work by making available innovative and scholarly resources that advance the liturgical and sacramental life of the Church.